Where There's Life . . .

Hilary Lawson and Adam Hart-Davis

Based on the Yorkshire Television Series

Where There's Life . . .

Published by Michael Joseph
in association with The Rainbird Publishing Group

First published in Great Britain in 1982 by
Michael Joseph Ltd
44 Bedford Square
London WC1
in association with
The Rainbird Publishing Group Ltd
40 Park Street, London W1Y 4DE
who designed and produced the book

ISBN 0 7181 2137 6

Designer: Yvonne Dedman
Indexer: Adam Hart-Davis

Text filmset by SX Composing Ltd, Rayleigh, Essex
Origination by Adroit Photo Litho Ltd, Birmingham
Printed and bound by
Hazell, Watson & Viney Ltd, Aylesbury, Bucks

Contents

Preface

About a year ago Hilary Lawson and I, along with the rest of the department, knew that during the summer of 1981 we had to produce a series of programmes of general interest in the broad area of medicine and human affairs. We talked to doctors, visited advisers, and invited consultants to our meetings – many long meetings – because before we could begin making programmes we had to decide what we wanted to do. Should we look at the latest advances in medical technology? At alternative types of treatment, such as acupuncture and faith healing? At the doctor-patient relationship? During the early months of 1981 we considered all these possibilities, and many others, and argued interminably.

Floating in the soup of ideas, a pair of newspaper stories caught our imagination. A teenager became so 'addicted' to Space Invaders that he spent all his time locked in combat with the electronic machines, and even stole money from his mother's purse to feed them. The same week we heard about Tim Freeman, a seventeen-year-old victim of cerebral palsy, who met a Space Invader machine and became fascinated, and determined to beat it. Within a couple of months he had achieved an excellent score, and suddenly he and his teachers found that he was able to concentrate in class. He could walk much better; he was catching up in maths; his reading age improved by five years; and best of all he could tie his own shoe-laces.

I went to see Tim and learned of his intensely personal experience of coping with the difficulties he faced. No one could suggest that Space Invaders can 'cure' cerebral palsy, but what we learned from stories like his was that personal experience can be enlightening as well as exciting. And that, perhaps, was how our ideas began to crystallize for the series – a series in which ordinary people told us about their experiences, about how they had overcome problems, about not giving up hope. In the end it turned out to be a series not about medicine, nor about doctors, but about people.

After the series had finished Hilary and I looked back over the programmes and chose sixteen stories which seemed to us to illustrate central problems of personal life today. I visited all the people involved to try and capture the events and the background in much greater detail than had been possible in the studio. Working with transcripts of these interviews, Hilary tackled the difficult job of turning long and sometimes rambling conversations into the stories that you see here, and setting each in context by means of an introduction.

Meanwhile I put together the 'What you can do' sections at the ends of the chapters. These are intended to lay out options – to suggest possible ways forward. The truth is that for most of the problems there are no simple solutions. There may be places where these sections seem to be saying 'This is the answer'; I hope that my suggestions do not give a false impression of being definitive – I am trying only to provide signposts towards potential sources of help.

I should like to thank first of all the people whose stories appear in the book. They not only gave me hours of their time and talked willingly of their most personal and sensitive problems, but also allowed me to take photographs, and plied me with tea and coffee. I have made many real friends. Equally I am grateful to those who helped me in just the same way but do not appear because their stories were squeezed out by lack of space.

In my search for sources of information, advice, and help, I ransacked several bookshops and libraries, and Erika Senior at Leeds City Library proved an invaluable ally. I must be one of the few people to have visited the Citizens Advice Bureau, the Samaritans, the Probation Service, and Marriage Guidance, all in the same week; each provided patient and friendly assistance. I telephoned many other organizations, and gratefully acknowledge the help they provided, especially the Mastectomy Association and the Patients Association. Finally Cathy Rutter and the ladies in the YTV duplicating office were immensely patient and efficient in typing interviews and other material.

Hilary Lawson is a philosopher, and was responsible for much of the thinking behind both the television series and the book; I am much more a practical compiler. We do not always agree, but I hope that between us we have produced a book that contains both truth and hope.

Adam Hart-Davis
Leeds
January 1982

Introduction

Human dilemmas have no easy solutions – there are often no right answers, but the stories in this book are based on the belief that to know what others have done, and to know what for them has been successful and unsuccessful, is not only to be forewarned, it is to be given advice . . . to be given hope.

A few decades ago technology allied with medical care looked as though it might solve most if not all of our problems. Here was the key to the future, here was tomorrow's world. The old killer diseases were apparently being tamed, and with the rise of new drugs and the constantly growing fund of knowledge the vision of an age without illness almost seemed possible. Such a dream now seems little more than an absurdity. In the last fifty years there has been only a marginal improvement in adult life expectancy, despite the fact that we now spend vast sums on our health.

So what happened? People no longer die from tuberculosis or smallpox, but they die nevertheless, only today it is from heart disease, bronchitis and cancers. Ironically our hospitals are full of cures for diseases we no longer get, while the beds are filled with patients for whom little can be done except to soothe and make things more bearable. We have become aware that the substantial improvements in health are due to better housing and sanitation. Of course great advances in medicine have been made: advances that improve the quality of our lives, and advances particularly in dealing with acute, emergency conditions. However, the chronic long-term illnesses that we are likely to suffer from have been left almost untouched. There are many treatments, and many ways of alleviating distress, but there are few cures.

Perhaps we are seeing the limitations of the framework within which science and medicine have operated since the end of the eighteenth century. A framework which has assumed that by looking at the body or society as a machine we will be able to understand, and to solve, its problems. Undoubtedly great strides were made by using this outlook but because of this advance we came to believe that it could be successful in almost every arena – and areas in which it was not very helpful simply became unimportant. The social and family problems that appear again and again in this book have been particularly intractable – whether it is a question of dealing with the handicapped, old, or mentally ill, coping with violence in the home and society as a whole, or facing personal emotional problems such as depression and bereavement. The scientific perspective led us to think that there must be an expert somewhere with the answer to any particular problem, and if there wasn't, there soon would be. We were on our way to a complete book of all knowledge. Given time the encyclopedias would be finished. It is in opposition to those beliefs, and the view that simple precise solutions are possible from a single perspective, that this book is written. If there is a moral to the personal stories found here, it is that while the mechanistic, reductive model of modern medicine is very powerful, it is not all powerful.

The growing recognition of the relative lack of success of medicine has perhaps been responsible for the increased interest in alternative or fringe medicine; as if having lost faith in science we seek faith in something else. But it is not a question of being in favour of one kind of medicine rather than another, or in favour of the abandonment of medicine altogether. For it is not the doctors and nurses, those heroes and heroines of the twentieth century, who are at fault, but the thought that they could do everything. Somehow we believed, and to a great extent still believe, that if we only spent enough money and trained enough doctors, we would be healthy. When a new clinic or hospital is opened, or the health budget increased, we applaud. But there is no clear relationship between more doctors and hospitals, and better health.

For although we think that we have given up witch-doctors our faith in the technological future has been mirrored by a faith in present treatment. We still believe in the magic cure, only today it comes in the form of a tablet. Such faith is leading only to disillusion instead. We have to come to terms with the fact that the medical profession never did have *all* the answers, and they are never going to.

Partly because we have wanted them to play at being God, doctors have assumed a position of omniscience they do not have – perhaps by seeing what they cannot do as well as what they can do, we will be able to move into a more realistic era. An era in which we will be able to use those with expert or technical knowledge, without believing that they have all the solutions, and without abdicating responsibility for our own lives. For the moment the doctor functions both as technician and priest. These are vital roles, but we should not confuse the two – you do not need faith in a mechanic. There is even a case for separating the two, so that the role of counsellor and adviser is not mixed up with that of the technician. To some extent this is already happening with the change in character of general practice and the increase in counselling services. However, in many of the situations dealt with in this book the best advice comes not from experts of any sort but from those with experience. For health is not simply a replacing of the broken parts in the machine, it is also to do with our well-being, our contentment, the balance of our lives – things for which we need wisdom rather than knowledge.

I hope this book provides information when it is helpful, but it is founded on the assumption that when you face some difficulty, some problem, or some illness, what is most helpful in addition to professional advice, is to talk to someone who has been in the same situation; to hear from them how they coped with it, how they fought with it, and perhaps conquered it. The power of information and science is very great, but it should be used when it is useful and abandoned when it is not. By turning to others with experience we may find that we learn more from them than we could from any textbook.

Hilary Lawson
Leeds
January 1982

Author's acknowledgments The book has grown out of a television programme, and although television is always a team effort this is particularly true of a series like *Where There's Life. . . .* As the editor of the series I would like to thank everyone on the production team – Elizabeth Brice, Mark Dixon, Irene Garrow, Annie Morgan, David Poyser, and Val Zabels – for these are the people who find the material and without whom there would be no show.

A special note of thanks to John Fanshawe, a producer on the series, who always has the answer to this week's panic, and, of course, to Duncan Dallas, the executive producer, who ensures that complacency is never an option.

I am grateful to Dr Mark Layton who made invaluable comments on the original draft and who did his best to help us avoid inaccuracies, to Penny Wordley who put up with continual chaos while attempting to type up the original script and to Georgina Evans, our Rainbird editor, for her painstaking efforts in turning the manuscript into a book, and for her advice and support. I would also like to make a general thank-you to the consultants, advisers, presenters of the show, and all those at Yorkshire Television who actually put the programme on the air.

H.L.

You and your family

1. When the baby isn't perfect
How it feels to face the reality we all dread

2. Children at risk
Baby battering: closer to all of us than we think

3. For the sake of the kids
When separation is better than staying together

4. The unspoken problems
Sex: perfectly natural but not naturally perfect

5. Death in the family
The daughter who didn't cry

1. When the baby isn't perfect

The experience of having a baby brings with it a time of great hopes and great fears. The hopes are for the future and for a healthy intelligent child; the fears we would often rather forget about. Almost all prospective parents ask themselves, 'Will everything go well? Will the baby be normal?'

Fortunately, most couples have perfectly healthy children who grow up into perfectly healthy adults. One hundred and fifty years ago roughly one baby in every three was stillborn or died in the first few months of life. Today, partly as a result of improved housing, sanitation, and nutrition, and because of advances in medical care, this figure has been reduced to about one in fifty. The unspoken fear of many parents is not so much that they will lose their child, terrible though that would be, but that their child will be born handicapped.

Babies can suffer from many different problems at birth. Many – minor bruising, for example – quickly disappear on their own; others are inconsequential and require no treatment. But there remain a few babies, twenty-five in every thousand, that suffer significant physical or mental handicap.

Modern medical care has much reduced the risk and can provide early warning of the problems. But however sophisticated our knowledge and techniques, children that are not perfect will continue to be born.

We all know it can happen but we never believe that it could happen to us. And it is just because we cannot face this possibility, that when it does happen, it is devastating.

Every cloud . . .

No one could have suspected that anything would go wrong with Linda's second child. Her first child, Sarah, was two, and since the pregnancy and birth had been straightforward, Linda and her husband, Paul, decided to have their second baby at home. At twenty-four, with a healthy family, Linda had every reason to believe that all would go well; she had even given up smoking for the duration of the pregnancy.

Her labour lasted all day; the midwife came and went twice. Finally, just before two in the morning, the baby's head was born. Paul, following the midwife's advice, put his knee into the small of Linda's back so that she could watch the rest of the birth. This was the moment they had been waiting for. But as the baby lay between her legs, with the cord still attached, the first chill ran through her.

Linda

'I noticed . . . I saw even before the cord was cut . . . in that moment of birth, that there was something wrong, something very, very wrong, something that didn't look right. It was very blue, and it seemed to have a very long tongue, with a thick neck and upward-slanting eyes. At that point I thought – I knew I suppose – that I'd given birth to a mentally handicapped child.'

That child was a mongol.

As a nurse, Linda had seen many handicapped children. But this was her child – nobody else's. She could hardly face it; she felt as if she wanted to wash her hands clean.

'I felt I had given birth to a vegetable. A cabbage. A child that would be no good to herself or anyone else for the rest of our lives. I handed the baby straight to my husband. I rejected her totally and completely. I didn't even want to touch her.

I remember lying there, looking at her, thinking, "This isn't really happening, it's a dream." I was watching the midwife clearing up, and I remember thinking, she's not going to leave the baby with me. She'll take it away with her . . . probably in a black plastic sack. After all, that's what you do with a reject, isn't it? You throw it away and you start again. So that's what I thought would happen. She would take Claire away with her. She wouldn't leave her with us at all.'

The midwife left. Paul and the baby fell asleep. Linda lay awake. The unreality, the bad dream, was fading, but the harsher truth was taking its place. No one was going to take the baby away. No one else was going to tell the relatives and friends. Linda could see the scene thirty years on, dragging this thing around with its glazed look, ankle socks and pudding-basin haircut. Faced with all this, Linda hoped it would all just end.

Perhaps . . . perhaps she could help bring it to an end . . .

> 'I remember lying there listening to her breathing and thinking . . . thinking that perhaps she'd stop; hoping that she'd stop. And then maybe, maybe . . . if I smothered her with a pillow – nobody would know. But more important still – the thought I couldn't shake off that night was that nobody would even care.
>
> Nobody would care that I had ended this life within its first few hours, because it would be of no use to anyone. I felt that I just couldn't face the burden of it all. There were moments when I even thought of throwing the baby out of the window . . . I think I would have done if the windows had not been louvered and high so that I couldn't reach.'

Very early the next morning a friend, their neighbour Eileen from next door, called in. Linda could hear her talking to Paul downstairs. What would she say? What could she say? All she wanted to do was hide.

> 'I saw the midwife's car in the middle of the night. You must have had the baby . . .'

Eileen had reached the bedroom door. There was no way out, it had to be said.

> 'I've had the baby – it's a little girl . . . But don't come in. It's a mongol.'

Eileen didn't seem to take it seriously.

> 'Rubbish, that doesn't happen to people like you and me.'

She had reached the cot. The baby was in her arms.

> 'Oh, look at her. She's beautiful.'

For Linda, this was the moment when the horror ended.

> 'For the first time in that very long night I really did take a hard look at Claire. I noticed her lovely ginger hair, her pink face, and chubby little hands, and I saw that she was beautiful. The blueness had gone and she was in a peaceful sleep. She was no longer the baby I had rejected just a few hours ago.'

It was only now – now that Linda could see beyond the handicap to the baby – that her affection burst through.

> 'I was suddenly filled with an all-pervading sense of love. A need to do, a need to give. I held her close, and wept tears of pure joy: I knew then that

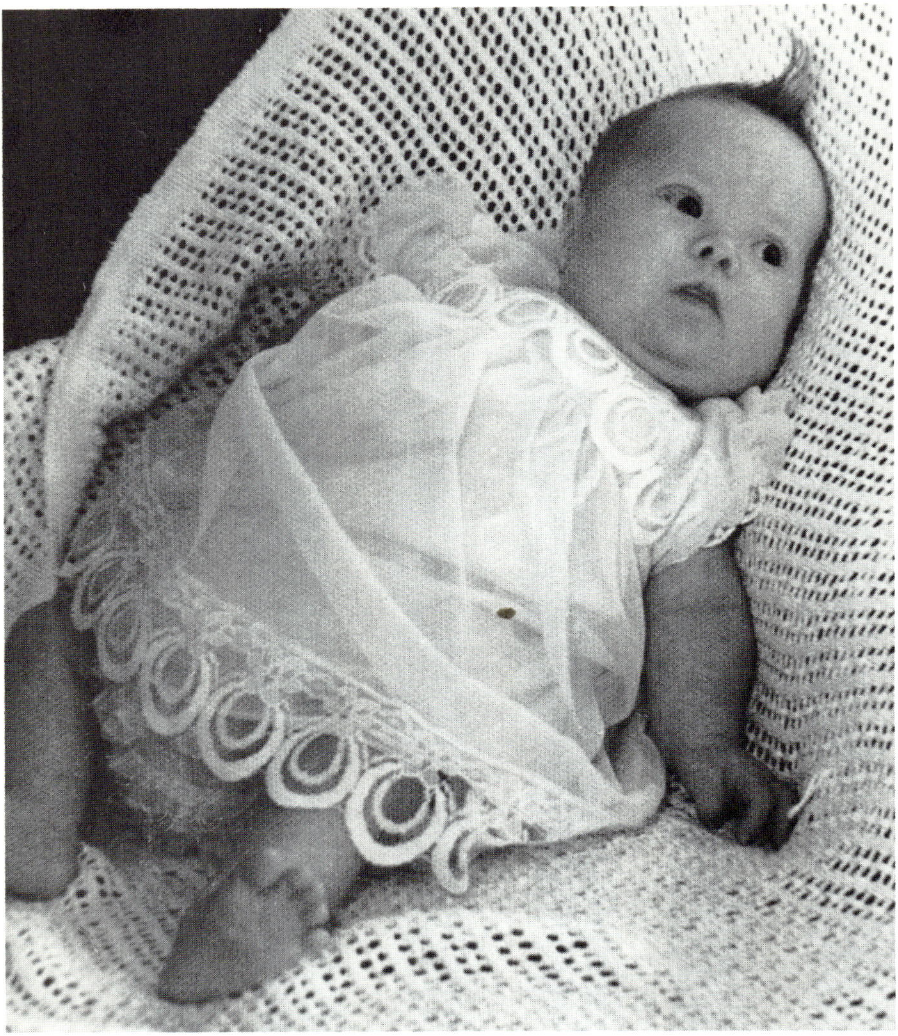

Claire was a pretty baby

even though Claire was handicapped she was now part of the family, and would get her fair share of love. I felt a tremendous amount of guilt over my rejection of Claire, but when I tried to look at it logically, what I had rejected was the handicap. I had got what I wanted and that was a baby.'

Later that morning Linda and Paul were visited by their doctor and a paediatrician who told them what mongolism would mean and that there is no medical treatment available – although there is for some problems associated with mongolism. Specialist education can be a help but that is all.

Normally, once the doctors have left, the parents are on their own. Isolated and frightened of the future, they just want to escape, to have someone else take the burden away; consequently our children's homes and adoption societies are filled with these unwanted babies.

In Southend, where Linda and Paul live, it is very different. A group of parents who have had handicapped children have made it their business to share their problems and experiences with people like Linda and Paul.

> 'Within thirty-six hours of Claire's birth we had been contacted by the leader of the group. They didn't come with sympathy; they came with compassion, and with concrete help – and this is just what we needed. Because as far as we were concerned we were lonely and desperate. We were the only people that this could ever have happened to. We felt that we had been singled out . . . that this burden had been dumped on us, for some reason.
>
> And then somehow it all changed. I felt I wasn't alone any more . . . I wasn't alone at all. It had happened to other people, and that made me feel very, very strong . . . There was now courage where there had been none; I had hope where all I had had was despair. I could take Claire out into the community. I could talk to people about my handicapped child. I could be proud to bring her up.'

By talking to others in the group Linda and Paul were able to face their worries and learn how to overcome some of the problems. They learned to have confidence, in a society that has no confidence in the weak and unsuccessful; to be open, in a society that tries to hide.

> 'It was strange. We used to take Claire out in the pram and I'd be walking down the street and Sarah would be sitting in the pushchair or on the front of the pram. And people would come along and they would speak to me, and they would speak to Sarah. And they would completely ignore the pram and the baby in it. And I would say, "Here is Sarah, here am I. We have a handicapped child in the pram. Please talk to her. We want you to talk to her. We want you to get to know her as we know her." And amazingly, it worked. Everyone became very interested in Claire, and now if she escapes out of the front door everyone knows. "That's Claire . . . that's Claire running down the street."'

Mongol babies sleep a lot, which makes them easy to look after, but they develop slowly. Linda and Paul therefore kept Claire awake as much as possible, and when she was awake they bombarded her with information. They tied bells to her feet to encourage her to move, and Linda carried her around the house on her hip, talking to her incessantly. Above all they played with her continually. There is great variation in the abilities of mongol children but with the help of physiotherapy and attending school from the age of two, Claire has developed, not as fast as Sarah, but faster than the average mongol.

Looking back, Linda will never forget the day of the birth:

> 'On the 12th of May 1972 I thought that life had ended. But of course it hadn't . . . it had begun. Life changed, for the better, that day. There are a great many joys . . . a great many joys. It's difficult to try and categorize

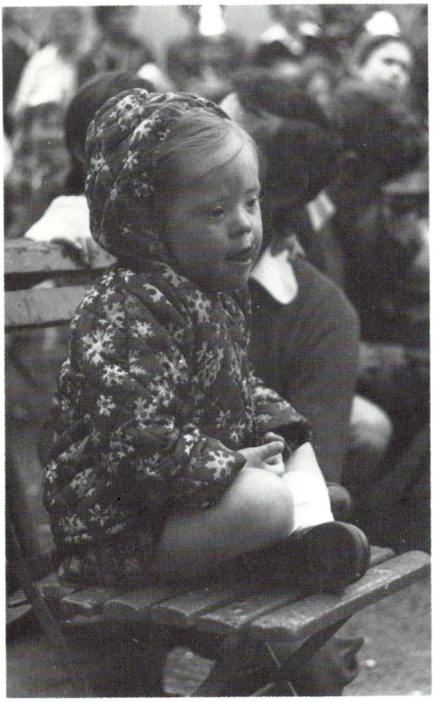

Above : Handicapped children can cause severe stress in the home, but Claire and Sarah are part of a happy and well-balanced family

Below : For Linda and Paul, Claire is a constant source of joy

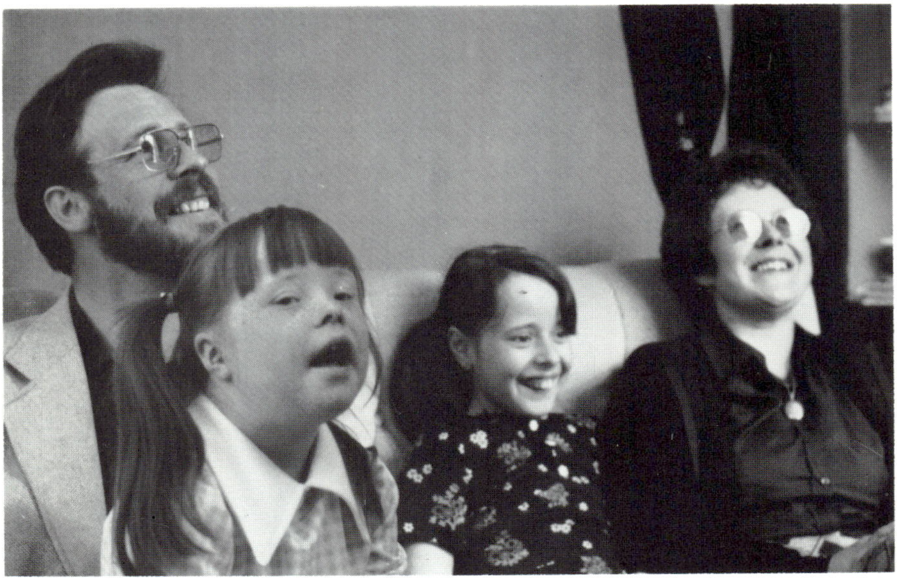

them. Her laugh is a joy for both of us all the time. Her development has been startling; she's a happy, lively girl and hopefully we are a happy well-balanced family. Life changed for me completely that morning . . . I now know for the better.'

But, of course, not every tale has such a happy ending, as Linda – now part of the group that helped her – is well aware. Handicapped children put great stress on the rest of the family, since the other members of it must necessarily receive less attention. And not all handicapped children develop so well, no matter how much attention they receive. Indeed, not all of them survive. Every couple must make their own decision, but Linda is sure it is worth helping handicapped children to live and to lead as full a life as possible.

'A little while ago some parents came to the group to talk about their child who had been born with severe heart problems. Without an operation the child would die, but if she was operated on there was only a 25 per cent chance that she would survive. The parents talked to us, to family, to friends, and went for surgery. The child died. At the funeral the grandparents came up to me and said, "Thank you" for all we had done. "But there's one thing we don't understand. How is it that the parents can talk about this baby the way they do? My daughter says she'll only remember her smile." And the parents came over and said, "Don't you see, the group taught us to talk, it taught us to accept, it taught us to live one day at a time. We only had her nine months, but they're nine months we wouldn't be without for anything in the world, because she gave us so much and she taught us so much." As far as I am concerned, if parents can say that in death, how much more is there to be said in the *life* of the mentally handicapped?'

What you can do

Every couple wants to know how to avoid having a handicapped child in the first place. There are no foolproof answers but there are precautions that can be taken.

- First, you must get good antenatal care. The evidence is that the earlier and more regularly you go for antenatal care, the greater chance of a normal, healthy pregnancy and a live, healthy child. Antenatal care is free in this country, and is available in clinics to which you are referred by your family doctor, or from him directly. The examinations in the months before the birth include blood tests from which some abnormalities in the foetus can be determined. But more detailed tests such as amniocentesis (analysis of the fluid in the womb) and ultrasound (a sort of sound 'X-ray') are not usually normal procedure unless there are further indications that there could be something wrong.
- Secondly, you must eat well throughout pregnancy. During World War II pregnant women were given priority in their food rations and the number of stillbirths dropped by 25 per cent. There is no one special diet; just eat well. When you are pregnant your demands for protein will

increase, and one cheap, good way to get protein is to drink milk. But what should you avoid? In general, if something affects you it will affect your baby, and if possible you should avoid all drugs, especially in the first three months, and attempt to do so throughout pregnancy. In particular, cut down on alcohol and cigarettes – preferably give them up altogether.

• Thirdly, if you are in a high risk category – if you are under 14 or over 35, if you have already had one abnormal child or if you carry an abnormal gene – you should have a blood test at about 16–18 weeks, plus an examination of a sample of the amniotic fluid (the water surrounding the foetus). There is a small risk attached to this technique, and it should, therefore, be done only by properly trained staff, and preferably together with ultrasound. Ultrasound can be used on its own and is on present evidence perfectly safe. It provides a picture of the baby in the womb and can often give warning of some types of abnormalities. At the same time it provides simple but useful information about the position of the baby, and indeed the number of babies.

A foetal stethoscope is used to listen to the heart of the foetus during an examination at the antenatal clinic

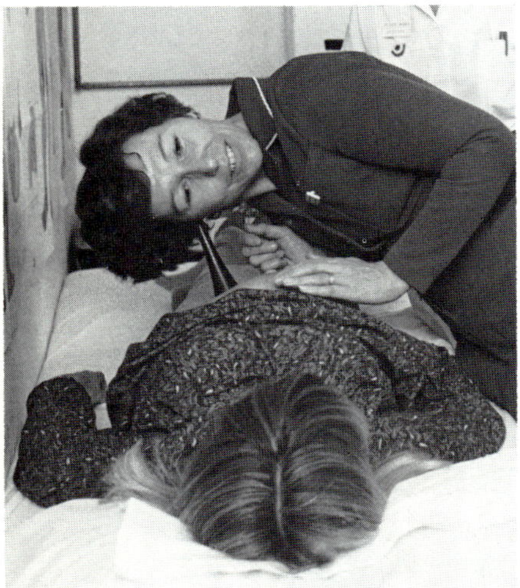

The routine blood sample will be used for several tests, including one for Rh factor. One in seven people are Rh-negative, and if this includes you, you will need to have further tests to see if your body's own defences are attacking the baby. This need not be as bad as it sounds as there are techniques that can help to protect the baby and preventive measures which lessen the chance of the problem rising.

Despite all of these precautions, some women will carry abnormal babies. If the abnormality is discovered in time, you may wish to consider abortion. Take advice from your doctor, but in the end it is you who should decide.

If you do give birth to a handicapped child unexpectedly, there are many groups that you can contact similar to the one that helped Linda and Paul. If you have already given birth to an abnormal child you should talk to your doctor about genetic counselling; this may help you decide about having more children.

Organizations If you want to talk to someone quickly, telephone the Samaritans (see the telephone directory for your local branch).

For general information about pregnancy, its risks, precautions to take, and abortion, contact one of these organizations, either by telephone, or write with stamped, addressed envelope to:

• The British Pregnancy Advisory Service (Head Office), Austy Manor, Wootton Wawen, Solihull, West Midlands B95 6DA; tel: 05642 3225. There are many local branches; look in your telephone directory.

• The National Childbirth Trust (9 Queensborough Terrace, London W2 3TB; tel: 01-221 3833) encourages methods of preparation that help women to have their babies consciously and free from fear. They can put you in touch with a local branch or an individual helper.

• The Pregnancy Advisory Service, 40 Margaret Street, London W1; tel: 01-409 0281.

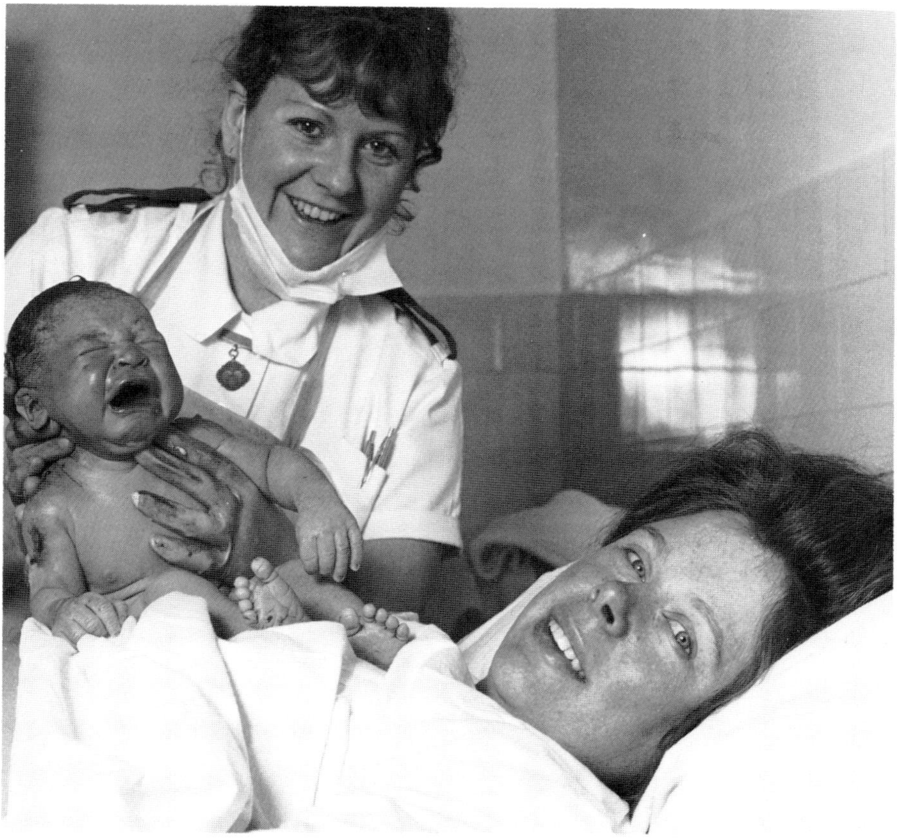

The happy minutes after birth

Other associations you may be able to use are:

- Society to Support Home Confinement, 17 Laburnum Avenue, Durham; tel: 0385 61325.
- Association for Post-Natal Illness, 7 Gowan Avenue, London SW6.

Books on pregnancy etc. There are many books available about pregnancy and its risks. Angela Phillips and Jill Rakusen, *Our Bodies Ourselves* (Allen Lane, 1978, and Penguin, 1978) is direct and practical. So is Christine Beels's *The Childbirth Book* (Mayflower, 1980).

The Spare Rib Dairy (obtainable from *Spare Rib*, 27 Clerkenwell Close, London EC1R 0AT) has a directory of information and services relating to pregnancy, childbirth, and so on.

To find out what medical help you are entitled to see Gerry and Carol Stimson's *Health Rights Handbook* (Prism, 1978, and Penguin, 1980).

Handicapped babies – organizations For information about the Southend group for handicapped children and groups in other areas of the country, write direct to: Mrs Linda Wonnacott, 117 Stornoway Road, Southend-on-Sea, Essex SS2 4NX; tel: 0702 64865, or to: Mrs Barbara Crowe, 19 Avenue Terrace, Westcliff-on-Sea, Essex SS0 7PL; tel: 0702 41096.

There is a similar group in Edinburgh called ADE. Contact Kenneth U. McDonald,

13 Lovedale Road, Balerno, Midlothian; tel: 031-449 4100.

Your local Citizens Advice Bureau (CAB) will have information about groups in your area, and the Patients Association (11 Dartmouth Street, London SW1 9BN; tel: 01-222 4992) produce a booklet listing the groups around the country.

The Voluntary Council for Handicapped Children (The National Children's Bureau, 8 Wakeley Street, London EC1U 7QE; tel: 01-278 9441) has published two excellent books, *Shared Care*, and *Parents as Partners*, which describe the different forms of help available throughout the country.

There are many associations that help families with handicapped children. If any of those in the list below sound as though they might be helpful, telephone them, or write with a stamped, addressed envelope, and ask what sort of information or services they can provide:

- Association for Spina Bifida and Hydrocephalus, Tavistock House North, Tavistock Square, London WC1; tel: 01-388 1382.
- Association for All Speech-Impaired Children, 347 Central Markets, Smithfield, London EC1A 9NH; tel: 01-236 3632/6487.
- Contact a Family (31 Tooley Street, London SE1; tel: 01-403 0969) aims to bring together families with handicapped children, and especially to provide early support.
- Cystic Fibrosis Research Trust, 5 Blyth Road, Bromley, Kent BR1 3RS; tel: 01-464 7211.
- The Down's Children's Association, Quinbourne Centre, Ridgacre Road, Birmingham B32 2TW; tel: 021-427 1374.
- The Haemophilia Society, 16 Trinity Street, London SE1 1DE; tel: 01-407 1010.
- In Touch (10 Norman Road, Sale, Cheshire M33 3DF; tel: 061-962 4441) arranges meetings between parents of handicapped children, and produces a newsletter.
- Handicapped Adventure Playground Association, Head Office, Fulham Palace Playground, Bishop's Avenue, London SW6; tel: 01-731 2753.

Spina bifida is an abnormality of the backbone and spinal cord. In severe cases the child is paralysed from the waist down.

• Invalid Children's Aid Association (126 Buckingham Palace Road, London SW1 9SB; tel: 01-730 9891) provides a postal information service, and helps of all kinds for parents of handicapped babies.

• The Lady Hoare Trust for Physically Disabled Children, 7 North Street, Midhurst, West Sussex GU29 9DJ; tel: 073-81 2696) will give advice and help for all physically disabled children.

• The Leukaemia Society, Hamlyns View, St Andrew's Road, Exeter EX4 2AF; tel: 0392 30032.

• MENCAP National Centre (Royal Society for Mentally Handicapped Children and Adults), 123 Golden Lane, London EC1Y 0RT; tel: 01-253 9433.

• Muscular Dystrophy Group of Great Britain, Nattrass House, 35 Macaulay Road, London SW4 0QP; tel: 01-720 8055.

• National Elfrida Rathbone Society (11A Whitworth Street, Manchester M1 3GW; tel: 061236 5358) provides social facilities of various kinds for families with educationally subnormal children.

• The National Society for Autistic Children, 1A Golders Green Road, London NW11 8EA; tel: 01-458 4375.

• The Nottingham University Toy Library (Nottingham; tel: 0602 56101) provides helpful information about both toys and how to cope with handicapped children.

• The Shaftesbury Society (112 Regency Street, London SW1P 4AX; tel: 01-834 7444) provides special residential care and teaching for all physically handicapped children, especially those suffering from spina bifida or muscular dystrophy.

• The Spastics Society, 12 Park Crescent, London W1N 4EQ; tel: 01-636 5020.

• Thalidomide Society, 19 Upper Hall Park, Berkhamsted, Hertfordshire HP4 2NP; tel: 04427 4717.

• Toy Libraries Association (Seabrook House, Wyllyotts Manor, Darkes Lane, Potters Bar, Hertfordshire EN6 2HL; tel: 0707 44571) provides advice and information about toys for disabled and other children.

• Association of Parents of Vaccine-Damaged Children, 2 Church Street, Shipston-on-Stour, Warwickshire CV36 4AP; tel: 0608 61595.

Books for parents of handicapped children

• Dorothy M. Jeffree, *Let Me Play* (Souvenir Press, 1977).

• Dorothy M. Jeffree and Roy McConkey, *Let Me Speak* (Souvenir Press, 1976).

• *A Guide for Parents of Handicapped Children* is obtainable free from The Scottish Education Department, Palmerston House, 6–7 Coates Place, Edinburgh.

• Janet Carr, *Helping Your Handicapped Child* (Penguin, 1980) is a very practical step-by-step guide to everyday problems.

• Cliff Cunningham and Patricia Sloper, *Helping Your Handicapped Baby* (Souvenir Press, 1978).

• Ann Purser, *You and Your Handicapped Child* (Allen and Unwin, 1981).

• Phyllis Willmott, *The Consumer's Guide to the British Social Services* (Penguin, 1967) contains useful information about the types of services that are available.

• Elizabeth M. Anderson and Bernie Spain, *The Child with Spina Bifida* (Methuen, 1977) is a rather academic book, but it clearly explains how the disease affects the child, what problems are likely to arise, and how to cope with them. It also has excellent lists of sources of information and assistance of many kinds.

• Lindy Burton, *The Family Life of Sick Children* (Routledge and Kegan Paul, 1975) concentrates on cystic fibrosis, but is helpful for other illnesses also. Again this is an academic book, but there is an excellent and very useful self-help section at the end.

• Marian K. DeMyer, *Parents and Children in Autism* (John Wiley, 1979) is also an academic book.

• Sheila Hewett, *The Family and the Handicapped Child* (Allen and Unwin, 1970) describes the author's study of how one hundred and eighty families coped with spastic children.

TUG-BOAT

2. Children at risk

Every day in Britain two babies are murdered by their parents, resulting in a frightening several hundred deaths each year. These numbing statistics cause most of us to feel horrified and repelled. Primarily there is the sensation of disbelief – how can parents inflict such pain and distress on their own child? How can they continue to batter it, not in a single fit of rage but in a continual process of abuse which eventually leads to the baby's death?

Only recently have we become aware of the full extent of this problem. A problem that is more pronounced in areas of deprivation but which extends across all sections of society and involves fathers as well as mothers.

The first step towards understanding is to recognize that given sufficiently difficult circumstances baby battering is closer to all of us than we dare to think. Some parents who abuse their children were themselves abused when they were young, but in general the crucial factor that leads to child abuse is the gradual building up of stress. The baby may be particularly difficult in the first place; the parents' relationship under strain; perhaps there is violence there too; financial pressures can mean that everything is a battle. All that has to happen then is for an additional unexpected problem to be added to these underlying stresses. At that point the parent cannot cope with the crying, demanding child – it is all just too much, and in an outburst of fury the child is assaulted. From then on, unless something is done, it is a dangerous downhill path. The first horror of assaulting the child is overcome – it becomes an increasingly easier outlet for the stress that will not go away.

Counselling by social workers and others may reduce the problem but any long-term solution can only come from within the parents themselves. It is all too easy for us to imagine the baby batterer as a horrible person, an ogre that has nothing to do with us. We must stop pretending that child abuse is simply a social problem that affects other people; we must face the fact that it is something we might all be capable of. Once we have realized that, we have come a step closer to avoiding becoming baby batterers ourselves. Few parents have not felt so exhausted and infuriated at a child's behaviour that they have lost their temper. It is vital to recognize when the tensions and stresses have built up to such an extent that we are at breaking point . . . and anything might happen. Unfortunately we so ignore and hide away from this awful possibility that when it is about to happen we very often fail to realize it until it is too late.

Pat

The last straw

After the event you can always look back and find reasons and causes – things that until then appeared to have no lasting significance at all.

'When I was a child I broke my nose badly and I had a real hang-up about it – I even talked my mum into letting me have plastic surgery. So I had this wretched operation but it didn't really make things better . . . I think it wasn't my looks I wanted changed but my personality.

Well . . . it sort of goes back to when I was adopted. I never knew who my dad was, and at the back of your mind you can't help thinking that your own mother gave you up. If people can walk out on you how can you possibly be worthwhile?'

By the time she was twenty Pat had married, and she and her husband had a delightful little girl.

'Susie was marvellous for my ego. I'd married this good-looking man – which I never thought I would – and now I had this exceptionally pretty baby . . . you know, I just felt marvellous.'

To see Pat and Susie together you would never have believed that anything could go wrong. Susie was a very good baby – even-tempered and easy to bring up – and Pat doted on her.

There was one problem, however: Pat wanted a boy. So a year later she and her husband decided to have another child.

'I'd hoped that Susie was going to be a boy – not that I was disappointed when she was born. So when John was born I felt fantastic – this was it –

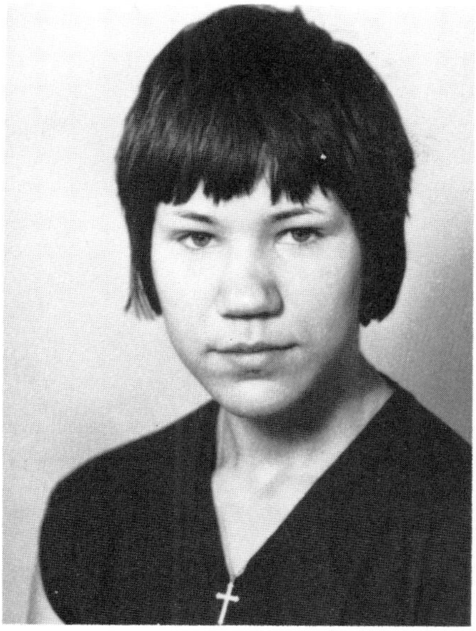

Plastic surgery straightened her nose but could not solve her deep-rooted problems. When she married a handsome man Pat began to feel that life was looking up.

I'd arrived; husband, pretty little girl, and now this handsome little boy. It was wonderful, it really was . . . for the first half hour.'

However, all was not well. The consultant returned to tell Pat that her little boy had breathing problems – he would have to stay in hospital for some time.

'Suddenly, I hadn't done as well as I thought I had. I felt inferior again, as I saw all the other mothers who had their babies with them.

The first real problem was that I wanted to breast-feed him, but I wasn't allowed to – he had to be kept in incubators and things. I'd breast-fed Susie, and it had been an enjoyable experience; it gave me a nice, close, warm feeling. Since John had been taken away from me I didn't feel the warmth towards him that I thought I should do . . . I suppose I thought breast-feeding might establish that warm feeling. I probably would have been mistaken. Maybe I wouldn't have enjoyed feeding him at all, because there wasn't the closeness, there wasn't the bond. But in my mind that was all I wanted to do. And I couldn't.'

John was taken to another hospital with better facilities, but this meant that Pat saw even less of him – gradually he ceased to be her baby at all.

'I desperately wanted to breast-feed him. I even said to the nurses, "Could I send my own milk to the other hospital?", and they just laughed. When he did finally come home he was a stranger. It was as if somebody had said, "This is your baby." But it didn't feel like my baby at all.

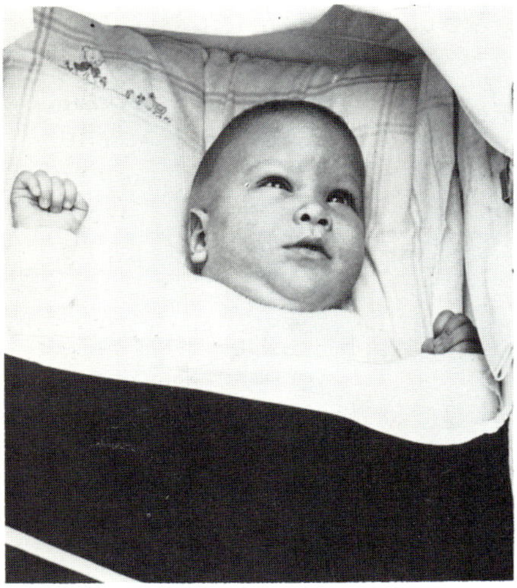

John, the son Pat had longed for, turned out to be less of a triumph than she expected, and soon she was taking out her frustrations on him.

The next best thing to breast-feeding John, I thought, to get him to love me and show my love for him, was to get him to take as much food as possible. But it took hours to feed him with the bottle. What made it worse was that other people seemed able to get him to do it. I was just so uptight the whole time, and then John would go very tense and stop sucking. The whole performance took so long that by the time I'd finished it was time to start again.'

Pat never had to think about her relationship with Susie; it just happened. With John it looked as if it was never going to happen. From the moment, half an hour after his birth, when he was taken away, whatever warmth there had been gradually seeped out. As the warmth went so the tension and worry rose; secretly Pat knew that things were not right.

'Had he been my first child I don't think I would have had a clue. I would have thought that all first-time mothers feel this way. But I'd had a good experience – I knew something was wrong. I felt tense all the time, and I was worried because of these feelings that I had for him – or didn't have for him – they were just so very different from those I'd had for Susie.

I'd try to feed him and he'd choke, and I'd think, I know it's ridiculous, but I'd think he was doing it deliberately . . . deliberately, even though he was only a two-month-old baby. I suppose I tried to put the guilt of my feelings onto him . . . it was his fault . . . he was being difficult . . . he was the one to blame.'

If everything else had been all right Pat would probably have mended her relationship with John. But the happy family was turning sour . . . for the time being there were only a few signs.

'My husband had been so proud of his daughter. She used to be the centre of attention, and that made me the centre of attention too. All of a sudden his attention switched to his son. The only topic of conversation seemed to be John . . . always John. I don't know why but it made me feel resentful – it made me feel inferior – as if it drew attention to the fact that I hadn't done well. But it also made me disgusted with myself. Why did I feel like that? What was the matter with me? And of course it was John that got the blame. I felt nothing for him. Well, at the best nothing. At the worst, hate.'

The tension in the household grew as Pat and her husband became more antagonistic towards each other.

'I don't think we were a couple that communicated at all. We weren't the sort of people that could sit down and talk about their feelings. There was a certain amount of violence within the marriage . . . both of us physically attacking each other when tempers got frayed. None of that helped.'

The perfect life that Pat had once had in her grasp was now beginning to fall apart. Finally after she had fed John one day Pat could take it no more.

'I sort of picked him up, and I just shook him and shook him. All my temper and frustration came out. John really howled and normally he was quite a passive child, but at least I felt he was acknowledging me. I got a funny perverse sort of satisfaction – he could no longer just ignore me.

Initially there was a release of emotion but then afterwards I felt tremendously guilty . . . and thought I'm sure other parents don't carry on like this . . . I wondered whether I was going mad or something.'

By shaking John, Pat thought that she was venting her anger in a safe way – but in fact shaking is very dangerous as it can result in damage to the baby's brain. It was not long before Pat was regularly taking her frustration out on John.

'It just went on and on . . . the shaking progressed to slapping him and throwing him onto the bed . . . and then I actually hit him and bruised his arm. When you've ill-treated a child once it becomes easier to do it a second time. The child becomes an object – it's no longer a person any more . . . I certainly didn't think, "This is flesh and blood." You are just faced with this irritating *thing* . . . it's not till afterwards when you see what you've done that you think, "Good grief, it's a person . . . it's my child."'

Eventually Pat's guilt led her to call in the National Society for the Prevention of Cruelty to Children (NSPCC).

'At that point I really did feel bad and wicked. Quite honestly I expected a man in uniform to arrive and either take me away, or take the child away. I was at an all-time low . . . I think I was really past caring.'

The man from the NSPCC turned out to be very helpful. He visited Pat regularly to talk to her and discuss her problems and feelings. Pat stopped taking everything out on John. After eighteen months of help and understanding from the NSPCC it was suggested that it was not necessary to keep up the same number of visits.

> 'It was about that time that my marriage was finally breaking up and I said that I really wanted them to carry on but they just suggested Marriage Guidance. I couldn't face starting from scratch again, and when he left the old treatment just returned. In fact it became worse than it had ever been before anyone called.'

By this time John became not only a focus of Pat's anger, but a means of getting back at her husband.

> 'I just couldn't cope with the strain of it all . . . John as always was the one to suffer. After a little while it was actually beginning to make him quite ill . . . it was a way of getting my husband's attention. I passed from a grey area through to a black disturbed area where the whole aim was to make John as ill as possible so that my husband would notice and come back and live with us. To a certain extent it worked – he came and went three separate times. In the end I went too far.
>
> My husband was saying that he was going to go and live with his girlfriend – but he hadn't gone, and he wouldn't say what he was doing, and I couldn't stand all the not knowing . . . I was annoyed with him not making up his mind. I just got hold of John and punched him out of frustration – it was the culmination of the mixture of emotions that had dragged on for months. For some time violence had been a common event. To start with I'd taken John off somewhere – to the toilet or the bathroom, and given him a sly whack in there, but in the end I was past caring where I was or who I was with.'

When John arrived at nursery school with a black eye, the school called in the authorities, and John was taken to hospital.

> 'I didn't feel relief, or upset, or even fear, just a numbness really. But although I didn't love John I still didn't want anybody else to have him. There was always that conflict – a bit of me that was maternal.
>
> When I went up to the hospital I was horrified. Inside, I felt absolutely sick. I couldn't hide from it any more. It was the awful little things that hit me . . . the photos of his injuries, that later were used in court . . . it was like . . . like a nightmare.'

Once in court Pat's overwhelming feeling was to try and keep John, even though at another level there was no reason for her to do so. Pulled in opposite directions Pat believed what she said at all times but her answer to one question often contradicted her answer to the next.

> 'When I realized that they might take John from me, I had this terrific indignant feeling: "How dare they! This is my child they're talking about taking away." At that point I'd forget about all the awful things. Instead all

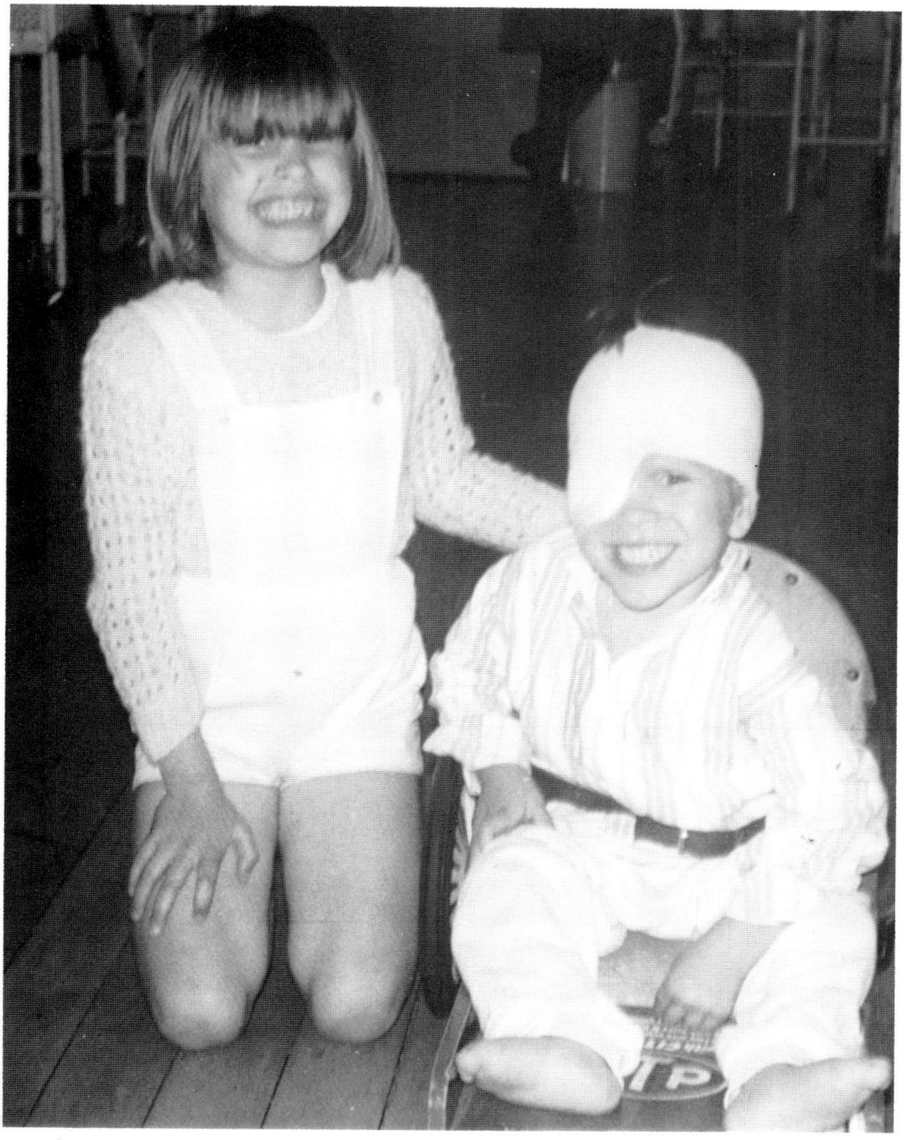

In the end John was taken to hospital

I thought was, "I don't want this to happen . . . I don't want it to happen. If they could just let me have him back – I'll never do it again, I've learned my lesson. How dare they suggest taking him away; I know it's not going to happen again, I know I'm not going to do this any more."

As the photos were passed round I would have to look at them to identify John. They were terrible photos – photos of his injuries. All I could hear were the odd words, really scaring words, echoing round and round. Was this real? And I'd look down at these pictures and they might just as well have been holiday snaps – someone else's snaps at that. I had no feeling about them, it was as if they had nothing to do with me. It was a numb, unreal time – I was very disturbed.'

Pat denied everything and appealed against the decision. It made no difference. She was separated from her son and it was seven years before the Care Order was revoked and he was returned to her. During this period Susie, her daughter, had begun to behave very strangely, and it was suggested she went to a special school. The idyllic scene had completely collapsed. Pat's husband had left, John had been taken away, and Susie was no longer the charming little girl. The court recommended psychiatric help.

'The good thing was that I got to see a psychotherapist, and I finally broke down and confessed. It was only then that the enormity of what had happened came home to me. I said that it had all been my fault – and that I'd been lying . . . it all came tumbling out. Oh, it was such a painful time – all of a sudden you wake up and have to face what you've done . . . to know that you did all these things.

You feel a bit like somebody who's lost their memory and suddenly it comes back and you find you've done a murder. It is like a giant flashback. Within half an hour I saw the terrible truth of everything. I was spared nothing. I had nothing to fall back on, no excuses – it was all there, raw. I just cried all the time, in fact for almost two weeks. There was so much pain you know, so much pain.'

That was the turning point. From then on everything that Pat did was positive.

'I decided to go and see the social worker and do the "true confession" bit. It was agony – like being outside the headmaster's office. But it was a move in the right direction. There was more pain and more hurt from the time that I confessed than during all the time when I was actually doing things and lying. It's really strange. But I did feel relieved. It was years before I could feel good about myself, but there was enormous relief and not having it on my conscience. Somehow I had always known that it was hanging over me like a great weight. It didn't come out, but it did show in other ways – I slept badly and ate badly, things like that. While I was telling the lies and saying that it wasn't me I lost three or four stone.'

Some years later when Pat had regained her self-confidence she set up a group called Parents Anonymous. It was based on the idea that a parent in trouble could telephone and have someone on the other end of the line to talk to about their problems – someone who is not going to be shocked by what is said, someone who may have experienced similar feelings.

'I think people's lives are like giant one-armed bandits. For most people the wheels are whirling all the time, but for some, because of their childhood, or present circumstances – housing or unemployment – some of the wheels are set. Two plums are already showing, and as a result the last one is going to come up more often than for the rest of us. It could be anything. For me, the day I gave John a black eye, I think it was a power cut. For other people it could be the milk boiling over or the dog running away. For most of the parents who ring us up it is like that – two of the wheels have jammed, and they know the odds on the third are too high.'

The most dangerous thing is to pretend nothing is happening. Fear of the shock of others, and fear of admitting it to yourself, make it all too easy just to deny that anything is the matter. From her own experience and from all those that have been helped by her organization, Pat is sure the only answer is to be as honest and open about it as you can.

'As a parent you know that something is wrong – even if you can't articulate exactly what it is. Whatever you do, tell somebody – I can't stipulate who. For some, talking to us anonymously on the phone is best, for others a relative. You must pluck up courage, and talk, talk to somebody. Don't be fobbed off, as I was, by people saying, "Yes, I feel like that," or "I know how you feel." You need to say, "I'm not just depressed, and I'm not just getting angry, but I've actually shaken my child, or smacked her too hard, or bruised her," or whatever. You've got to be honest. It may shock the person you are telling – especially if it's a relative – but you can only solve the problem by admitting that it is happening. Until you have done that, nobody is going to be able to help. It is very difficult, but it is a lesson I had to learn the hard way.'

What you can do

Child abuse is not confined to broken homes, nor to families in slum dwellings; it happens in ordinary middle-class households, too. It could happen in yours.

When the stresses of life build up, do not take it out on the baby; talk to someone instead. The only way to solve the problem is to admit that it is happening; until you have admitted that, nobody is going to be able to help you. You then have six different options.

- First, can you talk to a relative? Your mother, your aunt, your sister? This is bound to be difficult; no one likes to admit, even to himself, that he could even consider battering his own baby – but it may be worth it. There will be disbelief, shock, and perhaps disgust, but if you have the courage to get through that then a relative who knows you, and the family background, may be able to give you the support you need.
- Secondly, you can obtain immediate help on the telephone without anyone knowing who you are. Call Parents Anonymous in London, Birmingham, Nottingham, or Coventry (in the telephone directory under 'Parents'). Or contact the Organization for Parents Under Stress (OPUS, 29 Newmarket Way, Hornchurch, Essex RM12 6DR; tel: 04024 51538) who will give you the name of a group in your area. Or call the Samaritans. In each case there is a 24-hour service, and you will get a friendly, non-critical, sympathetic listener at the other end – not someone who will be shocked at what you have

done, or thought about doing, nor someone who will try to tell you what to do, but someone who will try to understand. Parents Anonymous is run entirely by people who are experienced and know what the pressures are like.

• Thirdly, you can telephone the National Society for the Prevention of Cruelty to Children. The NSPCC exists to prevent injury to children, and it attempts to protect children not by separating them from their families, but by listening to the problems of the parents with sympathy and understanding. Call them at any time, day or night (see under 'National Society' in your telephone directory). If you do not want to give your name they will not insist, but they do like to meet parents, and they will usually get someone round to meet an urgent case within twenty-four hours. When there is no panic they will arrange a meeting within a few days at a time that suits everyone concerned. The 'inspector' who visits you will be an ordinary person, without a uniform, in an ordinary car – no painted or labelled vans – and will chat to you for maybe an hour, trying sympathetically to understand your problem. The first aim is to reduce the stress and the strain, and to make sure the child is not at risk; they have power to put children in care, but never do so except in the very last resort. They will refer you on to a specialist if they think necessary, but if possible they will treat you at home, with the welfare of child and family in mind.

• Fourthly, you can contact the Social Services. Consult the telephone directory (see under e.g. 'Leeds City Council, Social Services') for the number and address of the nearest office. You can either telephone or visit them in person; the offices are generally open from 8.30 a.m. to 5.00 p.m. during the week, and in many areas there is a 24-hour telephone service – look for the emergency after-hours number. Tell the Duty Officer that you are under stress and are worried about your child. You will not be required to give your name and

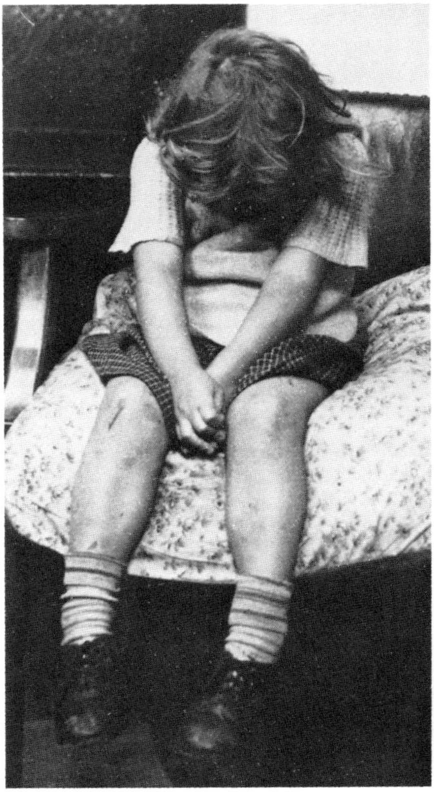

The NSPCC provides immediate help for some 50,000 children in this country each year. This child was emotionally abused and neglected until her spirit was broken.

address before anyone talks to you. From then on, the service will be similar to that provided by the NSPCC; you can visit them yourself, or a social worker will call on you at home; no uniform, no labelled van.

The Social Service Department may be called in by the school, by the doctor, or by any public services department, if they think there are serious domestic problems that put the children at risk.

The social worker's first aim will be to discuss the problem with you and see what help can be provided; perhaps he or she can suggest a day nursery or a child minder, help financially by explaining what benefits you might be entitled to, put you in contact with a psychologist or psychiatrist, get in touch with your doctor, or the school. The last thing they want to do is make you more unhappy.

In cases where there is a great deal of stress, the social worker may suggest that the child would be happier in care, perhaps for a week or two. 'Care' generally means a foster home – somewhere pleasant and friendly, with another family. You might find this a considerable relief, and if you agree, the arrangements will be made to suit everyone. You will be able to visit your child, and you will not be deprived of any parental rights. There will be no court hearing.

When a child has clearly been injured, the social worker will ask the parents to allow a medical examination; if the doctor believes that the injury is non-accidental then the child may be admitted to hospital. If the parents refuse to co-operate the Social Service Department may get a Place of Safety Order from a magistrate, which gives them the right to remove the child from danger; if necessary they will return with the police to ensure this. Within twenty-eight days of a Place of Safety Order, or if the child seems to be in danger, there will be a court hearing, at which the Department will apply for a Care Order. The parents may go to the court; they have the right to be represented and they have the right of appeal against the decision. If they lose, then the child will be committed to care.

Taking a child into care is the last resort. The social worker will try everything possible to help before suggesting care, and will provide continuing support.

- You do not have to become involved with social workers; instead you can go to one of the counselling services, such as Marriage Guidance (*see* page 218) – they are helpful in all family problems – or a local Family Crisis Centre (look under 'Family' in your telephone directory, or call the Citizens Advice Bureau (CAB) to find out whether there is one in your area). You will have to make an appointment, and then spend an hour with your counsellor, perhaps once a week. This represents quite a commitment but you may well get the assistance you need to sort out the family.
- Lastly, you can seek medical help. If you have injured your baby go at once to the accident or emergency unit of your nearest hospital, or call your family doctor. Tell the truth, if you can, about the cause of the injuries, for, apart from anything else, that will help you to obtain the best treatment. Otherwise talk to your own doctor, or to the health visitor, or to the staff at the baby clinic.

Money and other problems You may be able to relieve the stress indirectly by tackling some of the other causes. Are you short of money, for example? The CAB will tell you about any benefits or assistance you may be entitled to, and will also give you, free, simple financial advice, such as the best place to borrow money.

Shelters Battered wives can always find a refuge. Telephone the Samaritans, or WIRES (0742 755290).

Books you can read There are two American books which explain how baby battering starts, how it continues, and how difficult it is to prevent. These are:

- C. Henry Kempe and Ray E. Helfer, *Helping the Battered Child and his Family* (J. B. Lippincott, 1972)
- Ruth S. Kempe and C. Henry Kempe, *Child Abuse* (Open Books, 1978, and Fontana paperback, 1978).

Although American law is different, parents and children have much the same relationship to one another as they do in this country.

- Jean Renvoize, *Children in Danger* (Routledge and Kegan Paul, 1974, and Penguin, 1975) and *Net of Violence* (Routledge and Kegan Paul, 1978, and Penguin, 1979) discuss the origins of family violence.

3. For the sake of the kids

There is nothing new about wanting divorce; indeed the ancient civilizations – of Babylon, Greece, and Rome – all had extensive provisions for the breakdown of marriage. Only with the phenomenal spread of Christianity did separation become a problem. Marriage was then incorporated into the Church and became an aspect of Christian belief. This resulted in ideas of absolute monogamy, faithfulness, and indissolubility – 'till death us do part'. Marriage was no longer a business contract, probably arranged by relatives, but a romantic union backed by the power of the Church. By the sixteenth century no marriage was valid unless conducted by a priest, and in Catholic countries the bond of marriage once undergone could not be broken. Divorce was banned.

Over the last hundred years the weakening of the influence of the Christian Church has inevitably led to a return to more flexible views on marriage and a greater incidence of divorce. The number of broken marriages has now reached what we would once have considered epidemic proportions. For every three couples who marry in Britain this year, one couple will get divorced, and for those who marry under the age of twenty the figure is one in two.

Marriage is defined as the legal recognition of sexual union, and its social function is largely a matter of legal rights, obligations of the parties, and questions of inheritance. But these are not the issues that concern most parents when considering divorce. The break-up of a marriage inevitably causes great distress, both to the couple and to those close to them, but especially to their children.

Who is going to look after them? Where will they stay? Will the children be unhappy separated from one of their parents? Lurking in the background is the spectre of delinquent children from broken homes. These questions and fears are often sufficient to persuade couples to stick together and try to patch up their shaky relationship.

The evidence suggests that a broken home in itself rarely causes harm to a child; what matters far more are the living conditions and the attitudes of the parents. Bad housing or a breakdown in the child's relationship with the parents, through erratic or overstrict discipline, are often the causes of any long-term problems.

There are of course no simple answers and any decision must take into account the age of the children, the circumstances of the parents, and obviously the state of the marriage. The central concern will be for the well-being of the children, and it may not necessarily be the best course of action for their parents to stay together. For caught in a battle between two incompatible people the distress caused to a child can far outweigh the damage done by the parents separating.

However, provided the children are old enough there is probably no more sensible place to start than to discuss it with them.

People not children

Elizabeth was fifteen. Exams were coming to an end and the summer holidays were on their way.

> 'I was sitting around at home with my mother, and she said to me, "I want you to keep the day after you finish your O-levels free, because we're going out." She'd mentioned it before; so I knew it was some kind of mystery excursion – I was really quite excited about it. So I said, "Mum, Mum, tell me where we're going." She turned round to me, looked me straight in the eye and said, "Don't you know?" Well, I hadn't got a clue . . . I mean how was I to know? It began to take on all sorts of ominous overtones – there seemed to be more in it than a day in the country or whatever. But, it still never occurred to me that this was anything serious.'

Elizabeth soon forgot about the conversation; the last thing she was concerned about was what her parents were up to.

> 'You know what it's like – I was obsessed with myself and my boyfriend; at the time I was hopelessly in love, all I could think about was this guy.
>
> The night I finished my O-levels we went out for a little celebration. We sneaked into the pub as you do, and the following morning I had an enormous hangover, slept in late and got up about twelve. I can't remember why

Elizabeth

but I went into my mother's bedroom and out of the window I saw my mum putting things into the back of the car. I couldn't work out what she was doing taking loaves of bread from the house to the car rather than the other way round. I thought well, there's something a bit odd here . . . but I couldn't work out what the hell . . . so I thought I'd better get to the bottom of this.'

Elizabeth went downstairs to find her mother putting ornaments into a packing case. It still did not occur to her what was happening – somehow it wasn't an option she had considered.

'Exasperated, I said, "Mum, what are you doing?" She turned round and said, as if it was a commonplace remark, "We're leaving your father." My mother was quite calm. I sort of just stood there – in a way it didn't surprise me, in a way it did. I wasn't shocked that she wanted to do it, but it's always a shock when it actually happens.'

A few minutes later her younger sister, Helen, returned from school, and on hearing the news burst into tears.

'I remember thinking it was odd at the time; I couldn't work out why she was crying. All I wanted to know was where were we going. As long as I could carry on seeing my boyfriend – that's all that mattered. I phoned him up and told him that something very odd had happened, and he said, "You're not going to finish with me are you?" You see we were hopelessly in love. Of course it all fell apart two weeks later and we weren't really in love at all, but at the time that was all I could think about.'

Elizabeth's mother finished the packing; she left her husband's tea in the oven, and put a note on the television set where he could not help seeing it. The girls and their belongings were bundled into the car, and driven to the other side of London to stay with a man they had never met before – a man they had no reason to be with, no reason to like.

'I could understand my mother not wanting to be with my father, but I felt that if she was going to be with any man at all it should be him; he was the only real man that had any right to her. Because I sort of felt she was ours, it wasn't fair that she should be anybody else's . . . I suppose I was jealous in a way . . . I never rationalized it to myself – you don't like to think of yourself as jealous, but I was.'

Elizabeth had left their home and her father with reluctance but with no great emotional shock. It was not until that evening, when she finally asked her mother why she had left, that the force of what was happening came over her.

'I'll never forget it . . . I was sitting on a climbing frame outside the house, and my mum said that the reason she'd left my dad was that she wasn't entirely happy where she was, but more importantly because she had met

> somebody else she wanted to live with. I couldn't take it – I felt angry . . . angry that my mother should bring this stranger into our lives. He was sitting upstairs waiting to be met, but I wouldn't go and see him.'

The first few weeks of living with 'Mum's new man' were particularly difficult. He went out of his way to be good to Elizabeth and her sister, but it wasn't the same; and then there were all the little things that he didn't know about, or that didn't mean anything to him.

> 'About a year before my parents split up I bought my mother a little present – it was because I felt guilty really. I felt guilty because my mum had tried to talk to me about her problems and I just didn't want to know. But afterwards I felt guilty and so I got her this cruet set. I wrapped them up and left them in my mum's bedroom with a note saying, "Mummy, please cheer up." Well, within two weeks of moving in with this new man, he had broken both the things – the salt and pepper. So I went out and bought her another – but it wasn't the same. It was one of those things that cuts you down the middle.'

Children take for granted the emotional ties they see between their parents. They look at their parents not as separate individuals who choose to express their warmth for each other but rather as a single unit that just happens to behave like this. Your own parents are always the standard by which everything else is judged – no matter how eccentric they really are, to you they are never other than normal.

When a parent forms a new relationship this forces the children to see both their parents as separate people making their own decisions, and that in turn can undermine the certainty of their lives. Elizabeth's mother was particularly careful not to show too much affection for her boyfriend too soon.

> 'Mum was thoughtful, she didn't do it overtly, not for months and months, if ever in fact. They were obviously very physical, very much in love; that, I later came to accept, but I don't think I could have handled them snogging in the sitting room, or anything like that – I just don't think I could have handled it. They both appreciated that but in a way that was awful itself, I mean dealing with us with kid gloves, choosing the right thing to do. But my mum had it all planned, she'd thought it out so carefully, every eventuality – even how to behave in front of us.'

Not surprisingly, Elizabeth soon decided she would like to see her father.

> 'I discussed it with my sister, and then we went up to Mum and said, "We'd like to go home now please." It was obviously very traumatic for her, but she took us back – she dropped us at the bottom of the road. We trailed up the road, my sister was carrying an enormous teddybear that went with her everywhere at the time, and duvets were stuffed under our arms. We arrived at the door like two little waifs and strays and my dad said, "Hello." That was about it. But we both stayed.

Elizabeth and Helen had always assumed that their parents and their home were forever.

We had to go to him; he was the hurt party. We couldn't let one of our parents be hurt. She had "him" – that was the thing – so we had to go and look after Dad in case he was unhappy, in case he wasn't getting enough to eat. It's very odd really.'

Elizabeth stayed with her father for a few months; she looked after him at a time when things must have seemed pretty bleak for him. But after a while she realized she missed her mother too, and although she was still angry with her she was prepared to see that perhaps it was for the best.

'The fact that they slept together, and it was obvious they slept together, wasn't too hot. I don't know, though, I couldn't see how they could have done it better and still been happy in themselves. They'd obviously left their respective spouses and wanted to be with one another, so it was absolutely ridiculous for me to expect them not to sleep with one another . . .'

With the memories of how cold things had been at home the present arrangements seemed to make more and more sense.

'Dad had never cuddled Mum; of course we took it all as the normal way for things to go on, and we were astonished when we saw it could be different . . . and I'll never forget the rows . . . actually they weren't quite rows, just tension in the air.

Once they had made the break it appeared the obvious thing to do. Mum was in love – she'd told us so, she'd always been straight with us. We wouldn't have wanted her unhappy; we wouldn't have wanted her to go back. All his relatives cut her off, which was a shame because they were so fond of her really, and she was fond of them – you know all the maiden aunts he had and that sort of thing. Funny really. But I don't think either of us ever wished they'd get back together. Not at any stage. I mean why the hell should they? People always used to say to me things like, Don't you wish you mum and dad . . .?" Well, no, just no. Not at all, too much water under the bridge. Once it's done then that's it.'

One of the fears that most parents feel if they are breaking up is that the children will become attached to one parent or the other, but if Elizabeth is anything to go by it is not quite like that.

'I phoned my dad up last night and he poured his heart out to me because he's had a little rift with his lady. But the fact that he turns to me is very comforting because he's a fairly unemotional guy. It's like that with my mum too. I love my parents, I think they're marvellous. They were never suited to one another, but I'm very glad they got together because otherwise I wouldn't exist. But above all you know I get on great with them . . . I love them.'

Elizabeth and her sister were fortunate: because of good relationships with their parents they were able to cope with the break-up of their marriage fairly easily. If the children are younger, or the parents less considerate, or the circumstances harsher, the effects on the children can be damaging. But Elizabeth has no doubt about why parents should or should not stay together.

'It depends on how unhappy you are. I don't think it's sensible for anybody to be flagrantly unhappy in any situation. I don't see that it's going to benefit anyone at all. I can't see what is gained by hanging on. I don't see that people need be unhappy – children or otherwise. If the children are unhappy you've got to do something about it, and it doesn't necessarily mean that you have to stay together if that means that you'll be unhappy instead. If you're unhappy you've got to do something about it before it starts getting through to the kids.'

What you can do

The advice that follows is written for married couples. Almost all of it applies just the same to partners who are not married, except that the legal constraints of marriage are well-defined; so for 'marriage' read 'partnership' and for 'divorce' read 'separation' if you wish.

Every marriage is different, and the causes of strain are different in each case – from too much work, too much drink, too many lovers, to apparently simple things such as divergence of interests and constant nagging rows about meal times and the children's homework. It may look as though one partner is entirely to blame, or both may accept responsibility. In the end none of that matters a great deal. What does matter is that you are realistic about the future. However terrible life looks now, there is always a way forward; in fact there are always several, and it is important to choose a good one.

Children take for granted the ties between their parents

The children, if you have any, make all the decisions both more urgent and more difficult. Two people alone can fight, separate, come back together again, and on the whole hurt only one another. But children suffer too, all the way through, even though none of it is their fault; and that is why, while you are trying to decide what to do, your prime aim should be to protect the children. It is not to hide them from reality; not to lock them away; but to spare them from endless uncertainty and pain. Getting a divorce takes courage, but a destructive relationship does not do anyone any good, and the worst thing you can do is hide behind the children, stay together for their sake, and burden them with the feeling that all this bitterness has to be endured just for them. At the other end of the scale you and your partner may have drifted apart, and find it easy to leave one another, but difficult to imagine leaving the children. In that case you may have to think seriously about how you can rescue the marriage in order to stay with your children. Only you can decide which of these cases is more sensible.

Be realistic. Everyone wants rules for how marriages should work – and for how they should fail. There are none. Your marriage is a unique mixture of arrangements and agreements, and *you* have to sort it out. Only you know what it is really like from the inside, and conversely you do not know what any other marriage is like. Do not fall into the trap of comparing your marriage with a fairy tale – with the happy marriages that you imagine your friends, relations, and neighbours have. Marriage is not happy-ever-after bliss, whatever you have seen on the movies. Everyone has conflicts, and all you know of other people's marriages is what they choose to tell you, or let you see. Don't think that because you quarrel you are unusual.

One of the problems is that most of the time things are okay, and you do not bother to think about how the marriage is working, nor about the neighbours. Then suddenly a storm comes and you feel quite isolated. Everyone else's marriage looks wonderful, simply because you cannot actually hear them shouting at one another at that moment.

Do not underestimate the children. They are rarely as dim as their parents seem to think. They will know that you are unhappy, and they will know about divorce, since some of their friends' parents will have been divorced. So talk to them about what is going on and how you feel, and what you are planning to do. After all, it is their home and their family too, and if you try to cover it all up you are likely to give them the idea that there is something shameful to keep secret. Much better to say, 'We've been having terrible rows; we're unhappy together; we're going to try living apart for a bit; but we both still love you,' than to say, 'Everything's fine, but Mummy's going away for a few days.'

Most important, talk to your partner about what you really want to do. Not about what you ought to do; that is another trap to avoid – trying to do the right thing. Stop sniping at one another for a little and try to come to some sort of understanding about what you want, and what the children might want. Involve them in the decisions if you can do so without laying any 'blame' on them.

Professional help Some people find talking extremely difficult, particularly in the frosty atmosphere of a crumbling marriage, but you have to talk if you are going to reach any sort of sensible arrangement. There are professional counsellors who can help; first you should try Marriage Guidance (MG) (see under 'Marriage' in your telephone directory; *see also* page 218) or the Catholic Marriage Advisory Service. At MG you will find a sensible, down-to-earth person, who will listen, understand, and help you to look objectively at what is going on. MG's main aim is not reconciliation, but to find the best solution, whatever that is. They will give you time to get in touch with your emotions, space to allow relief of your anger, and a constructive atmosphere in which to clear away the dead wood and get near the truth about what you want.

Some people think marriage is an intensely private thing, like money or sex, that should never be discussed with anyone else; that if you have problems you ought to sort them out on your own; and that it is feeble to ask for help. Of course you can work it out yourself if you want;

but no one thinks any the worse of you for hiring an electrician, or a surveyor, when you need their professional expertise. That is what MG is there for – to help you help yourselves.

Family and friends are often too close for comfort; you may not want to talk to them about your marriage, and they are likely to take sides, rather than an objective view. There are other possibilities if MG does not work. The local Probation Service should be able to provide you with counselling. There may well be a local family counselling service, with a name like Family Network, or Family Crisis – look under 'Family' in the telephone directory or ask the Citizens Advice Bureau (CAB). Or try a social worker (*see* page 87). Again, tell the children what you are doing.

How to get a divorce If you are both sure that your marriage is doing more harm than good, and are determined to go separate ways, start making plans for separation. There is no need for one of the partners to move out of the house that day, or anything dramatic; be realistic, keep talking, and make plans so that the changes are brought about with as little pain as possible.

Beware of going to a solicitor immediately, unless your partner refuses to co-operate. You may need one in the end, but if you start with a solicitor you will probably cost yourself a great deal more pain and money than if you set out on your own. The problem is that once a solicitor is asked to act it is his duty to get the best deal for his client. That inevitably means pushing for rapid separation of the couple, demanding custody of the children, making extravagant financial claims, and acting out in court all the bitterness that has accumulated in the family. This can be terribly destructive, particularly to the children. Of course, there are good solicitors and bad solicitors, and none of them would deliberately harm the children, but additional trauma is a probable result of the solicitor's early involvement.

The best thing you can do to start with is come to a voluntary agreement with your partner over the terms of the separation, one that covers the most important matters: the house, the property, the money, and the children. When you are agreed, write letters to each other spelling out the terms. Don't try and make them sound legal; just simple. For example:

> Dear Margaret,
>
> I agree that you should stay in the house until the youngest of our children is eighteen. I will pay the rates and the mortgage, and will also send you once a month one-fifth of my salary. I should like to see the children at least once a week, preferably at weekends, and more often if they would like to see me; but otherwise I agree that they should stay with you . . .

Letters like this are not legally binding and cannot do you any harm at all when it comes to making a real legal settlement, but they can, if you both still agree, form the basis of a legal settlement. More important, they begin to lay down the ground rules for your separation. Provided that you both keep copies, you can see, three months later, what you actually agreed about the car or the dog. There are two things to remember about letters like this. Bitterness and aggravation are likely to develop during separation, even if it is not there already; you will gain considerably if you can get these letters written when you are still amicable and on speaking terms. It is much harder when you are not. Do not wait for a crisis to develop. Secondly, do not ask for things you do not want; most people tend to feel that they ought to ask for custody of the children, even though they would hate to be one-parent families. This applies in the court too; ask for exactly what you want, and do not ask for what you think you ought to want.

At this stage, also, it is important to get the bitterness out into the open; accept that your marriage has gone wrong and do not use the children as weapons. Avoid at all costs the sort of twisted reasoning that says, 'I don't love our daughter any more; in fact I never did; and that's because you always spoiled her; it was your fault that we had any children in the first place. . . .' You must accept that you two partners have made a mess of your partnership; the children are not to blame. You can only make the whole trauma much worse for them if you insinuate that it is all their fault.

If you cannot agree, or find it hard to talk, try the help of a counsellor. MG may help, or the family services mentioned above. In addition there are conciliation services in many parts of the country – not reconciliation services to try and bring you together, but counsellors whose aim it is to help you through the process of deciding what you both want from the separation. Ask the local County Probation Service or the CAB whether there is one in your area.

This is not a legal process; the end results will have to be ratified by the Divorce Court. The idea is to go to the court with a reasonable deal already worked out for the whole family. Other possible sources for help are the Divorce Court Welfare Staff, or the Probation Service – the latter is, however, required to write a report for the court, and will therefore necessarily be involved in the process of making the decisions.

Provided you can come to an amicable arrangement, there is no hurry about going through with divorce, unless one of you wants to get married again.

If you do want a divorce, the procedure is explained in a booklet *Undefended Divorce*, which you can obtain from the CAB or from a divorce court (ask the CAB for the address of the nearest, or look in your telephone directory). Basically what you need to do is get a petition form (three copies, or four for adultery) from the court office, fill it in, file your petition, along with signed statements of arrangements for the children and a copy of the marriage certificate, plus the court fee.

The court will send on to your spouse (the 'respondent') copies of the petition and the statement of proposed arrangements, with notice of the court proceedings. Any co-respondent (your spouse's new partner) will be involved at this stage. You will then be sent a form of affidavit of evidence, which you complete and take to the solicitor or court for swearing.

Once all the papers are in, the Registrar considers the evidence. If he is satisfied he issues a certificate, and fixes a date for the pronouncement of the decree. Where there are children he also fixes an appointment before the Judge for the children's arrangements to be considered. Neither party need attend the court for the pronouncement of decree nisi – copies will be sent to them. The petitioner, however, must go before the Judge (in private at the court) to settle the arrangements over the children.

Six weeks after the decree nisi the petitioner completes a form of application for decree absolute and sends it to the court office. If the Registrar is satisfied he makes the decree absolute, and the court sends copies of the certificate to both parties.

The process of divorce takes several months; it is no good expecting to have everything settled in a week or two. You are unlikely to have to go to court more than twice, and then only for brief appearances. You do not need to involve a solicitor at any stage, unless there are still disputes or disagreements between you and your partner, or questions about, for example, the grounds for divorce.

Conditions for divorce in England and Wales You cannot file a petition for divorce within three years of the date of marriage. At least one party must be either legally domiciled in England or Wales (Scottish law is slightly different), or must have been resident there for at least a year.

The only ground for divorce is that the marriage has broken down irretrievably. This can be established on the basis of adultery, intolerable behaviour, two years' desertion, or separation for two years with consent or five years without. The detailed rules governing these are complex, and you should read the booklet mentioned above. You will need proof for adultery, or intolerable behaviour, and if your spouse is not prepared to confess, then you will probably need legal advice. You will also need legal advice if the divorce is defended.

Go to the CAB or to a local Law Centre and ask for their advice before you go to a solicitor; there may be no need to let yourself in for heavy solicitor's fees. Ask about the Green Form scheme, which is a system operated by most solicitors to give simple advice cheaply.

The one-parent family After separation you will have lost half of what made the family work. If you are looking after the children then you are a one-parent family and you have a series of logistic and financial hurdles to face. Who will collect the children from school if you go to work? Who will pay the grocery bill if you don't? The CAB can help a good deal here, since it knows about the services available, and what benefits and so on you can claim. In addition there are some organizations set up specifically to help one-parent families:

- Gingerbread is a national self-help association, with at least four hundred local groups. They provide advice leaflets on finance, housing, legal rights, etc. Write for information to Gingerbread, 35 Wellington Street, London WC2; tel: 01-240 0953.
- The National Council for One-Parent Families (255 Kentish Town Road, London NW5 2LX; tel: 01-267 1361) is a national charity which provides advice and information on all the problems that may arise.
- The Scottish Council for Single Parents, 44 Albany Street, Edinburgh EH1 3QR; tel: 031-556 3899.

It is important to be with your children

Books Anne Hooper, *Divorce and Your Children* (Allen and Unwin, 1981) is a detailed and helpful book which takes you step by step through the psychology and practical details of separation and divorce. There is plenty of sensible advice on how and what to tell the children, and on what they are likely to feel; there is also legal information and advice; and there are addresses of organizations that may be able to help you.

- Dr Lee Salk, *What Every Child Would Like Parents to Know about Divorce* (Harper and Row, 1978) is helpful about the feelings of children and parents during the break-up of marriage. It is an American book: the law is, therefore, different. You may, however, find the psychology helpful.
- *On Getting Divorced* (Consumers' Association) has helpful practical information.
- Jack Dominian is a psychiatrist, and his *Marital Break-Down* (Pelican paperback, 1968) is mainly about the reasons for divorce. It may help you to understand your own feelings about your marriage.

4. The unspoken problems

Sex has ceased to be something we do not talk about. Quite the reverse: today no woman's magazine is complete without at least one article about some aspect of our sex lives. From every advertising hoarding and bookstall, in every film and every television play, the importance of sex in our lives is repeated. But for all the interest in sex, we still keep our sexual problems to ourselves, and sometimes we avoid even recognizing them. In fact the apparent openness with which our society now looks at sex hides and sometimes even contributes to the basic insecurities which are found in almost all of us.

Sex may be perfectly natural, but it is not naturally perfect. In fact it is a peculiarly difficult – if exciting – aspect of our lives. As we grow up we learn to copy those around us, and if we do not get things quite right, we can correct our behaviour by comparing it with that of others. If we don't speak normally either someone will point it out, or we will notice the mistake ourselves. But with sex it is different. No matter how promiscuous you are you never have anything like the same knowledge of the norm, or of the range and diversity of behaviour, that you do in almost every other sphere of human activity. This is made worse by the secrecy that surrounds our sex lives and our sexual habits. As a result, we rely on the fictional and media stereotypes that we read about and see on the screen – and if we don't come up to the romanticized picture of how things should proceed, we keep quiet about it.

Problems with your sex life often lead to more than frustration in bed. For, just as a close relationship is made much stronger by sex, so it can begin to crumble when sex no longer works. It is because these problems, once started, are difficult to talk about with your partner, let alone anyone else, that they often escalate, causing much suffering on both sides.

The extent of the problem is immense: it is estimated that 50,000 couples every year in this country find their sex so unsatisfying that they wish they could find help. Masters and Johnson reckoned that one couple in two has sexual difficulties. There are sex counsellors but the number is relatively small. Doctors are in general not qualified to deal with sexual problems; they are probably as embarrassed to talk about them as you are but they are able to refer you to people who are specialists of some sort. In addition they can rule out the possibility that there is a physical problem, which should obviously be considered first before it is assumed that the difficulty is an emotional one.

The most common complaints in men are impotence (the failure to achieve or maintain an erection or reach orgasm) and premature ejactulation (when the orgasm happens much too quickly). In women the problem is primarily one of satisfaction, and in some cases of positive dislike resulting in physical difficulties such as vaginismus in which the involuntary contraction of the vagina makes penetration painful. It is obvious that these problems are not simply the man's problem or the woman's; a difficulty for one partner is just as likely to be related to the behaviour of the other, as it is to some inner psychological problem.

Sexual problems are not usually due to the psychological hang-ups of one person, but the joint failure of two people to treat each other in such a way that they both enjoy sex. The last thing that any couple should do if either of them feel unhappy about their sex lives is to keep quiet about it. The solutions to one partner's difficulties can best be solved by the couple together. However, our prejudices and worries about sex run very deep, and just talking about it may not help. You may simply be unable to talk about it. In these circumstances outside help may provide the answer . . . if it does, it can save an otherwise shaky relationship, and possibly turn misery into happiness.

Just too old?

Iris had always been rather shy – that is what attracted Len in the first place. It was three years before they were married, in June 1960. They had two children, and their relationship seemed to get better as the years went by. To start with sex was fun, something they took for granted, but then their problems began, problems that were very difficult for either of them to deal with, but particularly for Len.

> 'We'd been happily married for ten years, but over the next ten our relationship suffered.
>
> We used to have sex two, three, four times a week perhaps, but it deteriorated so gradually we hardly noticed it. These things creep up on you – like your children growing up, others can see it happening but you can't. I only realized there was something the matter when I couldn't do it any more . . . well, I was never able to maintain an erection long enough to perform, you know, the normal marital procedures. It got so bad that intercourse became an annual or bi-annual event.
>
> The strange thing was it wasn't as if I was getting past it. I would go to bed and would feel excited and randy, and capable . . . until I actually started. Ninety-nine per cent of the time I'd fail, I would just lose the erection, after two or three minutes I couldn't carry on . . . it just went. Completely.'

Normally if you are suffering from a disability or illness you can expect some sympathy and encouragement from your friends. Impotence is not like that: not only do you have to put up with the difficulty, but most men have to face it in secret. Moreover, rightly or wrongly, they feel it is an undermining of their manliness . . . of themselves.

Len and Iris were married in June 1960

Their troubles began after their second child

'It's like having to tell your parents you've failed your exams, but worse, because it's a very personal exam. I was very embarrassed, we didn't talk about it, and I certainly wasn't going to tell anybody else. I suppose I was a bit disgusted with myself . . . at my inability. I felt it was a reflection on me, on my masculinity. It is the sort of thing that happens to other people and not to yourself. It was an awful period in my life.'

It may have been tough for Len but it made Iris's life miserable as well.

'It was very frustrating, going to bed and . . . it was as if we might as well not be married. Marriage needs sex, just as your house needs bricks and mortar to keep it together. I'd go to bed wanting to have sex and then either he wasn't interested, or if he was, nothing could happen. I would lie awake at night and cry myself to sleep . . . it was so frustrating. I got very depressed and agitated; in the end I used to cry over the slightest thing.'

Len's impotence undermined his confidence in himself, but in a different way it also undermined Iris's confidence. Was there something she was doing that was wrong? Why wasn't Len interested in her any more?

'Sometimes I would think it was me . . . there was something the matter with me. I thought perhaps I don't look so nice now I'm getting a bit older. Perhaps . . . perhaps it is my fault.'

Although neither Len nor Iris realized at the time, the origin of their problem had begun only a few years after they married.

'Originally Iris was much less interested in sex than I was, at least she pretended to be, but the trouble was that it didn't really work for her. Anyway, on one occasion when we were trying out some rather lusty experiments, suddenly it all happened. Iris had found a position where she was able to get some satisfaction . . . she, sort of, controlled me, and I let her. I think that was the beginning of my problems. You see, I found it rather uncomfortable, and for Iris to achieve an orgasm it was a very laborious job, and always took a long, long time. Well, about twenty minutes . . . it doesn't sound that long perhaps, but when you are trying to maintain an erection and prevent yourself finishing too quickly, it is really off-putting. It was a curious balancing act, on the one hand I used to think of all sorts of things to stop myself coming, and on the other, I had to maintain an erection sufficient for penetration . . . and for long enough, and that was the difficulty.'

As soon as Len started to have trouble the problems multiplied, problems that until then had not even been apparent.

'Well, I mean, I wanted him . . . I wanted him to make love to me, but I didn't ask him. I just couldn't. I daren't . . . I didn't think it would be right. I couldn't touch him either, because if I touched him and I started to make a play, and then he still didn't want me, it would look worse than ever. So I used to lie there and think . . . "If only he'd start something, touch me, or give me a goodnight kiss, or something like that." During the day when I was cleaning up I would think, "Tonight – should I say something? Should I start something?" But then I thought, "If he doesn't want me and he rejects me what shall I do then?" I can't tell you what it felt like . . . it was terrible.'

As with almost all sexual problems, once theirs began there was a spiral of worry that only served to make matters worse. Built on a misguided belief that she was being considerate, Iris's reticence simply helped to accelerate the deterioration.

'I used to tell Len that it didn't matter . . . that it was okay if I didn't have an orgasm, as long as he was all right. Then afterwards I used to cry. Len would finish and lose interest and I would be left having almost reached a climax. It was like being very, very hungry and somebody comes along and puts a lovely dinner in front of you, and then just as you pick up your knife and fork they take it away. I would get so upset, and then it would upset Len because he had not managed to wait long enough. Gradually it got worse and worse . . . he would want me to reach a climax and I would be thinking, "Oh, let it happen, let it happen. . . ." I wanted it so much. And of course it didn't, it just went further away. It got so bad that I could never let myself go, there would always be other things on my mind . . . I was never at ease.'

As Iris was distracted by failing to have a climax, so Len was distracted at the thought of failing to keep an erection. Their sex life had fallen apart.

'In the end I think Iris gave up expecting anything from me. I was so worried about it . . . I couldn't even begin without watching myself, and waiting . . . that's what made me incapable. I couldn't get out of my mind the thought of failing . . . failing again. I was annoyed and angry with myself that there seemed to be so little that I . . . it was all so hopeless. There was no point even starting something I couldn't finish. I couldn't see the point of talking about it . . . there was nothing to talk about. I accepted the blame.'

However, Len could face the end of their sex life more easily than Iris.

'Len was prepared to let it drift but I didn't want to let it drift. I felt I was missing something. I wanted a love life, and I didn't want to lose it.

I didn't want any other men, only my husband, but I did have fantasies. I used to think I wish somebody nice would come and knock on the door and say, "Come out to dinner," you know, and we'd go out to dinner and then . . . the fantasy would pass and I would wish Len was more like that. Sometimes in bed after Len had failed I would imagine that Jim Reeves had come to the house and that he was here in the bedroom making love. At least that way I could get to sleep.'

In desperation, Iris forced Len to see the doctor. It wasn't an easy thing for Len to do . . . it took him ages to get round to it . . . but eventually he ended up at the surgery.

'I told the doctor, and, well there was virtually no reaction . . . he showed no reaction at all. He wrote out a prescription for some tablets – which were totally useless – and said hardly anything at all. It was as if I didn't really have a problem at all . . . there was no interest, no concern, nothing.'

Over the next five years there was little incentive to go back to the doctor. Len and Iris staggered on; they didn't talk about the problem – they just learned to accept it.

It was a chance conversation that was to make all the difference. Iris was supposed to go to the family planning clinic every six months to have her cap checked and occasionally to have a cervical smear. Recently there hadn't seemed much point and as a result she had not been for two and a half years. When she did go the doctor said it was time she had a new cap. 'I haven't used this one yet' was the obvious comment. A few more questions and the whole story came out. It was a great release to be able to tell somebody. At least somebody else knew – and if they knew, perhaps they could help.

Two weeks later Iris had followed the doctor's advice and persuaded Len to see another doctor. After a brief examination they were told there was nothing physically wrong, and therefore nothing he could do, but that they should go along to the Marriage Guidance (MG).

'Len and I came out of the doctor's and we thought, "That's stupid, going to the Marriage Guidance Council. Our marriage is all right; it's sex that is the problem." Anyway, we decided to give it a try, as we had nothing to lose.'

Telling other people about their sex problems did not come easily to Iris, and for Len it was obviously potentially even more difficult.

> 'We thought it was just going to be a waste of time – everything else had been. We were both very nervous when we went along for the first time – we didn't know what to expect. But I suppose I felt that I would clutch at any straw. I think Iris felt the same, it was a sort of now-or-never attitude that we had to adopt.
>
> Things began to get better from the moment we started to talk to the therapist. She's the sort of person that makes anyone feel at ease, whatever the subject. All of a sudden sex was accepted as being normal and desirable instead of something to be hidden . . . it's easy to talk to somebody then . . . and, you're not on your own any more.'

At the end of the first session they were told not to have any sexual intercourse at all for a few weeks. They were to start by caressing one another, just touching faces, hands, feet. Nothing intimate. A warm room, a soft light . . . one of them first and then the other. Iris thought it was ridiculous.

> 'I said to Len, "It's silly this, I don't think we'll bother going again." It seemed so stupid, just touching each other's hands . . . after twenty years of marriage it did seem very, very, silly. Anyway we decided at least to give it a try. So we sat in the front room with a paraffin lamp on, with a very low light. It felt like touching a stranger at first, but then it wasn't . . . it was nice, very nice. It was like the beginning of courtship again – discovering

The therapy recommended by their Marriage Guidance counsellor began with touching one another's face and hands

each other for the first time. I felt like a girl on her first date. It was very strange after all those years, and there we were just touching . . . that's all, just touching.'

By caressing and talking to each other Len and Iris were gradually learning, learning for the first time, what each other liked, what each other wanted. At the same time Iris started to feel less guilty about sex.

'Until then we always had the light off. I couldn't bear Len to see me. I was so shy. I don't know why, I can't express it, but I thought there was something wrong in being able to say what I wanted. And when I found that I could satisfy myself, again I thought, "This isn't normal, you shouldn't do things like this." After we saw the therapist I felt reassured, other people talked about this . . . it was normal after all.'

The following week they went back to see the therapist. Slowly the mistakes, which compounded over twenty years, had destroyed their sex life, if not their marriage, were eroded.

'Each week we would talk a bit more, and have a few different things to try out. One week she said, "Have a bath together." I had never even got undressed in front of Len. The thought of being in the bathroom with nothing on, and then to have a bath together . . . it was terrible. I felt ashamed at the thought of it.

The whole week I spent thinking, "I'll have a bath now, and I'll ask him." And then I'd think, "No, I'll leave it until tomorrow." Finally, I shouted before I had the chance to change my mind again. I think it was the thought of having to go down to the clinic and tell the therapist that I hadn't done anything. When she's trying to help, you just had to do it.

Anyway, it took a while to pluck up my courage, but once I did it, it got easier and easier. Having a bath together was one of the real breakthroughs . . . we washed each other and I think it sort of justified being naked.'

Since they went to see the therapist Len's impotence has become a thing of the past. Looking back, Len now realizes that his impotence was only the overt result of deeper and more general problems.

> 'I think we were insufficiently aware, well, I was certainly insufficiently aware, of feminine anatomy. I suppose, well, we were doing it wrong. It sounds ridiculous after twenty years, but that was it. You don't automatically do it right, it doesn't just come naturally. Iris never used to complain to me, or tell me what she wanted me to do, and at the same time she appeared to be happy with what was happening. I ended up satisfying myself without satisfying her, but it didn't suit me either . . . and that was what it was all about.'

The whole course took ten weeks. The therapist had wanted to stop after eight but Iris had insisted on two more to help her get over her shyness. In those last two weeks she was given a book about women's sexual fantasies.

> 'I realized from the book that other women had thoughts like mine. Thoughts that until then I felt were wrong. I thought I was odd thinking things like this. There was also an educational part telling you what to do . . . of course I had no idea what to do. I used to go to bed first and read it and think, "Oh, I'll try that." And of course . . . it worked.'

Len and Iris have been married for twenty-one years and their sex life is now better than ever before, and that has helped Iris in unexpected ways.

> 'I used to go to the doctor once or twice a month with different ailments: headaches, pains in my arm or my side. They just kept telling me it was in my mind, but I never believed them, they were so real. I used to start crying for no reason at all. I couldn't think what it was, now I know it all boils down to nerves and stress from being frustrated . . . and worried.'

For Len and Iris it seems so simple, all they needed to do was to discuss it with each other. And yet, Len doesn't really think that was possible.

> 'Iris could tell me now, but at the time neither of us knew the cause of the problem. We were both considerate towards one another and didn't want to harm the relationship – that's why we didn't talk. I think if we had been too critical harm would have been done. In fact I think if Iris had said too much it would have probably ended the affair.'

Sex is so personal, and therefore so difficult, that when things do go wrong we may need an outsider if we are to avoid painful criticism. Unfortunately, just because it is so personal that is precisely the most difficult thing to do, but it can make all the difference.

> 'We only wish we had gone along to see someone ten years ago. Since we saw the therapist it's been wonderful. I would say to anyone who can't deal with the problem themselves, take up your courage and go down and see a therapist . . . immediately!'

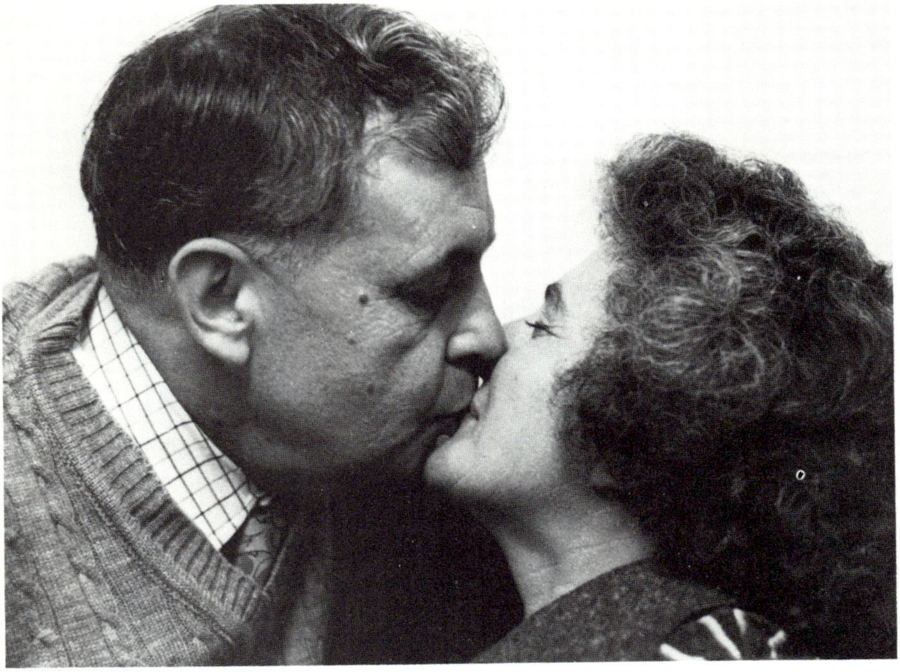

Today Len and Iris are happier than ever before

What you can do

There is no standard, no 'normal' sexual performance, and therefore no one but you can decide whether or not you have a problem; but if you are unhappy about your sex life you can probably improve it. The most straightforward way is to talk honestly to your partner about what you like and dislike, and to try resolving the difficulty together; but because sex is so difficult to talk about you may find it easier to approach someone else.

Professional help Occasionally there is a medical cause for any of the common sexual problems; you should therefore go first to your family doctor, or to a family planning clinic (see the telephone directory under the District or Area Health Authority) for a check-up. Most cases, however, have a psychological basis, and an excellent way to tackle this is with counselling. The best people to go to are Marriage Guidance (*see* page 218); their counsellors are trained in handling all types of personal problems, and they have special Marital and Sexual Dysfunction (MSD) clinics in most areas of the country. Their treatment is generally based on the Masters and Johnson technique of 'sensate focusing', and is essentially about learning to make love in a warm and relaxed way. The counsellors are not doctors, but ordinary people with their own sex lives, and often their own sexual difficulties. Treatment is absolutely confidential; no one else need ever know.

MSD clinics are for committed couples who want to improve their sex lives. Your first session will be used to find out what the difficulty is; the second will probably be devoted to history taking, and after that you will be asked to return for an hour of discussion perhaps once a week for at least three months. In addition you will be asked to do several hours of 'homework' in between sessions; so you have to be prepared to make a considerable commitment. However, the therapists are neither critical nor threatening – they will never laugh at you – and if you do make the effort you are likely to notice considerable improvement, for there is a high success rate.

If you cannot obtain help from MG, ask to be referred to a sex therapist either by the family planning clinic or by your family doctor. For a list of the sex clinics and therapists in your area, write with a stamped, addressed envelope to the Association of Sexual and Marital Therapists, P.O. Box 62, Sheffield, South Yorkshire. Or you can try a family counselling service such as Family Network. Look in the telephone directory under 'Family' (they have various names) or ask at the Citizens Advice Bureau (CAB).

Books You can borrow the books below from a library, or buy them from any good bookshop; if you don't want to go into a bookshop you can obtain them by mail order. The National Marriage Guidance Bookshop (Herbert Gray College, Little Church Street, Rugby CV21 3AP; tel: 0788 73241) will let you know the prices of the books you want, and send them when they receive your cheque; or you can use Access or Barclaycard.

You can order books by telephone from Blackwells (Broad Street, Oxford OX1 3BQ; tel: 0865 49111 and ask for the medical department), who will send you a bill with the books. Hudsons will also take telephone orders, and charge the books to your Access card (Hudsons Medical Bookshop, 12 Ethel Street, Birmingham B2 4BQ; tel: 021-643 8311). Do check the prices first; some of these books are expensive.

- Dr David Delvin, *The Book of Love* (New English Library, 1975, second edition 1981) is recommended by MG for basic information and advice about both the biology and psychology of sex.
- Bernard Zilbergeld, *Men and Sex* (Souvenir Press, 1979; Fontana paperback, 1980) concentrates on male sexuality.
- Women may be helped by Judish Silverstein, *Sexual Enhancement for Women* (Jay Publishing Co., 1978) and by Julie Heiman, and Leslie and Joseph Lo Piccolo, *Becoming Orgasmic* (Prentice Hall, 1977).
- Jane Cousins, *Make It Happy* (Virago, 1978; Penguin, 1980) is a practical down-to-earth guide to what sex is all about, written for young people, with a slight bias towards girls.
- Angela Phillips and Jill Rakusen, *Our Bodies Ourselves* (Allen Lane, 1978; Penguin, 1979) is a health book by and for women. It is clear and intensely practical on all aspects of female sexuality.
- Nancy Friday, *My Secret Garden* (Virago, 1975) is about women's sexual fantasies; this is the book that Iris found useful.
- Paul Brown and Carolyn Faulder, *Treat Yourself to Sex – A Guide to Good Loving* (Dent, 1977; Penguin, 1979) is a rather more advanced book with positive suggestions for revitalizing your sex life, but written in an unusual style that some may find off-putting. We don't all have the confidence to treat ourselves.
- Alex Comfort, *The Joy of Sex* (Quartet, 1978) is a well-known manual which glorifies the acts of sex with enthusiasm and line drawings. You may find it helpful, but don't let it put you off; the fact that he says something is fun doesn't mean that everyone will agree.
- David Mace, *Sexual Difficulties in Marriage* (National Marriage Guidance Council, 1972) is a very short and clear account of the most common sex problems and how counselling may help to solve them.
- For more detail on the biology and psychology of arousal, how it can go wrong, and how it can be put right, see

Helen Singer Kaplan, *The New Sex Therapy* (Bailliere Tindall, 1975; Penguin, 1978), or Fred Belliveau and Lin Richter, *Understanding Human Sexual Inadequacy* (Coronet paperback, 1971).

Contraception You can obtain birth-control information from your doctor, from a family planning clinic, from free leaflets provided by the Family Planning Information Service (27–35 Mortimer Street, London W1; tel: 01-636 7866), from the British Pregnancy Advisory Service (see your telephone directory), or from Family Doctor booklets sold through chemists. You can also go to MG to start with if you do not like the idea of talking to a doctor. The Brook Advisory Centres (see your telephone directory , or contact the head office at 233 Tottenham Court Road, London W1; tel: 01-323 1522) were set up specifically to advise young people on all sexual matters. Family planning clinics are happy to discuss the options with couples, and can also supply the contraceptives.

Sheaths can be obtained over the counter in chemists, from slot machines in public houses, and by mail order (there are advertisements in many magazines and newspapers). Contraceptive pills can are available only on prescription, but they and most other systems can be obtained free on the National Health Service.

Our Bodies Ourselves is extremely clear on the advantages and disadvantages of the various methods, and also on what happens at family planning clinics. *Make It Happy* has practical information on the different methods and how to use them. Carolyn Faulder's *Talking to your Doctor* (Virago, 1978) is a useful handbook intended to help women understand their gynaecological problems so that they can discuss them with the doctor.

Infertility Most young, sexually active couples will conceive within a year if they use no contraception. If you want a baby and you have waited longer than this, go to your family doctor; there may be a medical problem that can be solved. You may be referred to a special unit in a hospital. Your doctor may be paternalistic, and say, 'There, there! Let's leave it a bit longer.' Do not be fobbed off; be firm. There will be a specialist in your area. The British Pregnancy Advisory Service provide infertility help and treatment. There may be a local branch; look in your telephone directory or contact the head office at Austy Manor, Wootton Wawen, Solihull, West Midlands B95 6DA; tel: 05642 3225. You might like to contact The National Association of the Childless (318 Summer Lane, Birmingham B19 3RL; tel: 021-359 2113/4887), which provides information and counselling, and publishes a newsletter.

If you would like to consider adoption, the first stage is to contact the Social Services office, but adoption is a long, slow, difficult process.

Sexually transmitted diseases There are about a dozen diseases that can be passed from partner to partner specifically during sexual contact, including gonorrhoea and syphilis which are commonly called venereal diseases (VD). None of these sexually transmitted diseases (STDs) can be caught from lavatory seats or towels. The most common symptoms are painful or frequent urination, discharge from the penis or vagina, or sores and itching on or near the genitals. For recorded information about STD symptoms ring 01-246 8072. Some of these diseases can be serious if they are not treated, and almost all are curable. The important thing to remember is *Don't worry; do something.*

If you suspect you have an STD you must avoid sex, and seek treatment. You can go to your family doctor, but you will probably be sent straight to a clinic, and as you do not need a referral you may as well go straight to the clinic in the first place. Most large general hospitals have such a 'special clinic'. Either look in the telephone directory under 'Venereal Disease', or telephone the most convenient hospital and ask whether there is a special clinics for STDs. If they do not have one they will tell you where the nearest is; if they do they will tell you when it is open and where to find it. You do not need to make an appointment; just go along to the clinic.

Treatment at the clinic is free and totally confidential. You will be asked for your name when you arrive, but you do not even have to give your real one, and you may anyway be given a number for identification. You will have to wait for an examination by a doctor; you will then have blood, smear, swab, and urine tests. Preliminary results will be available within about twenty minutes, but you will have to go back again a few days later when all the tests will be complete. Treatment is usually simple, though it can take some time to work and the tests will be repeated to confirm the cure.

During your first interview you will be asked a number of detailed questions about your sex life, since the doctor must try to establish what you might have picked up and how. Later, if an STD is confirmed, the staff will ask you to help in alerting all your recent sexual contacts, so that they also can be treated. Otherwise, you will not be asked embarrassing questions, and you will not be criticized or condemned.

Our Bodies Ourselves and *Make It Happy* both contain useful information about STDs; you can get booklets from the Health Education Council (78 New Oxford Street, London WC1; tel: 01-637 1881) or from Women's Health Concern (16 Seymour Street, London W1H 5WB; tel: 01-486 8653). For more detailed medical information you should consult David Barlow, *Sexually Transmitted Diseases; The Facts* (Oxford University Press, 1980).

Homosexuality To have one or two sexual experiences with someone of the same sex does not make you gay, but about five people in a hundred find that all their close relationships are homosexual. You can read about lesbian perspectives in *Our Bodies Ourselves*.

You can obtain advice, information, and support on the telephone from a local Lesbian Line (the telephone number is available from WIRES; 0742 755290) or from Gay Switchboard (01-837 7324; 24-hour service).

Other sources of help The Albany Trust (16–18 Strutton Ground, London SW1P 2HP; tel: 01-222 0701) provides a counselling service on all types of sexual problems. SPOD (c/o RADAR, 25 Mortimer Street, London W1N 8AB; tel: 01-637 5400) provides information, advice, and counselling for disabled people with sexual difficulties.

The Spare Rib Diary is an extremely useful source of information for women's issues in general, and for health and sexual problems in particular. The monthly magazine also provides many addresses and telephone numbers. Diary and subscriptions from *Spare Rib*, 27 Clerkenwell Close, London EC1R 0AT.

Most women's magazines, and many national newspapers, have columns devoted to answering sexual questions. Some will provide personal replies. You can always write and ask; the advice you get will almost always be sensible.

For further information about women's health, and menstruation in particular, *see* pages 120–24. For information about childbirth and abortion *see* pages 19–22.

5. Death in the family

In the sophisticated, technological world of the West we have tried to forget about death: we avoid discussing it, or thinking about it, and when it happens we cover it up as quickly as possible. Perhaps this is because death forces the painful recognition that all our sophistication and technology is only of so much use.

In other societies, and in the relatively recent past in our society, death has played a more central role. But today death has become an unpleasant event at the end of life; of course, it is more than that for it is the way in which our lives are given their perspective. As our society hides from death we have lost the rituals that used to help us to deal with it and, therefore, when someone close dies we are not sure how to react. Commonly people feel that they ought to want to cry; if they do not cry they feel guilty; and if they do, they are embarrassed about crying in front of their friends because somehow that would bring the whole question of death to the surface.

This uneasiness about death is not restricted to the bereaved. If you know that someone's husband or mother has died, what do you do? Most of us find it easiest to avoid the subject. We do anything but allow the conversation to turn to the obvious, and justify this to ourselves by saying that the person wants to forget about it, and would rather think about the good things. But whatever we actually do, most of us are extremely embarrassed in this situation because we know that emotion is dangerously close.

It is a mistake to think that you will forget about the death of someone close; you will never forget, but your emotional reaction changes. After the initial shock and the numbness that comes with it, the second stage of grief usually brings waves of emotion and uncontrollable tears, and only after that has passed does a period of calm set in again.

The death of a close relative may well be the most stressful event that you will ever face. It can lead to deeper and deeper depression, a depression that is fuelled by the denial of death that is now almost universal. We are all aware that at some time we will die and that those closest to us will die. It may do no harm not to dwell on such thoughts. But if when a close relative or friend dies, we try to pretend that it has not happened, or that it can be simply forgotten about, the effect can be very destructive, at worst it can result in us losing our own will to live.

Mary always felt like Daddy's girl

Learning to cry

Somebody special – that's how Mary thought of her father.

> 'He was very tall and very handsome and always smiled a lot. I was . . . I suppose I was always Daddy's girl, it was quite important, I always saw myself as Daddy's girl. I always asked him things and he always explained them to me; I wanted to know about everything, and I would ask questions all the time and he'd always tell me, he always knew. That's how it felt – he always knew. I thought he was wonderful.'

Mary's father was a businessman; they had a beautiful home and the material advantages that success can bring. But for Mary her father provided the solidity around which everything else moved. He supplied the certainty, even when he was not there.

> 'He was strong and capable – people liked him . . . he always taught me things, showed me things, explained things to me. I looked forward to being alone with him – it was our time, a time when we'd talk, talk about everything – about politics, about life . . . we didn't talk about Mum, or the family . . . it was almost like a secret – being alone with him, there were the others but I felt special . . . I liked it.'

Growing up is a strange process; one moment you are a child and the next you are not. Many children feel trapped by their parents: trapped into always being children and treated as such. But Mary's father provided the framework within which she grew up; he was the judge of her progress.

> 'It was my fifteenth birthday, and my dad was to take me out to lunch as a special treat. I got dressed up, I wore a suit and hat and shoes, and a matching handbag, and felt very grown up, and he took me to this very

Mary's father used to take the family everywhere, and she particularly looked forward to their private times together

posh restaurant in London. All the waiters called me "Madam" and I felt really grown up – that was all – he just treated me as if I was grown up. Which was very nice, because I was fifteen and I wasn't grown up at all.'

In the middle of the summer holidays Mary had made a special trip to London to help a friend organize a party. It was a perfectly ordinary afternoon, but an afternoon she will never forget. The conversation has in retrospect gained a dream-like significance.

'We were sitting there talking – who were we going to ask to the party and so on – and for some reason we talked about some friend of hers she knew whose father had just died, and we talked about how awful it must be because we were the same age – we were both fifteen – and how terrible it would be if you didn't have a father.'

Mary realized she was going to be late; so she rang her mother just to let her know. As the phone rang all she was thinking about was which train she had to catch.

'My mum answered and I just said very quickly, "Mum, I'm really sorry but I think I'm going to be a bit late. . . ."

But there was something that wasn't right. Mum wasn't saying anything or . . . she was just making a funny sound . . . so I said, "What's the matter?", and she said, "Something's happened darling . . ."

At that moment I was in an absolute panic; I felt sick, completely sick. I had that buzzing in my ears. "What's . . . what's happened?"

"It's Dad. . . ." The conversation seemed to slow, "He's . . . he's had a heart attack."

And I said, "He's all right though, isn't he, he's all right?" But I understood that he wasn't – I had to ask, "Is he dead?" and she said, "Yes . . ."

I just panicked. I put down the phone and picked up everything and ran out. I tried to get a taxi home – the first taxi driver wouldn't take me and I burst into tears, it was miles away, but all I could think of was, "I have to get home, I have to get home." In the back of the taxi I thought, "I mustn't cry, I mustn't cry, I've got to look after them, I've got to look after the family, I've got to pull myself together – I'm the responsible one; that's what Dad would want, I've got to look after Mum." And I sat in the taxi – and I didn't cry.'

Mary's father had died abroad, and as a result she never saw the body. Instead of a full funeral the family had a memorial service.

'We sat in the service and some vicar said that he was a wonderful person, not that he bloody well knew; and I cried because it was a very sad and sombre occasion. There you are sitting in the front row, and at the end of the service the family walks down first – and everybody's looking at you, and some people were crying and you notice who's crying and who's not crying and you know they are all watching you. My mother cried a lot and

There was no one that Mary could talk to about her father's death

stopped and talked to people and held people's hands, but I just wanted to get out . . . I didn't want to be with any of them . . . it was nothing to do with them.'

Afterwards at the reception Mary used the practicalities of the social event to avoid the emotions that were churning beneath the surface.

'It was such an awful scene – everyone standing around, and they're all there because they love somebody but it's still everybody's private grief. It was too personal – I did not want to share it with anybody. So I made jokes, and topped up the glasses and handed round the peanuts. My mum talked a lot about what kind of man he was, and the good times, and the bad times, and how she wished she'd done this, and how she wished she'd done that. My mum is a very lucky person, she can just talk and talk and talk; her emotions are always on the surface. I made sure she went to bed and had her tranquillizers, and that she was okay. And I didn't cry . . . I didn't cry at all.'

Mary went back to school – it was as if nothing had happened. Only the closest of her friends knew – and they had no idea what to say. Mary had not allowed herself to think about her father, but now the memories began to return, and with them anxieties and guilt – emotions that would eventually tell on her health and began by keeping her awake.

'I hadn't seen much of my father that summer, but I kept remembering one day when we were swimming . . . my father had trained as an Olympic swimmer before the War, and I was a strong swimmer too – he had taught me to swim. Swimming had always been something I'd taken seriously, he'd always taught me, and that summer he taught me somersault turns . . . it was a very sunny day and we were standing by the pool. I was looking forward to a swim with him, we'd probably have a race or something – he always won . . . and I remember him starting to shiver and clutching his chest. He wouldn't jump in; so I tried to push him in, and he said something like, "The water's cold," and I said, "No it's not; no it's not," and I'd try to push him in again. I first thought about it the very day that he died because I remembered people had said that when there's something wrong with your heart you're frightened of cold water because it's a shock. The memory kept on coming back, and I felt I'd almost forced him in and maybe. . . . The image of him standing there shivering kept on returning; I mean Daddy swam always, whenever he could. And there he was, not wanting to go in, and me trying to push him. And maybe he went in even though he didn't want to get into the cold water. It made me feel terrible . . . terrible.'

Guilt is one of the common reactions we have when someone close to us dies. Perhaps if we had been kinder to them . . . perhaps if we'd only just paid more attention, if we hadn't had that argument, if we had tried to understand, perhaps somehow it all wouldn't have happened. At school, things just began to get worse, so Mary went to the doctor and was given sleeping pills, and then more sleeping pills; then tranquillizers and more tranquillizers. But no one ever talked to her; she was left with her memories and her private world.

'That summer I hadn't been getting on with my father so well because I had this atrocious school report. My father had no education at all, so he really wanted me to do well. I knew I ought to do well, but for the previous year I'd done nothing except smoke a lot, and get drunk occasionally, and have a good time . . .'

Mary had been regularly caught missing lessons – she was just a very rebellious fourteen-year-old. After one particularly bad report her father wrote her a long letter . . .

'It was all incredibly sympathetic, I mean it wasn't a strict dad saying you know, "Pull your socks up, and get on with it – what am I paying your school fees for?" It was just, "Of course I understand, but it's not doing you any good." But I carried on, and at the end of the summer term it happened again and he was even more upset about it . . . and that made me feel doubly guilty.

I really loved him and I would think, "How could I do that to him?" I was letting him down and I felt terrible – it was just that; I was letting him down. He was so nice; other people's dads would have hit the roof; they'd have been thrown out . . . but I still didn't do anything about it. No. At the time I thought, "I'll do what I want." I was making my stand, but when I looked back on it, I could only feel terrible.

Of course, I didn't think that I'd actually killed him . . . when I looked back on it I didn't think that he had died because I pushed him into the swimming pool, or because my school report was bad . . . but I half thought that . . . yes I half thought it . . .

I suppose it wasn't at all logical, but I did feel awful – when I got back to school that term I worked my guts out. Somehow I felt if I worked . . . it wouldn't bring him back, but it would take away my guilt. I felt very guilty.'

Although the thoughts of her father were gradually destroying Mary, she never really talked about him, or openly expressed her feelings in any way. As a result there was a pretence that bit deeper and deeper into Mary's psyche as time went by.

'I wish somebody had made me talk, had really made me talk. It is difficult though, your grief is private – you can't help feeling that it's private. I did see my godmother once – she made me cry . . . I hated her for making me cry. She'd say he was wonderful, and that I loved him very much . . . and she'd try and make me remember. I did start to talk, but then I didn't see her again for a long time.

Looking back, I wish somebody had come and said, "How are you feeling about your father?" But of course nobody interferes.'

The sleeplessness, the depression, and the insecurity did not go away. The full extent of Mary's inner bitterness only came to the surface four years later. The underlying feelings about her father's death had been covered over by the relationship with her boyfriend. Nick had lost his own mother and so could have sympathy for Mary, but somewhere there . . . there was the seed of the problem.

'I suppose I always expected him to look after me and make everything all right – I didn't have a father and he would look after me instead. I suppose I wanted him to be my father really . . .

One sunny afternoon we had this rather funny conversation about how much we loved each other but that we weren't ever going to live with each other permanently. My world completely fell apart. I'd thought he was going to save me and we were going to live happily ever after . . . and it wasn't going to be like that at all.'

So long as there had been someone else around, Mary had not ever fully faced what the loss of her father had meant. Suddenly, with no one else to take his place there was nothing left.

'I didn't have anything . . . I didn't have anything at all to live for. Ever since my father had died, there had always been a man there and I always thought that he was going to save everything. When it went wrong there was absolutely nothing.'

In desperation Mary went to a psychiatrist. She saw him for an hour a day, four days a week. He just listened . . . and she talked, and talked. After six months Mary started to talk about the things that really mattered to her, the things that really hurt. But then there was a moment when everything changed . . . she was telling a story of how when she was only four she had left a doll on the beach and it had been stolen.

> 'I adored this doll; my mother had tried to get me another, but it was never ever the same again. And that was the moment . . . that was the moment that I really cried. I had realized what I'd lost . . . my father had been taken from me and it had never ever been the same again.'

From that moment, instead of avoiding the death of her father, Mary was able to talk about how she felt. She used to feel angry – why had she lost her father, why did this have to happen to her? She now felt sad, not only for herself, but also for him – for the life that he didn't have, the things he didn't do, or didn't complete.

> 'I used to feel that it was so unfair, so unfair that I shouldn't have a father. I felt, "Poor me – everyone else has a dad." But that day I just felt terribly, terribly sad. And since then it has been much easier to cry . . . now I cry all the time. You feel so much better after you've cried – you look different, you feel different, it's over, it's something that's finished with. If you don't cry it's never finished with, it's always with you.'

We are all guilty of conspiring to contain grief. The damage that we do is to be found in the psychiatric wards of our hospitals. Our sterilized society does not allow for death, and for those who are close enough not to be able to hide from it, the resulting pressures can be too great to handle. Crying, or expressing our feelings about death, does not make those feelings go away but it does stop them becoming destructive. It is now ten years since Mary's father died.

> 'Sometimes I feel so sad, I really miss him . . . I still miss him . . . and I still cry. But when that moment's gone, it's gone, and I ring a friend and have a laugh.
>
> I still hate talking about it, but I accept it – I do accept it. I didn't accept it at the time; I didn't accept it until the moment that I started crying . . . it was terribly important for me that, because that's how I accepted it. I love him and I accept that I've lost him . . . and that is my story.'

Mary today

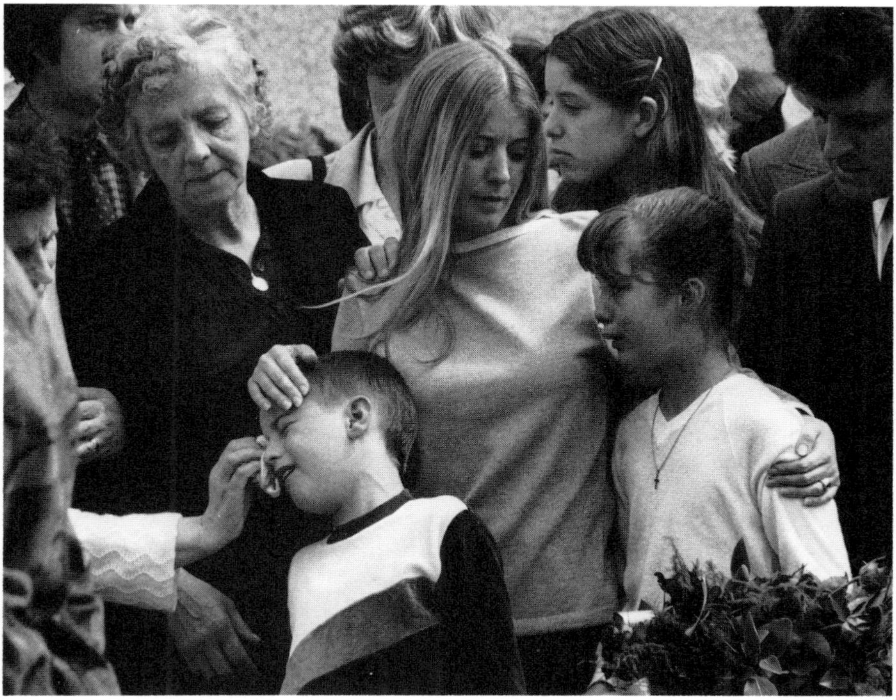

Never be ashamed to cry and to express your grief

What you can do

The moment of death is hard to accept. The family will probably find it comforting to be present; to sit quietly at the bedside, and to touch or kiss the dead relative. Physical contact helps to bring home the reality of death – something you have to accept.

Young children do not usually understand the finality of death, and partly as a result are often better able to deal with it than we expect. Let them see how peaceful the dead person is; explain what is going to happen before the funeral; encourage them to discuss their feelings; but do not force them to go to the funeral if they do not want to.

Use your family and friends. They will come to you to offer support; talk to them about the dead person, and what you feel; don't hold back your tears. Someone has died, but that is not the end for you; your life does go on.

There is a real danger that widows especially can feel, that when their husband is gone they have no future. Do not underestimate yourself and your value as a person in the community. Do not allow the breakdown of the old routine to mark the end of your active life. Look for new interests: go to evening classes; consider voluntary work. One positive first step is to talk to an organization such as the Citizens Advice Bureau (CAB) or the Marriage Guidance Council (MG) – they are extremely helpful in discussing all sorts of personal problems. (*See* page 218 for details.)

The perpetuation of the dead person's existence should be avoided. The mother who keeps the bedroom of her dead child intact for years, with his cot made up and his toys on the shelf, is storing grief for all the family. You must accept the fact of death – and this is another good reason to talk about it.

A sense of guilt after a death in the family is very common and very destructive. There is also the thought that you cannot enjoy yourself because to do so would be to devalue the dead person's memory. This is nonsense. Life does go on; you must learn to enjoy it again; if the dead person had a choice they would surely want you to be cheerful?

Practical details When someone dies you can get advice from your doctor, from a social worker, a nurse, the Social Services Department, the CAB, a solicitor, or a funeral director. But the first thing you must do is to deal with the immediate practical details: contact the family doctor, and the nearest relative; also the police if the death is violent, accidental, or unusual.

After a death in hospital the ward sister or another official will advise you about the necessary arrangements. Occasionally, especially in a case of unexpected sudden death, there is a request for organs for transplant. As next of kin you will have to decide what to do about this. Furthermore if the dead person wanted to donate their eyes, telephone the nearest eye hospital. The hospital doctors may ask you to allow a post-mortem examination in order to discover more about the disease involved.

At home, provided the doctor has attended the dead person during the last illness or seen the body soon after death, you will be given a medical certificate, free of charge, showing the cause of death, and also a formal notice telling you how to register the death with the Registrar of Births and Deaths. The doctor will tell the coroner about deaths that are unusual, accidental, alcohol-related, or if the cause is uncertain. A post-mortem examination, and perhaps an inquest, may be arranged.

You should register the death with the Registrar (get his address from the telephone directory, the CAB, the doctor, or the local post office) within five days of the death, or when the coroner tells you that you may do so. When you go, take with you the medical certificate of the cause of death, the dead person's National Health Service (NHS) medical card, any War Pension order book of the dead person, and the Pink Form if the coroner has given you one.

Ask the Registrar for a certificate for disposal, which you need to give to the funeral director. You also require a certificate of registration of death to give to the Social Security office if you want to claim the death grant and/or widow's benefit. You will also be given leaflets on State benefits and income tax for widows, form PR48 on the procedure for wills, and you can obtain extra certificates for the will, pension claims, savings bank certificates, and premium bonds. You will have to pay for these.

For more details on all aspects of what to do, ask for DHSS leaflet D49 *What to Do After a Death* at any Department of Health and Social Security (DHSS) office (see telephone directory under 'Health') or at a main post office.

The funeral Do not make any arrangements until you are sure that the death does not have to be reported to the coroner. You should then choose a funeral director. Funerals are expensive and there is a danger that grief-stricken relatives will accept the first suggestion that is made, letting themselves in for great expense. It is, therefore, better for someone else, such as the executor or a trusted friend, to make

the arrangements, and in particular to obtain at least two written estimates to compare. A basic simple funeral will not cover the church or crematorium fees, flowers, or notices in the local paper. The funeral director can arrange these, but he will charge you for them.

The funeral can usually be paid for by the estate of the deceased although their bank account will be frozen. You will probably be entitled to a death grant – a small cash payment which depends on the dead person's age and National Insurance contributions. Complete the form given to you by the Registrar, and send it to the Social Security office. You are eligible for a cash grant if you are arranging the funeral and are getting supplementary benefit, or if you are working only part time.

There are two options for disposal of the body: by cremation or burial. The deceased may have specified a preference; so consult the will or ask the solicitor, the executor, and the next of kin.

For cremation an application form signed by the next of kin or executor is required, in addition to a cremation certificate signed by two doctors, or one from the coroner, and a certificate signed by the medical referee at the crematorium. No one can be cremated until the cause of death is definitely known.

Most crematoria are run by local authorities. The charges usually include the medical referee's fee, the use of the chapel, and the chaplain's fee for a short service.

The ashes can be scattered in a garden of remembrance, or a favourite spot of the dead person, buried in a churchyard or cemetery, or kept in an urn.

If burial in a churchyard is preferred consult the vicar or rector and discuss whether you want a funeral service. Or you may prefer burial in a cemetery. In either case you will have to pay for the grave space if the dead person has not already done so.

A will A will states what the dead person wants to happen to their property. It may also appoint one or more people as executors who will be responsible for paying the debts and dealing with the money, property, possessions, and also looking after any children. The executor must obtain form PR48 from the Registrar which will clearly explain the procedure.

If there is no will the nearest relative must apply to the probate registry for 'letters of administration'. The Registrar will explain the details.

Visit your nearest CAB or the local council if you do not have enough money to live on. You may be entitled to supplementary benefit, Family Income Supplement, or help with rent and rates. The CAB will also advise you about a number of other benefits to which you may be entitled.

Useful publications

- *What to Do when Someone Dies* (Consumers' Association, 1978) is clear and helpful on the practical details and the arrangements you have to make.

Other books you may find useful include:

- *What Should I Do When Someone Dies?* (Oxfam).
- Richard Lamerton, *Care of the Dying* (Technomic, 1976, and Penguin, 1980) has a useful chapter on grief and how to handle it, and helpful advice on the process of dying.
- Rosemary and Victor Zorza, *A Way to Die* (Deutsch, 1980, and Penguin, 1981) tells the intensely personal story of how their 26-year-old daughter died of cancer, and the way in which they all came to terms with her death, slowly, but before she died.

Associations You may wish to contact:

- The National Association of Widows (c/o Stafford District Voluntary Service Centre, Chell Road, Stafford, ST16 2QA; tel: 0785 45465 (24-hour service) or 56532) is run by and for widows, and provides help and support through a nationwide network.
- Cruse, the National Association for the Widowed and their Children (126 Sheen Road, Richmond, Surrey; tel: 01-940 4818 or 9047) provides help and support to widows and widowers, and publishes books, pamphlets and a newsletter.
- The Compassionate Friends for Bereaved Parents (Mrs B. Trimmer, 2 Nordon Road, Blandford, Dorset, DT11 7LT) offers comfort and consolation through meetings and visits.
- The Foundation for the Study of Infant Deaths (3rd Floor, 4 Grosvenor Place, London, SW1X 7HD; tel: 01-235 1721) runs a support and counselling service for those who have lost children, and produces leaflets about cot deaths, and how to handle them. Please send a stamped, addressed envelope.
- The Stillbirth Association (37 Christchurch Hill, London, NW3 1LA; tel: 01-794 4601) has a national network of parents who help. It also produces leaflets; send a stamped, addressed envelope.
- The Family Welfare Association, 501 Kingsland Road, London E8; tel: 01-254 6251. There are also branch offices throughout the country. The association provides welfare services and it also produces publications such as *A Guide to the Social Services*.

You and yourself

6. Depression
When drugs are no solution you have
to find the answer in yourself

7. Serious illness
Can positive thinking make any difference?

8. When fear is everything
When you don't even dare to go shopping

9. Every 28 days
The female problems that are often ignored

6. Depression

One in three women, and one in five men, will at some stage in their lives suffer from depression badly enough to need outside help.

Each of us knows what it is to be depressed; indeed a general lowering of spirits must be regarded as a perfectly normal reaction to unpleasant circumstances, but when depression is excessive in both intensity and duration, it is not a mood, it is an illness. This illness is a primary cause of suicide, and one of the most common reasons for people to seek psychiatric help.

The feeling of depression most of us have experienced following the death of someone close, or the break-up of a relationship, or the loss of a job, is predominantly a sense of unhappiness. Although this is not something that we should normally regard as enjoyable it is nevertheless an active feeling: we feel strongly; we may want to cry; we will in general want to express our emotion, by talking to others, by telling them about it. But depression in the medical sense, while it may originate in these feelings of unhappiness, is in many ways a non-feeling rather than a sad feeling. There is a general apathy, a loss of energy, of appetite, of sex-drive, and of undisturbed sleep. The victim withdraws and wants to do nothing – until the feeling has gone on too long, and then they may think about suicide.

All interest in the outside world is lost: there is no desire to do anything, not even to talk to others. As a result the effect is crippling and the person becomes less and less able to lead a normal, social, life.

We are inclined to think of depression as a new phenomenon. More than two thousand years ago, however, in the time of classical Greece, Hippocrates described the condition. He called it melancholia and it was thought to be caused by 'black bile', one of the four 'humours' by which the ancients understood disease. Our present understanding is different but little more helpful. Depression has been divided into two main types. The first is an extreme version of the normal human reaction: it goes under a variety of names such as depressive neurosis, or reactive depression. The second type, known as depressive psychosis or endogenous depression, represents the other end of the spectrum of depressive illnesses in which there is often no stimulating factor and no apparent cause for the distress. There is often a family history of other depressives and it is sometimes thought that there is a physical cause with an imbalance of chemicals in the brain. This category includes a number of more specific illnesses such as manic depression in which the person alternates between bouts of great elation (the manic phase) and periods of severe depression and persecution (the depressive phase). These categories may have long and precise-sounding names but the distinctions are not clear-cut; people often seem to have evidence of both elements in their depression.

The causes of depression are almost as vague as the categories but we do know that it is possible to inherit a predisposition to depression – if your parents are liable to depression you are also at risk. It is most frequent in the age group 45–60, and it is about twice as common in women as in men. Childhood, most would agree, plays a vital part, especially in reactive depression, but if you say much more than that disagreement abounds.

Given that we understand so little, it is hardly surprising that there is no simple treatment. A large number of anti-depressant drugs are available and their success varies enormously from patient to patient. Drugs have been most effective in endogenous depression. In really severe cases drastic treatments like the controversial Electro-Convulsive Therapy have been used with some success. More often, however, it is found that non-technological solutions such as counselling, reassurance and support are more effective.

Ultimately if a solution is to be found, it is probably to be found in the person themselves – with the vital aid of those supporting them. Not every depressive finds a solution, for, of all severely depressed people, one in seven take their own lives. It is never enough to say to someone who is depressed, 'Snap out of it,'; they need help, and they can be helped, by themselves and by other people. Whatever else we may know, depression is more than a mood.

The end of feeling

There was no single cause of Anne's suicide attempt, no desperate disaster, no immediate problem. It was not a defiant gesture, nor some sort of statement; it was simply a rather nondescript decision not to live.

> 'I'd thought about it so many times, actually. Should I or shouldn't I? I'd rehearsed it, I'd been through it, and there was nothing particularly dramatic about it really. It was almost as though every day was the same day. I'd had a row with Robert – the bloke I lived with – but that was nothing out of the ordinary. . . . That was just common. A common occurrence. I can't remember that it was any particular day, it was just another day like all the others; one more day – there was always another day – no end to it. So that was it. I sort of just . . . decided.'

Where did it all begin? Her mother was an alcoholic and unable to look after the family, and Anne's unhappy childhood was spent in a succession of children's homes. She has few memories and even those show the doubt and uncertainty that later perhaps played a part in her depression.

> 'My earliest memory is my brother falling into the river. I can see it so clearly. I was angry with my father because he didn't just jump in. He took off all his clothes and put his swimming trunks on. My brother was a year old . . . floating in the river.

Anne

At home with my father and stepmother, it was as though we were living in a drama. We were play-acting at being happy families. There was no substance to it – just convenient smiles and the odd greeting. There was no real physical contact between us – at the most a forced quick kiss on the cheek. You didn't dare to be really angry or to really show any affection . . . I think we were just afraid to rock the boat.Whenever I did show anger it would be killed quickly with a remark like, "Would you rather go back to the children's home? I don't know why we took you away." That would kill it. Kill it dead.'

The effect of childhood on adult life is always obscure but in Anne's case one thing it clearly did not do was help. Depression is a disease of adulthood; children are unhappy, not depressed. It is almost as if somewhere in our adolescent years we discover emotion and with it the possibility of no feeling.

'I think probably the first depression I had was in my teens. At school. The first real depression. The funny thing about depression is people ask you how you feel, when the point is that you don't have feeling. You don't feel like crying, you don't feel like being angry, it's a bit . . . a bit like being alive and yet you feel dead.'

Anne did well at school, and with her O- and A-levels behind her she planned to go to university. During the holidays she went to stay with some friends of her father. She was to have a wonderful time, but ironically it made things worse in the long run.

'Suddenly I was in a normal family situation; people were just being spontaneous, warm, loving, open, honest. Interested in life. Just normal human beings. It may seem dramatic but I literally hadn't experienced this

Everyone else thought Anne was having a wonderful time at university

in my life. I'd read about it; I'd seen it on TV or on the films; but I had no experience of it. It was very much of a shock – a very pleasant shock – it was so marvellous the way they accepted me. It was my first experience of being a real member of a family. The trouble was that when I had to go back home it made the contrast seem very stark. I never went back to live at home after that.'

Outwardly, Anne seemed to be having a marvellous time at university. She had a large number of friends and lots of boyfriends. Her course was going well. It would have been difficult to believe that here was somebody heading for trouble. But beneath the whirl of her social life she felt she was losing all sense of her own personality – this is one of the symptoms of depression.

'I wasn't isolated – I was taking a very active part in the life of the university – but inside me, I was getting more and more a feeling of being lost . . . a feeling of, "What was it all about?", "What was I doing?". It was a bit like the feeling in my childhood of playing happy families, only now I just had this awful feeling of playing at being a happy university student. It's strange – it's as if I was one step removed from all that was going on. Things just happened around me – like a scene in a film. You're an observer, but you're not safe, it can draw you in – and yet you're distant from it all. And when that feeling gets hold of you it just gets worse and worse and worse.'

These are feelings that many people have at some point in their lives. But characteristic of depression is that not only do you feel an observer of somebody else's world but you see no point in taking part.

'I just lost interest in myself. I didn't eat. I couldn't sleep. I put up a good front – in order to survive I suppose, but it was to survive; I didn't want to do it.'

People who are depressed often wait a long time before seeking help. If you see no point in living what good could help do? Why do you need help anyway? And if you do see a doctor it is often with some other complaint.

'I went to the university doctors because I had a problem with my periods. As I was to realize later it is a common thing when you're depressed – sometimes my periods stopped completely.

I was referred to a psychiatrist . . . at first you think this is absolutely marvellous because they take an in-depth history of your childhood. But once they've got it all sewn up, and they've got you in their little box, neatly categorized in the right file, then the long probing interviews stop. From then on it's a ten-minute job and, "You're depressed – take these tablets." Still it was a relief in a way that someone knew I was depressed.'

The treatment of depression depends on the diagnosis: on what type of depression it seems to be, most importantly whether it is seen as a reaction – a more extreme and extended form of the normal human response – or as a psychosis in which the depression is of a qualitatively different order. There are many different types of drug treatment which can be successful for some. Most people find drugs helpful in the initial stages.

'You tend to go through a phase of pills. You're charmed by them at first, and then you become a bit obsessed by them. But for people like me, in the end, they don't work. Nothing has changed in your life. None of the questions have been answered. None of the causes of your depression have been removed.'

Shortly afterwards Anne ended up in hospital. She had been to see her psychiatrist again and he decided this time that she was probably suicidal and suggested to her that a stay in hospital might help.

'I'd never been inside a large Victorian mental hospital before. It was just like a nightmare. All around there were people who were very very sick. Some living in their own world, so depressed they couldn't talk at all. Others, dancing madly, and wildly jumping about.

I remember being particularly upset by one woman who kept coming in and watering my flowers with the urine from her potty. And then there were fights . . . people were forceably restrained . . . it was very frightening.

For some reason I was put in a side ward with all the most disturbed people. I felt I'd been put there because I was one of the worst. I suppose they wanted to keep an eye on me but I felt I was one of them . . . one of the worst of them.

I became much worse, and just retreated into myself . . . anybody could have done anything with me. My parents came down and said they were taking me home. It was the last thing I wanted to do, but I went. I would have gone anywhere . . . I would have done anything. It was as if I didn't mind what happened to me . . . I did mind really but I felt incapable of doing anything about it, incapable of having any control of the world I found myself in. I felt like a puppet, a puppet that had the disadvantage of being alive.'

Depressives are not easy people to live with or look after. Either they will not talk about what is the matter, or if they do, it can seem insuperable. Just as things seem to be getting better they can, for no apparent reason, become as despondent as ever. The most difficult thing is that nothing seems to be effective. At times everything you do seems to be wrong. If you are trying to help, you are helping in the wrong way; if you are trying to be optimistic, you are failing to understand; if you are ignoring it, you are unconcerned.

For the person who is depressed, an unbridgeable gulf looms between them and everyone else. No one understands, and everyone avoids talking about the things that really matter. These are not just delusions, for most of us hide from problems we cannot deal with and we hide precisely because we do not know how to deal with them; talking can help, but it is no simple panacea.

'My parents were obviously very concerned. But they were sure that it was just that I'd done too much at university . . . It was as simple as that. I needed a rest.

They brought me meals and just treated me like a sick person. I can remember thinking, "Nothing is ever going to change really; it will always be the same." I just became more and more depressed inside.'

Anne forced herself back to university. After successfully completing her course she became a social worker. But there was always the possibility that her depression would return for a few days or weeks. Most of her relationships quickly fell apart – somehow she had decided in advance they would not work since no one could know her or really love her. There was one man with whom she lived with for a long time but that was a relationship based on her needs rather than her wants.

'He was very much a father-figure to me. In fact I was in love with somebody else. He was there in the background – he picked up the pieces when they needed picking up. He was marvellous to me – he gave me presents all the time. I couldn't be depressed with the place full of flowers; he'd never send one bunch, it was always a dozen.

I often think that he never . . . sort of really loved me. He did, but then I had this feeling, maybe depressives always have this feeling, that nobody ever really knows them, just because they never let anyone get to know them. For him, I suppose, I was somebody who needed looking after.'

For a couple of years Anne drifted out of social work and back into it again while the spiral of her depression got deeper. The cycles of blankness came more frequently and when they did come they were even more empty. There is nothing dramatic about depression. There is no intensity. If you decide to end it all, the decision comes almost from boredom, from the dullness of living. Life is not sharp and unbearable, for that would at least be something; it is nothing.

> 'For a couple of years I really didn't do anything. I would spend days and days in the flat, not going out at all, not eating, and hardly sleeping. I would spend them in bed. Lying in bed. No, not even watching television. I was still taking barbiturates, and much of the time I was in a daze – not even thinking. It was just a sort of state of apathy . . . of complete apathy. I . . . I know that I never cried.'

Anne had reached the point where she decided to bring this non-existence to an end. It was not on any particular day, or at any particular time, or indeed for any particular reason.

> 'I just decided, I suppose, that I didn't really want to face another weekend. When it came to taking my sleeping tablets at night I decided that I might as well take the lot. Which is what I did.'

Anne should have died, but her boyfriend Robert returned unexpectedly. Hospital is not much fun for those who have attempted suicide – the staff are overworked anyway, without having to deal with people who have been unsuccessful at killing themselves, and as a result, there is little compassion for people like Anne.

> 'I know that I can't remember much sympathy. I really can't. I suppose I remember people being annoyed with me. But I didn't really care – I just didn't care what happened to me.'

But it was her experience in hospital that was to give Anne a new determination to live.

> 'I sat up in bed and by accident I caught sight of myself in the bedside mirror. It was as if it wasn't me, and it was someone I don't think I liked very much. Seeing this wreck made me feel that I wanted to make myself a human being once more. It was in a way not so much a decision to live, but a decision to come back to life.'

Things were better for a while, but there was no immediate recovery. It was a long, slow progress – a progress regularly interrupted by setbacks.

> 'Robert was shattered by what I'd done. He made a very big effort. He stopped drinking for a start . . . for months. It made quite an impact on me, because I knew how important it was to him. It was okay for a few months. But then I'd get depressed and go back on the tablets.'

One of the most important things for someone with depression is to have some evidence that they are something and matter to somebody, that they are able to achieve things, and can be of some help. For Anne it came in a rather ironic way. She found a job she could do, a job she was good at – as a psychiatric social worker. She had mentioned it to her psychiatrist as a joke but he took it seriously and encouraged her.

'He said, "I think you'd be very good at the job." I couldn't believe it, but he kept repeating it, and I thought, "Well, perhaps I should." So I did.

I haven't looked back because I simply found that I did the job well. It brought out a lot of my skills – not just being able to empathize with people in distress, because not everybody is depressed anyway – but it turned out I was a very good organizer, good at getting things going, and generating change. I have made a lot of friends and I enjoy my work enormously.'

Depression takes years to develop and lasts for many more. Indeed, in so far as it is caused by your childhood and by your personal character it never really goes, for those you cannot escape from. But what will help you through are all those things that make you into a person, that make you somebody rather than something.

'There wasn't a dramatic turning point. It was a gradual build-up of self-esteem. Finding that I was good at my job, that my relationships were a lot better, that I was making friends more easily – proper friendships, not just acquaintances.

Coming off the drugs was difficult; I was so terribly addicted to them. Giving up barbiturates I had to pretend I was ill, and I took four or five days off work.

My growth of independence led to my break-up with Robert. He had provided me with support. He had never not been there. He had saved my life. But it was my old life – I had to begin again, and begin without him. It was difficult, but I'm sure it was right.'

Today Anne has a future to look forward to

Throughout this period Anne had counselling from a social worker once a week. She was fortunate in being able to talk to others who had been through similar problems – for when she realized she was not alone, she knew she had something valuable to offer others.

'The crucial thing is not to try and do it on your own. It need not be psychiatric or medical help – for me the real help came from other quarters, from counselling . . . and from self-help groups. Being with other people who have experienced the same problem is absolutely invaluable. You certainly need some kind of help if you are going to get through it. But you also have to accept that if you are a depressive then you are going to be one for the rest of your life. You must learn to live with it rather than seek a miracle cure. But I'm not the only one, the only success story, if that's what I am. You can win. Yes, of course, you can win.'

What you can do

Recognizing that you are depressed is the first and essential step to a solution. Depression is not a feeling of unhappiness about your circumstances, or of worry. These are more likely to be signs of stress and anxiety rather than depression. The warning signs of depression are a lack of interest in anything, often combined with sleeping badly, and the symptoms mentioned earlier in the chapter. If you feel like this, and you cannot sort out the problems with the help of friends and relatives in two or three weeks, then you should accept the fact that you are depressed, and you need help.

How to get help The simplest way of seeking treatment is to see your family doctor. He knows you, your background, and something of your medical history. But you should be aware that general practitioners are rarely skilled in treating depression. They are given little training in how to handle emotional problems, and although yours may refer you to a psychiatrist or the Social Services, many doctors have a tendency to prescribe tranquillizers for anyone clearly suffering from mental anguish.

Tranquillizers are designed to calm you down when you are agitated. They can help considerably in cases of anxiety, but they do not lift the dead, non-feeling of depression; they may even make the condition worse. So if you think your problem is depression talk to your doctor, and ask whether you should have anti-depressants rather than tranquillizers.

If your bouts of depression are mild and infrequent, drugs may well be the answer for you. They will undoubtedly make you feel better, and that may be enough. But many depressives find that pills cannot provide a long-term solution; they only help you through the worst patches.

In the end the only foolproof solution is in you yourself. You have to find ways of building up your self-esteem, of becoming an important person again. You will need someone who can listen and talk to you, understand your difficulties, and who is also sympathetic but tough when it is necessary.

You may find such a person close to you already – an aunt, perhaps, or a friend – but you may prefer to go to a professional, someone who has been trained in counselling. You have at least two options: a psychiatrist or a social worker. Do not be afraid or ashamed to talk to either. A

Talking to others with similar problems can be extremely helpful if only because it breaks the feeling of isolation

psychiatrist is a medical doctor who has chosen to specialize in illnesses that affect the mind rather than the body. And the social worker is the official community helper. Local authorities have set up Social Service departments throughout the country with the specific aim of helping people in need. You have every right to make use of these services.

Psychiatrists If you wish to see a psychiatrist, ask your family doctor for a referral. You will probably be sent to the psychiatric department of the nearest general hospital, where you will first see a general psychiatrist. The psychiatrist will assess you on your first visit; he may then ask you to come back, or refer you to a specialist, such as a psychologist, a psychotherapist, or a child psychologist. It is, of course, important that you get on with your psychiatrist. If you do not, go back to your family doctor and ask to be sent to someone else.

Social workers Your family doctor may refer you to the Social Services, but if you wish you can contact them direct and ask to see a social worker. You can find the office through a police station or the post office, or by referring to the telephone directory under your local council, e.g. 'Leeds City Council, Department of Social Services, Area Offices'. It is advisable to visit the Social Services office personally where you should ask to see the Duty Officer. After your initial interview you may be invited to return for another session; or you may be sent to see a doctor; or arrangements might be made for a social worker to call on you at home.

Other ways to get help If you have difficulty getting help, contact your nearest MIND office (see your telephone directory or page 219). MIND is the National Association of Mental Health, and gives expert advice and information about where to get help. It also provides some counselling.

Group therapy may sound rather alarming to anyone who is not very keen to meet people. In fact it often proves exceptionally helpful to those in trouble. In a group where everyone is encouraged to talk about their problems you will find not only that many other people share the same types of experiences and feelings but also that some of them have found ways to help themselves which may in turn help you. Even to talk over your problems with someone who has experienced similar ones can be tremendously helpful.

If you hate the idea of going to any sort of meeting write to the Depressives Anonymous Self-Help Centre, 83 Derby Road, Nottingham, NG1 5BB. It has groups throughout the country, and produces a regular newsletter, written by and for depressives, which allows people to share experiences without revealing their names. Please send a stamped, addressed envelope with any enquiry.

Books Finally, you may discover that books can help you to understand more about your own feelings or those of someone you are trying to help. Useful books about depression and its treatment include the following:

- Andrew Stanway, *Overcoming Depression – Sympathetic Advice for Sufferers and their Families* (Hamlyn paperback, 1981).
- Ross Mitchell, *Depression* (Penguin, 1975) – a MIND special which looks at the causes, treatment, and understanding of depression.
- George Winokur, *Depression, the Facts* (Oxford University Press, 1981).

There are many other books and booklets which you can see in your local bookshop, or learn about from MIND. It may be you are helped by some books that also seek to explain some other aspect of human behaviour. For example some people regard most depression as repressed anger, and you may find useful Anthony Storr's *Human Aggression* (Atheneum and Pelican, 1968) or Claire Weeke's *Self-Help for Your Nerves* (Angus and Robertson, 1962).

The MIND Bookshop (155–7 Woodhouse Lane, Leeds LS2 3EF; tel: 0532 453926) can supply all MIND publications and advice on others.

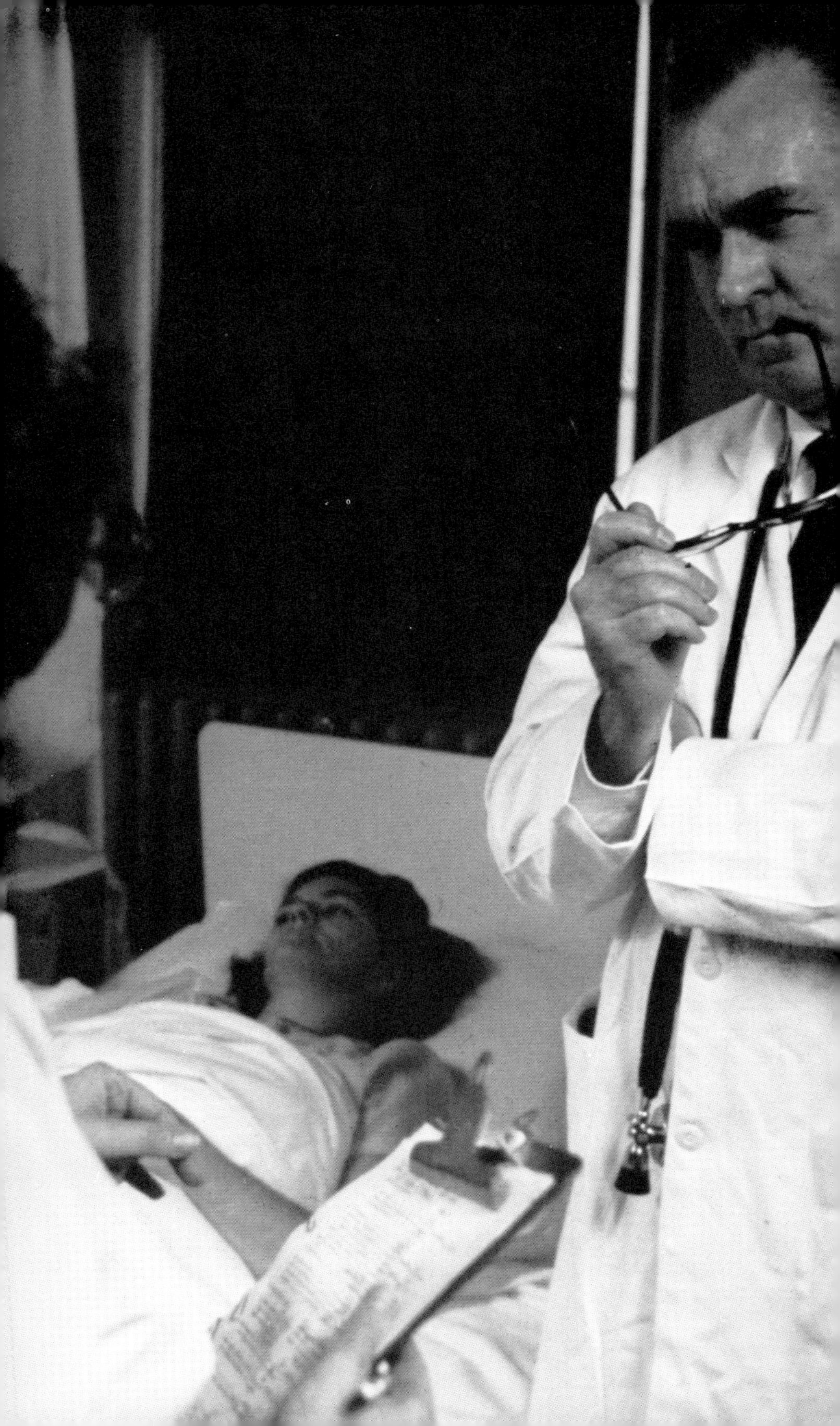

7. Serious illness

Health is something we do not think about until it is no longer there. We take it for granted because it is essential to our normal lives, and it is for that reason that when we fall ill everything becomes different.

Serious illness calls everything into question; family, job, plans for the future – they are all placed in shadow. People go to work, children go to school, the world outside carries on; but that is what it is – the world outside – because when you are ill you move into a new world of your own. And it is not only you, for visitors will treat you differently – you are no longer one of them. This probably happens because serious illness reminds us of the possibility of death, and as a result everything that makes up our normal lives is put into perspective; people who are not ill try to avoid thinking about it.

Medicine has made great strides during the last century, and coupled with effective public health has dramatically reduced the danger of death from infectious diseases such as smallpox and influenza which used to kill millions. However, there still remain a number of chronic diseases for which medicine can do very little. Treatment may alleviate symptoms and make the illness more bearable, but for real killers such as cancer, bronchitis, and heart disease there are no simple cures and no proven treatment. Of course some people recover, and the right treatment may be vital to that recovery, but there are many for whom there seems to be no cure. Despite all the advances in medicine, the span of human life is still in the region of threescore years and ten.

Medical theory today regards the body as a machine; parts that break down or wear out are repaired or replaced. But what about the mind? Can how we think have any effect on how the body works? For three hundred years, ever since Descartes separated the workings of the mind from those of the body, the relationship between the two has remained an enigma.

Most of us instinctively think that if we are miserable and feeling low we are more likely to fall ill, and in old age, when people give up the will to live they do indeed die. These commonplaces suggest that there may be some sort of link between mind and body, between how we think and how we feel. In medieval times this was how people thought of illness. The body had four humours – phlegm, blood, black bile, and yellow bile – and not only did good health depend on their presence in the right proportions, but they directly affected temperament. Ideas like this can also be found in Eastern religions, and today in the United States there is a growing number of people, including doctors, who believe that illness can be effectively treated only by considering the whole person, rather than by only treating the body – the machine.

How could thoughts, or outlook, affect physical well-being? At present we have no answer to that; indeed so long as mind and body remain separate entities it is difficult to see how there ever could be an answer to it. For the moment perhaps the best we can do is to suggest that the mind might have some control over the effectiveness of the body's defences – the immune system – and that in turn plays a central part in our health. The key question is, 'Can you actually improve your health by positive thinking?'. 'If you are ill, can you really help yourself to get better by adopting a determined and positive attitude – by deciding you are going to recover?' There is no hard evidence one way or the other, but there are some who believe that outlook plays a vital role in illness.

Whether or not our attitude affects our health, the way we think will certainly affect the way we feel about the illness, and it is a salutary thought that learning to cope with serious illness is something most of us will have to face at some time in our lives.

Making the most of it

May and her family were looking forward to Christmas. Five years earlier they had emigrated to South Africa but that did not work out, and when they decided to return they lost their home and most of their belongings. For four dreary years they had been putting their life together again, and now at last things were improving. But the happy Christmas holiday they had hoped for was not to be.

The first innocuous signs that something was the matter passed almost unnoticed:

> 'I started to get this bruising; it was pretty minor and I automatically assumed that I must be backing into some of the rails at work. But then the odd thing was . . . it didn't seem to be going away. I didn't feel ill, that was the strange thing about it.
>
> I remember the 16th of December. We had been invited to a works dinner and I had to try on various dresses to avoid showing these bruises, and in the end I had to go out and buy a dress specially – with long sleeves.'

Eventually May's husband, Horace, persuaded her to see the doctor, who gave her a simple examination and asked for what seemed to be a routine blood sample.

> 'I thought no more of it . . . it was just nothing. I wasn't worried, I wasn't the least bit worried about it – and of course I just wasn't ill.
>
> A couple of nights later the doctor was on the phone. He said they were rather anxious about the blood test, and could I go and see a specialist?'

Two days later May was in hospital for further tests, but it was not for another ten days that she found out what was wrong with her.

May had been looking forward to a happy Christmas

'Three doctors came up to my bed, they drew the screen curtains around and then one of them asked if I knew what was wrong with me. So I said "No." They were all standing to one side of the bed – it all seemed so ordinary. The doctor said that they'd done most of their tests, but there was still one to come – it had to be sent off to London. He looked up at the ceiling, he looked so casual, and said, "There is a name for it." Even then, I thought he was going to come out with some remote Latin term. He looked down at me and he said, "They call it leukaemia."

I just looked at his face. Everything was still. I felt cold . . . as if every little bit of air had been pumped out of me. I could almost feel the shock. It seemed as if the moment would never end as his words, "they call it leukaemia . . . they call it leukaemia", echoed in my head . . . they almost seemed to be written on the walls.

I don't remember them leaving – just the sound of footsteps retreating.'

May was left in the small hospital ward, looking out of the huge picture window to the city below. A city of people doing ordinary things. A city of streets she had walked along. A city she now felt no part of. And her life too – her home, her youngest daughter Pam, all the things she had loved, it all tumbled out before her.

'I sat there on the side of the bed, and I just looked up at the sky and I thought . . . I thought . . . "God, this is terrible." I thought about Pam and Horace, and I felt, "It's too ridiculous." I thought about my painting too and embroidery and all the things I wanted to do. Millions of things that I still wanted to do. I felt cheated . . . cheated out of the one thing I had relied

May wondered whether she would ever see Pam grow up

upon, my good health. It was terrible. It was the end. There was an elderly person next to me and I remember just collapsing on the bed and crying.'

One of the first reactions, when you are told that you are suffering from a serious illness, is to deny it. A mistake must have been made. It cannot be happening to you. May was no exception.

'Then I thought . . . "I'm not ill; I'm well. I want to go home. I want to talk to my husband." Within the space of ten minutes I'd got my little case out. I was going to calmly walk down and tell them I was going home. I didn't feel ill. I couldn't accept it like that. I dressed and packed and walked towards the door of the ward. The nurse looked at me disapprovingly. "You're doing the wrong thing – don't you realize you're ill?" "Well I don't feel ill," I said. "I'm sure you've got things mixed up somewhere along the line. I couldn't do what I'm doing now if I was ill – I've just had a very, very, busy Christmas. I've been working in the store, I've been cooking and dashing out for presents. I do all my own washing, ironing, and looking after the family. I couldn't be ill and do what I'm doing now. It's impossible."'

Neither the nurse, nor the doctor who appeared, could stop May returning home. It was New Year's Eve. Once she was outside, the truth of what she had been told came home to her.

'It was ironic . . . a day of hope for everybody, and suddenly I felt I had none. I looked at even the poorest people I saw and I envied them. I envied them their health . . . the things they did not even realize they had.

I got home to my family and I sat down, and I told them. The three of us cried together that day. My husband made me a meal and then the phone rang; it was one of the senior doctors, and he said, "You do realize Mrs Merton that you've got to come back?" So we only had the one day. We cooked a goose, and I tried to eat a bit of food. Was I going to see Pam grow up? If I could see her grown up – that would be enough. My older daughter had arrived for the meal. We had some wine . . . and we tried, we tried, to forget.'

The following day May's son took her back to hospital.

Leukaemia is a disease of the white blood cells – they provide the body's defence – and in order to treat it the abnormal white cells have to be killed so that the others can flourish normally. Unfortunately it is not always possible to destroy the abnormal cells without suppressing the healthy parts of the defence system. Treatment for leukaemia may be very debilitating before it can be effective – if it is effective. After the first treatment May was very weak.

'The very first injection was pretty dreadful. I came out in violent spots just like a measles rash. They let me home that first weekend and all I could do was just sit. I didn't want to do anything. It was beyond me to do anything.'

The treatment came in ten-day cycles, five days of injections and five days off. By the third cycle May had little strength left, and perhaps more important – little hope.

'I couldn't concentrate enough to read a paper. I couldn't even knit because of the drips in my arms. I couldn't see my family; they were too far away. My husband does shift work, and he couldn't make the long journey in every day.

I was very depressed . . . very depressed, because when you are in a ward where people are dying, and you know, you know that they've got leukaemia and they're dying, well, even though people are telling you that you're going to get better, you begin to doubt it, you begin to wonder if the treatment is really going to work.'

Every day May seemed to get weaker; the slightest thing would exhaust her; she began to feel there was nothing to live for. But then at her lowest ebb she was given some advice that changed her perspective.

'I'd formed a friendship with a lady Indian doctor; she used to come and chat to me, and I think she could see that I had become overwrought and that my spirits were going. She said, "You don't need any miracle treatment – just keep on repeating that you're going to get better . . . that you're going to see Pamela grown up." And I thought, "Yes, get back to work, see my customers again, that would be wonderful." She said, "Just think about what you want to do."

I found it very interesting, and when she'd gone I thought, well, there must be something in it, to will yourself better, to will yourself to carry on with life. And let's face it, there weren't any other straws around left for me to clutch on to.'

There came a point when May began to think positively

From that point on May tried to think of the future. She tried to force herself to do things. She tried to stop thinking of herself as being ill, as being different. There was no miraculous change in her condition but she did begin to feel better.

> 'I would say to myself, "I'm going to get better, I'm going to make it. I don't care what they say, I don't care what the books say, I don't care what the medical journals say, but I'm going to try." And instead of looking inwards, and generally feeling sorry for myself, I began to take an interest in other people. I listened to their stories, I sympathized with them, I helped the nurses on the ward. There were patients worse off than me – young people dependent on blood transfusions – and I took courage from their courage. I seemed to get energy from nowhere, and even though I still couldn't read or knit, I began to perk up.'

Three months later the doctors came in to see May to tell her that the leukaemia was in remission and she was beginning to get better. Perhaps May would have got better without her change in attitude – relying on the drugs alone – but she is convinced that it did help her.

> 'When I was in hospital, unable to read, I had this little aim: it was to return to the part-time job I had in our busy department store. I imagined myself just walking into the store, taking up my position, selling the coats and suits, talking to the customers. I didn't tell anyone about this, I didn't dare, my family would have probably laughed at the whole idea.'

But that is what May is doing now. She gets up at about 6 a.m. every morning, she makes breakfast for the family, and twice a week she goes to work. In a strange sort of way she finds the world is almost a better place than it used to be:

> 'I've learned to appreciate the world, learned to see the beauty in it, and that you must live your life and live it to the full.'

May knows that she is only in remission and she has not been cured. She recognizes also that the treatment was crucial for her recovery, but she also feels that thinking positively played its part.

> 'I think the important thing about illness is not to wallow in it. It's so easy to make yourself a semi-invalid. If you have something serious just don't listen to the pessimists. I'm not saying go and climb mountains, but aim for something, even if it's only a walk to the shops, or making a cup of tea. You must aim for something. I think it works.
>
> The whole point is, we all know we're going to die sometime or another, and I just think that whatever time you have, you must make the best of it.'

What you can do

When you learn that you have a serious illness, you are likely to go through periods of denial, misery, and optimism. You cannot do much to alter this, but you can concentrate on the practical. Avoid wallowing in gloom about the past; it is better, unlikely though it sounds, to think about the future.

Divide the future into two parts: long-term and short-term. The long term is more difficult, so begin thinking about that as soon as you feel strong enough and have accepted the fact that you are seriously ill.

Strategy You may like to find out about your illness; if so, ask your doctor specifically about it. The advantages of knowing are that you will get a better idea of what life is going to be like. You will also find out about the symptoms that may affect you, and even if the doctor is unwilling you may find it worth pressing him to tell you what symptoms could possibly crop up. You may have a bad half-hour when you hear the awful possibilities, but it can be well worth it, because once you have the information you cannot be frightened by what happens. (*See also* pages 200–201.)

Many people find it extremely helpful to talk to others who are suffering from the same illness. This often proves to be the most practical way of finding out both what might happen next, and how to cope with the problems. Your doctor may be able to put you in touch with another patient in your area, or you can find out whether there is a national association. There are associations for many illnesses including colitis, diabetes, leukaemia, heart disease, and multiple sclerosis. Ask your doctor, or your librarian, or your local newspaper; *see also* the end of this chapter and the index (page 221).

You might also find it worth asking your doctor about your treatment. Is it to cure you, to prevent the problem spreading, or just to make you feel better? What symptoms will it produce? Will it give you a headache, make you feel sick or tired? How long does the course take? Have you any options? Finding out about your treatment can help you to face up to it.

Some people even find it helpful to ask the direct, bald question, 'Am I going to die?' Most people think that no one should ever talk about death with the patient, and the books generally recommend that doctors and relatives should steer clear of the subject; but many terminally ill patients have found it much better to know the truth. There is more information about this in Chapter 15.

In fact the key question is not, 'Am I going to die?' but 'What are my chances?' Death is never certain. Your doctor does not know you are going to die any more than he knows whether he will cross the road safely on his way home. People have been given six months to live and have survived ten years. A lady from California had cancer operations at the ages of 42, 57, 90, and 92, and lived to celebrate her 103rd birthday. If you have breast cancer, you have a good chance of living another five years; even if you have lung cancer, one of the deadliest, you may be one of the lucky ones who survive.

Once you know the truth about your chances you can begin making realistic plans for the future.

Tactics In the short term, try planning your life from day to day. Don't just lie there sunk in gloom but work out a schedule for yourself. Set yourself goals, however simple they might be, and try to achieve something every day, and if possible achieve something new every day.

You should try to maintain a normal lifestyle for as long as possible. Do not allow yourself to become an invalid but at the same time use your knowledge of your illness to plan for changes in your routine. For example if you know that your treatment is going to make you tired in the evenings, plan to do what you want in the mornings. Even when your activity is cut down, stay as independent as possible: get up, get dressed, and go to the lavatory on your own.

Going into hospital Most patients are admitted to hospital after first attending as an out-patient. If you do not like the hospital your doctor sends you to, it may be possible for you to be sent to another one; ask your doctor whether you can change. You do not have the right to treatment by a particular hospital or a particular consultant unless you are a private patient and have arranged your treatment with that consultant in advance.

If you choose to be treated as a private patient you will have to pay weekly hospital charges and separate fees to the surgeon, the anaesthetist, and possibly the physician as well. Make sure you find out in advance how much these charges are likely to be, and that any insurance scheme which you subscribe to will cover them adequately. Alternatively you can pay for a private bed only, or (more cheaply) for an amenity bed, which will give you greater privacy, but your food, nursing care, and medical attention will be the same as those of non-paying patients. Paying for a bed does not give you the right to treatment by a particular consultant. You may not occupy a National Health Service (NHS) bed and pay for private treatment.

Every National Health Service hospital should provide a small handbook of information for prospective patients; ask for a copy if you are not given one. You should take with you into hospital your NHS medical card, details of your National Insurance number if you are drawing benefit, papers about any hospital fund or private insurance scheme which you want to use, any pension, supplementary benefit or Family Income Supplement book, and the name and address of your next of kin, or someone authorized to act for you. In addition you should take in night clothes, washing and toilet materials, a book or two, and a small amount of money to buy such things as magazines, newspapers, and stationery in the hospital. Write with a stamped, addressed envelope to the Patients Association (11 Dartmouth Street, London SW1H 9BN; tel: 01-222 4992) for a leaflet of advice and information on going into hospital.

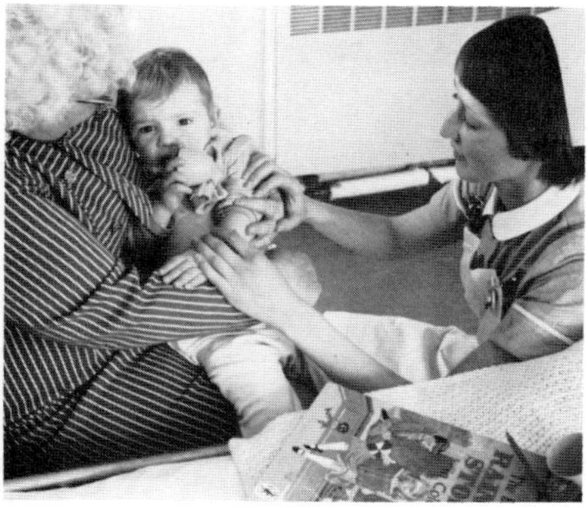

If your child is going into hospital, take his immunization record, and if the child is adopted take the necessary papers to show that you are the legal guardian. Also take toys and books – enough of the familiar things to provide a reminder of home. Visiting hours should be unrestricted. For advice and information, and for *Your Child in Hospital: A Parent's Handbook* write with a stamped, addressed envelope to the National Association for the Welfare of Children in Hospital, 7 Exton Street, London SE1 8UE; tel: 01-261 1738.

When you arrive in your ward or room the staff will probably do a series of tests: weight, height, urine, blood pressure, and perhaps also X-rays, electro-cardiogram, and blood tests. You may feel as though your body is being used as a pin-cushion, but do not worry. They are not taking these measurements because you are dangerously ill; they need to know about the state of your body and how it is working, both so that they can choose the right quantities and types of drugs and anaesthetics, and to enable them to monitor your progress. Do not be afraid to ask what is happening, and why.

Hospital routine starts early; you will probably be woken by the night staff before 7 a.m. and have your temperature and pulse taken and your bed made before breakfast at 7.30. The doctor generally does his round in the middle of the morning, and when he comes he may arrive with a group of students. This is the main training they receive in how to handle patients, and if you co-operate you are helping to teach the next generation of doctors. But if you are unhappy and if you want to talk to the doctor in private, tell your family doctor in advance, or tell the nurse or sister in charge of your ward, or even the doctor when he comes to see you.

Moving into the hospital world can be a difficult experience. You will find it easier if you can take a friend along with you for moral support; this is particularly true if you are at all uncertain about your illness or your treatment.

For more information about how to handle your doctor and consenting to operations, *see* pages 181–9.

If you are in hospital and you do not enjoy it, discuss with your doctor and your family the possibility of going home. You may not be able to get the same treatment at home, but perhaps missing the treatment would be worth it in order to be happier in familiar surroundings.

Illness at home If you are confined to your home, make sure you are in the best room and that you are not isolated from the rest of the household. Ensure you have company – friends, pets, television, and radio are all helpful. Don't forget the radio, which not only broadcasts twenty-four hours a day but is often less taxing and more agreeable than television.

Encourage your friends to visit you and talk to them; don't be embarrassed. They may well find it difficult to talk about your illness, and especially about the future. It is up to you to break down the barriers, but once you have done so you will find their presence a great comfort, even if they just sit and hold your hand when you do not feel like talking.

You may be able to get help or nursing at home; you may be entitled to laundry assistance (e.g. incontinence pads, plastic sheeting, and perhaps even the washing of bed linen), to nursing equipment such as

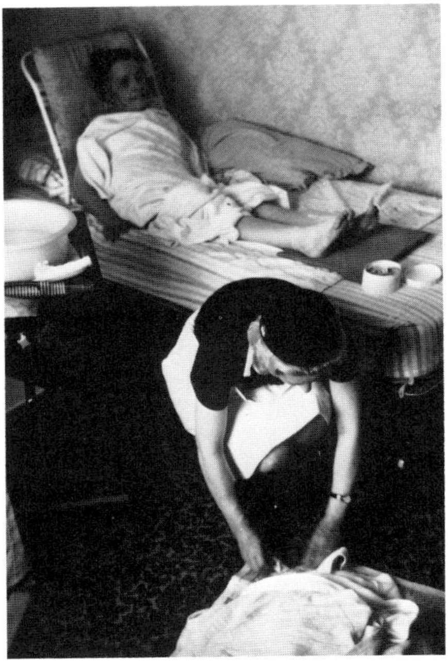

a commode, or even to adaptations to your home. You may also be able to use services such as meals on wheels and the mobile library. You can ask your doctor, health visitor, or social worker what services are available, or consult one of the books or organizations listed below.

If you are in pain, or in distress, tell your doctor about it. He may well be able to help in some practical way: by giving you drugs, or by showing you how to relieve aching muscles, or whatever. For example some people with serious illness feel nauseated at the sight of food, become constipated, or vomit after meals. These distressing symptoms, added to weakness and lethargy, can lead to increasing worry and depression. The future may be uncertain but additional treatment might help you to handle the present more easily.

Do not be afraid to talk about the possibility of death. Remember that for most people death itself is less frightening than the worrying and the uncertainty of not knowing what to expect. And most important of all, never give up hope . . .

Useful publications To find out more about a particular illness the first place to look is a medical reference book such as: *Black's Medical Dictionary* (A. & C. Black, 1976), the Reader's Digest *Family Health Guide* (1972), or Dr James Bevan's Home Medical Encyclopedia *Your Family Doctor* (Mitchell Beazley, 1980). Ask your doctor, or your librarian, if you need more information.

Bevan's *Your Family Doctor* contains a great deal of practical advice on how to look after patients who are seriously ill. You might like also to look at a paperback written specifically about terminal illness by Richard Lamerton called *Care of the Dying* (Technomic, 1976, and Penguin, 1980).

If you are nursing an elderly relative you will find one of these practical books helpful:

- Dr Muir Gray and Heather McKenzie, *Taking Care of Your Elderly Relative* (Allen and Unwin, 1980).
- John Agate *Taking Care of Old People at Home* (Allen and Unwin, 1979).

For more information about the services to which you may be entitled, see Phyllis Willmott's *Consumer's Guide to the British Social Services* (Penguin, 1978), which tells you not only what is available but also how likely you are to get it.

To find out whether there is a national association for people suffering from your illness, consult the booklet *Self-Help and the Patient* produced by the Patients Association (11 Dartmouth Street, London, SW1H 9BN; tel: 01-222 4992), or the *Directory of British Associations* (a CBD Research Publication) in your library.

Heart and chest diseases The British Heart Foundation (57 Gloucester Place, London W1H 4DH; tel: 01-935 0185) provides leaflets about heart attacks, strokes, angina, pacemakers, and so on, and strictly practical advice on how to cope with these conditions.

The Chest, Heart, and Stroke Association (Tavistock House North, Tavistock Square, London WC1H 9JE; tel: 01-387

3012) provides information and counselling service, by letter or telephone; also grants to help fuel bills, rent arrears, etc.

The Cardiac Spare Parts Club (Mr T. Davies, Four Winds, Beech House Lane, Bembridge, Isle of Wight; tel: 098387 4196) aims to support heart patients both before and after an operation.

Cancer For information on cancer, go to the Cancer Research Campaign, 2 Carlton House Terrace, London SW1Y 5AR; tel: 01-930 8972.

To obtain help, contact the Marie Curie Memorial Foundation (124 Sloane Street, London SW1X 9BP; tel: 01-730 9157), which runs eleven homes for the seriously ill, a rehabilitation centre for controlled cases, a night-nursing service for those ill at home, and a welfare service. They run a telephone-counselling service and know what services might be available in your area.

The National Society for Cancer Relief (Michael Sobell House, 30 Dorset Square, London NW1 6QL; tel: 01-402 8125) helps cancer sufferers in poor circumstances with small weekly cash allowances, practical home comforts, grants towards nursing, holiday allowances, and travelling expenses for relatives. Any request, however unusual, is always considered. They have built twelve hospices, which are now run by the NHS, but they concentrate on practical help, and have established home-care services. They always operate through the hospital social workers and the hospital is the simplest way to get their help but if you have difficulty you can telephone them direct for advice.

The Cancer Aftercare and Rehabilitation Society (CARE, Lodge Cottage, Church Lane, Timsbury, Bath BA3 1LF; tel: 0761 70731; or 29 Drum Brae Terrace, Edinburgh; tel: 031-336 8399) is a self-help organization of cancer patients who provide support for other cancer victims.

Other illnesses The associations listed below aim to provide support for patients, and to raise money for research.

- National Association for Colitis and Crohn's Disease, 3 Thorpefield Close, Marshalwick, St Albans, Hertfordshire.
- The Association to Combat Huntington's Chorea, Borough House, 34A Station Road, Hinckley, Leicestershire, LE10 1AP; tel: 0455 615558.
- The British Kidney Patient Association, Bordon, Hampshire; tel: 04203 2021.
- The Leukaemia Society, Hamlyns View, St Andrew's Road, Exeter EX4 2AF; tel: 0392 30032.
- The Motor Neurone Disease Association, 7 Lorimer Avenue, Gedling, Nottinghamshire NG4 4BS; tel: 0602 878700.
- The Multiple Sclerosis Society of Great Britain and Northern Ireland, and for the young, CRACK, 286 Munster Road, London SW6 6AP; tel: 01-381 4022.
- Action for Research into Multiple Sclerosis (ARMS, 71 Grays Inn Road, London WC1X 8TR; tel: 01-568 2255) raises funds for research, gives information, and also runs a 24-hour telephone-counselling service.
- Parkinson's Disease Society, 81 Queen's Road, London SW19 8NR; tel: 01-946 2500.
- British Polio Fellowship, Bell Close, West End Road, Ruislip, Middlesex HA4 6LP; tel: 71 75515.

Disability The Disabled Living Foundation (346 Kensington High Street, London W14 8NS; tel: 01-602 2491) gives information on daily living problems (not medical) of disabled people.

The Disablement Income Group (Attlee House, Toynbee Hall, 28 Commercial Street, London E1 6LR; tel: 01-247 2128/6877) provides a series of helpful leaflets on access to services.

Invalids-at-Home (23 Farm Avenue, London NW2 2BJ; tel: 01-452 2074) helps permanent invalids to live at home with grants, loans, and equipment.

8. When fear is everything

We all think we know what fear is: a reaction to danger; but it is a more complex and confusing emotion than that. Fear of the dentist or an injection seems straightforward enough but what about fear of the dark? There is no real danger associated with the dark; there may be slightly more chance of being robbed, or mugged, but that is not the root of the anxiety most of us sometimes feel. We are not frightened of anything in particular but we do have a sense of general unease. Even the dentist rarely causes real pain; the waiting is always worse than the treatment. None of us should think that our fears are simply rational.

For phobics, however, the extent of their fear makes its irrationality more obvious. Most of us will feel slightly concerned if we have to make a speech, or talk to the boss, but there are some phobics who are totally unable to meet anyone at all – because of their fear. We are inclined to label people suffering from these phobias as being wildly irrational but what is strange about their fear is not so much its irrationality but its strength. We all have to live with irrational fears, but phobics have to live with fears that can eventually dominate their behaviour.

There are four million phobics in the United Kingdom. They suffer from a range of apparently unnecessary terrors: from fears of spiders, and lightning, to extraordinary fears of apparently innocuous things such as cats, or clocks.

One of the most difficult problems for phobics is that we do not really take their fears seriously. We want to say: 'There's no danger.' 'There's no problem.' 'Come on, what's the matter?' Many phobics are afraid, quite understandably, of being thought mad. But once we see that these fears are not as much irrational as extreme it is easier to understand how they might develop.

At the centre of a phobia is often the fear of fear itself. This may seem absurd: how can you be afraid of fear? But fear, for all of us, breeds not on what is, but on what might be; it is in a way an emotion of the unknown. We are frightened before we give the speech, not during it; we are frightened of what that noise might possibly have meant, rather than of the burglar; and any director of a horror film is aware that the shadow of the murderer's footsteps is more effective than actually seeing the murderer. So for phobics, after an initial attack of anxiety, the fear of that fear returning provides the impetus for an ever-increasing vicious spiral of fear which may eventually be completely debilitating.

It is not surprising therefore that one method of treatment is to persuade the phobic to face the fear, either by gradually bringing the person closer to the thing that causes their fear, or by a sudden confrontation. This treatment has not changed significantly in the two thousand years since ancient Rome. Celsus, the first man to use the term phobia, described hydrophobia (fear of water) and recommended the following cure: 'Throw the patient unawares into a water tank. If he cannot swim push him under at intervals so that he drinks water even against his will; for so the dread of water will be removed.' Modern treatment is not so macabre, but the principle has changed very little over the centuries.

The only alternative to this approach was developed by Freud, and underlying it is the belief that a phobia stems from deep-rooted conflicts in the patient's personality. The aim of the treatment he advocated is to expose this conflict thus releasing the pressure that results in the phobia. Psycho-analysis, the name given to this outlook, tries to uncover the significance of the phobia by examining the past, the relationships and the emotions of the individual concerned. The success of the treatment is, however, as unpredictable as that proposed by Celsus.

Most of us take our day-to-day activities for granted. Walking to the shops or going to work in an office are not acts that worry us but for someone suffering from a phobia these simple tasks can prove terrifying. Quite simply, normal life can be made impossible.

Out in the open

> 'I was just walking through a shopping centre, and suddenly with no warning there was this feeling crushing me . . . I couldn't breathe, it was as if all the air was squeezed out of my lungs. And all I knew was that I desperately wanted to get away . . . just to get away, to get away to somewhere safe . . . but home was a good mile's walk away. I had a friend with me, and I just had to run, I just had to escape. I ran off crying . . . I remember thinking, I don't know what the hell's wrong with me – what's wrong with me, what's wrong with me?'

Maria was suffering from agoraphobia.

Agoraphobia is often thought of as fear of open spaces, but it really means fear of public places, or literally market-place phobia, after the Greek word *agora* meaning market-place. But there are many aspects of the illness which do not fall neatly into this description; often it appears closer to claustrophobia, in that sufferers have a fear of being trapped and unable to escape.

After her first attack Maria called the doctor.

> 'He just called it a panic attack – well I didn't know what that was – and he gave me some pills. I couldn't believe that it wasn't physical; it certainly felt physical. Then I was told that it was my nerves, but I thought the doctor just had to be wrong – it couldn't be my nerves. What I wanted to know was why was I like this, what was the matter with me.'

Maria

As the weeks and months passed the attacks did not go away; instead they became more frequent. Gradually all the daily excursions became great trials of will, even the simplest of tasks was daunting . . . but the shopping had to be done.

> 'I would be in a shop and all would be calm. I'd feel all right, and then I'd just be looking at the shelves and all of a sudden everything would seem to move, and it was as if the ground was going to swallow me up, as if it was enveloping me – I would actually feel dizzy and faint – and then things would go black as I was sucked in and engulfed . . . but you don't faint. Either I stand frozen, rooted to one spot . . . or, I want to run like hell. In fact once I nearly ran into a police station. I don't want to run anywhere in particular, I just want to run away – run away from everything. But normally I try not to run, because it makes you worse. You get more and more breathless, you breathe in too much oxygen and it makes you much worse . . . I don't know . . . you can't remember . . . it's as if you're not there. You carry on doing things but you're not there.
>
> Once I was in a shop and it was as if I had a total blackout. I don't remember anything at all and yet I got through the check-out, and paid. I came to as I was being shoved through out of the way.'

On our own in a lonely cottage at night almost all of us would occasionally feel a little uneasy, a little nervous. We are not anxious about any particular thing; instead our uneasiness stems from a more underlying uncertainty – an uncertainty of nothing in particular, a feeling of insecurity; we do not quite feel safe. The feeling of safety is not directly related to the existence of external dangers; it is more to do with our own inner composure. So with agoraphobia, the fear is often not of anything specific. The thought of having to do something can be horrifying, but exactly what it is that the phobic is frightened of is very unclear. The panic can strike at any time: it is as if it wells up and breaks out. But what is it a panic about? What is it that the sufferer is so terrified of? These questions seem obvious to the rest of us for whom the fears appear unfounded – even though our own fears are no easier to explain. In the case of phobics what matters is that the fear is out of control.

> 'If you are frightened of spiders – and I am absolutely petrified of spiders – you can always walk away from it . . . but you can't walk away from this . . . there is nowhere to go. I'm also frightened of wasps, but I can sling something at the wasp, or if I can't kill it, I can leave or keep out of the way. But if I've got one of these panics, how can I keep out of the way? The panic seems to be everywhere; there is no possible escape and that is just what is so frightening. All you are left with is fear. Fear that you can't run away from, fear that is so terrible just because there is no way you can run away.
>
> Sometimes I get what I call stuck – I feel stuck because I can't get out. Sometimes it is because I physically can't get out: there are people in front of me but that is just the beginning. If I see a wide, clear space I'll run for it. And run home. Once I'm home I collapse – it's so shattering. The attack completely exhausts me – I feel really done in. When the attack is really bad it just grips me; I can't see how it can ever stop; it just gets worse and worse. To be honest, I think I'm dying. I think, "God, this is it. I am going to die."'

The constant fear of an attack can eventually destroy your life. In the beginning Maria could not face going to the shops, but then she was not able to face visiting the post office, or the bank. Eventually almost any step outside the front door was a test of strength.

> 'Even to go to my mother's house I felt terrible. All I could think about was that I wanted to get home . . . it's silly because I wanted to see my mother and father but I got so scared. Once I got an attack in their house, and they called the doctor – they thought I was dying.
>
> Things like getting on a bus, going into town, or for a walk – I couldn't do anything like that. If somebody was to take me into town in a car and just dump me I wouldn't know what to do at all; it would be terrible – just thinking about it was absolutely horrible . . . I would try not to think about things like that.'

Maria's doctor gave her sedatives to control her panics. This treatment controlled the extremes of Maria's phobia but it did not in any way attack the cause, and as a result life continued to become increasingly difficult. And the doctor's explanation that it was 'nerves' certainly did not convince Maria.

'What I really thought was that it had to be physical: I'd got some awful disease, something wrong with my heart, or something like that. I couldn't believe that it was in my mind.'

Finally Maria was persuaded to see Tony, the organizer of the local Phobic Association. Tony started up the association after he developed agoraphobia himself. He remembers the determination of the early days with some pride.

'I decided that if nobody was going to help me, I was going to help myself. So I started to advertise for other sufferers because I found that the trouble is talking about it. The saying goes: "A trouble shared is a trouble halved." Well, getting the group together and talking about it has been fantastic. We spend our time talking . . . talking to people who understand, because we've all been through the same things. Talking really is the best therapy there is.'

Everybody in the association is a phobic – there are no doctors or professionals in charge and therefore no one feels pressured into doing something; no one feels that they will look silly, and no one feels, as they do all the time elsewhere, that they are the odd ones out.

'It is difficult talking to other people; they think you're crackers. You get labelled mentally ill – it's almost as if you are not quite human.

It's no good people saying, "Pull yourself together," because they don't know what it is like. You've got this fear, and you can't get out of it . . . but together with others you can go through it – but you have to go through it in the right way. With the right kind of help. With sympathy and guidance you can overcome it . . . but it takes time.

We have shopping expeditions, and a bus from the Social Services, and British Rail help us with our train therapy; we even have an aeroplane available for us. We don't force anybody to do anything, we just let their own conscience take over. If a person's frightened they'll stay back, but with the others doing it, in a few weeks they'll do it as well.'

One of the very effective techniques that the group has developed is to use walkie-talkies. People who had been trapped in their own homes for years were able to go out with the aid of a walkie-talkie. The sense that there was always somebody there at the end of the line made it possible to get into a car or go shopping.

'People lose confidence in driving, and so they can't get to work. So we have a walkie-talkie in the car, and we can talk them through their panic. One of our sufferers had never walked through the centre of Nottingham. So we gave her a walkie-talkie and I sat on the other end: and she walked for a few hundred yards, in the middle of the crowds. It was absolutely wonderful – she was over the moon.'

Maria had been with the group a few weeks and for the first time she had gone with them on a bus trip. It was time for her to try walking to the shops

Left and right: Tony's reassurance through the walkie-talkie radio helped to give Maria the confidence she needed to face her fears.

on her own. Tony handed her the walkie-talkie and walked round the corner out of sight. Maria waited . . . waited for the reassuring voice to come out of the machine. Already she was feeling that she had to get out. Why had she agreed to do this? Tony's voice broke through:

'Can you hear me all right?'
'Yes, Tony . . . yes.'
'Just take your time love, just take your time.'

Maria walked slowly along the street, gripping the walkie-talkie for security.

'Tony . . . I'm shaking like a leaf.'
'You will do. You will do. Just carry on. When you get to the shop I want you to look into the window.'
'Yes.'

Maria stood in front of the shop. Tense and trembling she was only aware of the constant pressure of feeling she wanted to leave.

'Maria, just look into the window, look at all the things around you. And realize that we are here waiting for you. Have a good look in the window. Now, I want you to go slowly into the shop and buy a box of matches. Have a look round, and say, "Could I have a box of matches please?" Okay?'
'Okay, Tony.'

Maria could hardly speak. Trapped by the thought of her fear she was quite unable to think about what she was doing – if she could only concentrate on achieving her task she might be able to forget the fear. Tony prompted her.

'Take your time now. Just go in. I want you to take your time. Occupy your mind by just looking round the shop. Look at the things on the shelf. Is there anything you want? Is there anything you like the look of? How about something for your little boy?'

Maria was in the shop but there was only a muffled answer from her. Tony was worried.

'Are you all right Maria? . . . Maria?'
'I'm wobbly Tony . . . I'm very wobbly . . .'
'That's normal . . . you are doing great. Absolutely wonderful. We are outside; you can come out whenever you want to.'

Maria didn't think she was going to make it.

'I'm getting the matches . . . I'm coming out.'
'Okay, Maria, your doing brilliantly.'

For Maria it was a question of just holding on until she managed to get through the door of the shop into the street outside.

'I've got the matches – I'm coming out now.'
'Just take your time. You're all right Maria, you're all right.'
'I'm coming out . . . I'm coming out . . . I've got, I'm out Tony, I'm out. I'm out of the shop.'

Over the next few months Maria began to show some improvement, but more important she began to believe in herself, to believe that she could make it.

The children have really noticed the difference in their lives since Maria joined the association

> 'For the first time in my life I've met other people like me. I've seen other people having the attacks that I have. I just couldn't believe that it happened to anybody else. When you see other people, and they talk to you and tell you what it's like for them, all sorts of things come home to you. For a start you realize that it isn't physical illness; and once you've accepted that, you know you have to do something about it, and you begin to get a bit better.'

One of the problems of agoraphobia is that the whole family suffers. As Maria started to improve the weight of feeling inadequate began to lift as well.

> 'I wasn't able to go out with the kids. Not on my own. They'd want to go out for walks. I'd have to make some excuse. They'd pester me: "Let's go to the pictures, let's go somewhere – everywhere." And I can't . . . I feel as if I'm not a proper mother . . . I feel guilty about that. But soon I hope I will be able to – that would be great.'

As an agoraphobic you have to put up with feeling separate, feeling that no one will understand. If you just want to leave, no one will believe you, they want you to explain, and you can't. The group has now opened a permanent centre and Maria works there every morning running the office. She has found that sense of belonging, that sense of ease that otherwise she only felt at home.

> 'People should just accept us as we are: we're not barmy, not at all. We're too sensitive really, definitely too sensitive. We don't need pity, we just need understanding. We all need understanding – without it you are on your own, and that is frightening . . . it's very frightening. When somebody understands, you know . . . you feel a lot better.'

What you can do

The most important thing to realize is that you are not alone. However bad you feel you can be sure there is someone else feeling just the same, or even worse. You are not going mad. You can get help.

How to cope with an attack An attack of panic is a wave of raw fear that surges through you, giving you hot and cold sweats, rapid breathing, palpitations, giddiness, and so on. Do not run away. Remember that the fear of fear is worse than the attack itself; if you fight it, or try to escape, you will only agitate yourself more than ever, and make the attack worse. Stay where you are, standing up or sitting down, and let time pass. The wave of fear will disappear more quickly if you don't fight it. Do not fuel the fear. Telephone the Samaritans if you are desperate to talk to someone.

Professional help Your doctor should be able to help you with the anxiety by prescribing sedatives or tranquillizers which will help you through the worst patches but they will not solve the underlying problem. Your doctor may also be able to refer you to a psychiatrist or a social worker (*see* page 86 for further information), or to a specialist clinic, such as the one run by Professor Isaac Marks at the

Institute of Psychiatry, De Crespigny Park, Denmark Hill, London SE5 8AF.

The Marriage Guidance Council (MG) (see your telephone directory under 'Marriage') may be able to provide useful support. They will certainly suggest ways in which you can get help. *See also* page 218.

MIND (*see* page 219, or your telephone directory) provides helpful advice to phobics. Telephone your nearest branch to find out what help is available in your particular area.

Self-help – books Even those who get professional help generally find that they have to do all the work; the best way to get help is by yourself. Many phobics have tackled their problems entirely on their own and have cured themselves. They work from books, and from tapes or records. The advantage of this is that you can proceed at your own pace; you are not pushed into anything; and no one sees when you make a mistake or fail. But it does require great self-determination, will-power, and persistence.

Professor Isaac Marks is an acknowledged expert on phobias, and his book, *Living with Fear* (McGraw-Hill, 1978), is an excellent account of the different types of phobia, and how to understand and cope with them. He provides case histories, discusses the effect phobias can have on your everyday life, and outlines medical and non-medical approaches to treatment.

Some of the best-known books are those by Dr Claire Weekes, who believes in treatment by desensitization – by teaching you slowly and gently to face the object of your fear, and stay calm. Once you can do that you are getting better. As this is not easy you have to approach the goal in easy stages, and she advises four primary ideas: face (do not run away), accept (do not fight), float (do not tense), and let time pass (do not be impatient). This is described in detail in Claire Weekes's *Agoraphobia; Simple, Effective Treatment* (Angus & Robertson, 1977). You may also find Dr Weekes's earlier books useful: *Peace from Nervous Suffering* (Angus & Robertson, 1972) is also primarily about agoraphobia. *Self-Help for Your Nerves* (Angus & Robertson, 1962) is a more general book about the relief of nervous tension.

Ruth Hurst Vose was an agoraphobic who became completely housebound in Lancashire. She tried all sorts of treatment before she was able to escape from her fear. Her book *Agoraphobia* (Faber paperback, 1981) is valuable both as a personal account of what agoraphobia feels like, and also as a source of information about the different types of treatment available, both medical and non-medical, and it explains how you can try homeopathy, hypnosis, or yoga, if you want.

You may also find useful Joy Melville's paperback *Phobias and Obsessions* (Allen and Unwin, 1979).

In order to obtain a self-help brochure called *Agoraphobia*, written by a former victim, write with 75p and a stamped, addressed envelope to Mr R. Peel, 3 Acacia Drive, Wakefield Road, Lightcliffe, Halifax, West Yorkshire HX3 8UF.

You might also like to read Joanna Johnson's *Working at Home for Profit* (Blackwell, 1980). This is a comprehensive guide to occupational opportunities for the housebound.

Self-help – tapes Another source of help lies in cassette tapes (or records), which tell you how to face your fear. There are several available; try the list below, or ask for advice from one of the self-help groups. Cassettes available by Claire Weekes are:

- *Hope and Help for Your Nerves*
- *A Goodnight Talk and a Good Morning Talk*
- *Nervous Fatigue*
- *Moving to Freedom and Going on Holiday*

In each case Dr Weekes speaks to you as though she was sitting beside you, and explains how you can cope with nervous problems. For full information send a stamped, addressed envelope to J. Skene

Keating, 16 Rivermead Court, Ranelagh Gardens, London SW6 3RT.

Mary Barfield's cassette *Relaxation for Everyday Living* has proved helpful to agoraphobics and others who live with stress. Write for information to Mary Barfield, 2 Toot Rock Coastguards, Pett Level, East Sussex TN35 4EW, enclosing a stamped, addressed envelope.

Laser Books Ltd (Denington Estate, Wellingborough, Northants NN8 2RQ) issue a tape on *Overcoming Agoraphobia* and another on *The Conquest of Fear*, as well as several on relaxation and meditation. Write to them for a full catalogue.

The Way to Peace of Mind is available from Doreen Darby, 174 Surrender Road, Brighton, Sussex BN1 6NN, price £4.50 including postage and packing.

Self-help groups The difficulty of working entirely on your own is that there is no one to encourage you, to spur you on when things are not going too well, or to congratulate you when you achieve a breakthrough. That is why the best solution of all probably lies in the self-help organizations that have grown up around the country. Most of these are non-professional groups, run by phobics for phobics, and they provide practical advice and support to those in need.

When you know that your fear is irrational you find it hard to talk to anyone about it, for you may well worry about being thought peculiar; but in one of these groups you will find others who have just the same sort of fears. You may find the prospect of meeting people appalling, but if they have the same sort of problems you will be able to share your own. Many phobics have found that group therapy, where everyone can talk about their own fears with other people who understand, is the most helpful first step; after achieving this they can even think about joining the rest of the group on a bus, or in a shop. Then they find they are helping themselves by helping others.

The Nottingham and County Phobic Association, founded by agoraphobe Tony Elliott in 1974, is one of the most active in the country. You can write to them at 1 Oban Road, Chilwell, Nottingham NG9 2TK; tel: 0602 412591 during working hours. It provides all sorts of therapy for phobics in the area, and also an information service about other groups and types of treatment available. Write for information, enclosing a stamped, addressed envelope.

The Phobics Society, founded in 1970 by agoraphobe Mrs Katherine Fisher, provides support and advice for sufferers all over the country. It produces regular progress reports, with details of new treatment, members' experiences, and methods of contacting people who might help. For full details send a stamped, addressed envelope to The Phobics Society, 4 Cheltenham Road, Chorlton-cum-Hardy, Manchester M21 1QN; tel: 061-881 1937.

Other organizations which you may find helpful are (write with stamped, addressed envelope):

- Mona Woodford, The Open Door Association, 447 Pensby Road, Heswall, Wirral, Merseyside L61 9PQ.
- Phobias Confidential, 1 Clovelly Road, Ealing, London W5 5HF; tel: 01-567 0262 or 01-840 3790.
- Mrs Annette Smith, Stepping Stones, 22 Harlech Walk, Throston Grange, Hartlepool, Cleveland TS26 0TN; tel: 0429 36941.
- Be Not Anxious, 33 Broadview Avenue, Rainham, Kent; tel: 0634 34262.

There may well be a small group in your area – ask the Citizens Advice Bureau (CAB), the Marriage Guidance Council, The Samaritans, or the area Probation Service.

THE SUNDAY TIMES

9. Every 28 days

Illness is not a straightforward matter. You may wake up one morning feeling dreadful, but unless you can put a well-understood label on this feeling you are not going to get much sympathy, let alone a day off from work. Feeling rotten, or under par, or miserable, is not enough to qualify for the special status of illness. You need in addition clearly defined symptoms which are accepted as being an indication of disease. Nor is it obvious which symptoms count. For being seen as having an illness sets you apart from others in a privileged although isolated way, giving you a status that is formally recognized in the doctor's sick note. Menstruation is a classic example of this. Are period pains sufficient to allow the special status of an illness? Our changing attitude to this question shows that illness is something that to a considerable extent we decide by our social prejudices and attitudes.

Throughout history, in almost all societies, menstruation has been regarded as a very special happening. Menstruating women have been thought to have unseen, almost magical power, and at the same time have commonly been ostracized and isolated from the community. Only in relatively recent times has the function of menstruation become known, and only during the last fifty years have the physical effects been studied in any detail.

Menstruation is the shedding of the lining of the womb. A fertilized egg embeds itself and begins to grow in this lining. If, however, the egg has not been fertilized the lining is obsolete and is lost in the resulting period. Traditionally any problems associated with menstruation tended to be written off as 'women's troubles'. Indeed it was not until 1931 that a name was given to the mental symptoms of irritability or depression that sometimes precede a period. Since then pre-menstrual tension has become more and more widely recognized. The other major symptoms that may affect women are the physical sensations during the period: these can vary from mild cramps to severe abdominal pain, bloatedness and backache. This condition is known as dysmenorrhoea and the cause is still not known. However, the pain usually diminishes as you get older, and also following your first child. Strangely, pre-menstrual tension often seems to become worse after the first or second child.

A quarter of a century ago if you went to the doctor with pre-menstrual tension you were told either that you were imagining it, or that this was an inevitable part of a woman's make-up. Either way, you were 'sent packing'.

Since then it has gradually become more accepted. In recent court cases juries have been prepared to return 'not guilty' verdicts because the women charged had been diagnosed by a doctor as suffering from pre-menstrual tension. However, the special status conferred in such decisions by regarding PMT as an illness is double-edged: for if a woman can be freed from murder charges on the grounds that she was unaware of what she was doing, another woman can also be thought to be unfit to hold an important job.

So while it would be foolish to ignore the symptoms of PMT, it is a dangerous answer simply to declare it as an illness. That menstruation is natural does not mean that the symptoms it can cause are non-existent or should be ignored, but neither does it mean that it should become an illness. Doctors tend to regard themselves as treating disease; as a result some are inclined to see anything they deal with as a disease – even pregnancy and birth, although recently there have been signs of change. It would be a sad mistake if the decline in the taboo surrounding menstruation and an increasing openness towards talking about it resulted in the medical profession turning it into an illness. We can treat ourselves without regarding ourselves as being ill.

Second-class citizen?

Until you are given a name, until you know that something might be wrong, the easiest thing is to assume there is nothing the matter.

> 'As a teenager I didn't know about PMT, so it didn't even occur to me. Looking back I think people used to accuse me of being miserable or irritable. I also used to fall asleep a lot, no matter how much I tried to keep myself awake. Now I know that it's one of the symptoms. At the time I didn't know anything. Nothing at all. I didn't know anything about, I mean, periods . . . you just didn't talk about them . . . my mother never said anything; it was all very much hidden away, never really spoken about.'

The taboo surrounding menstruation is one of the reasons that PMT often goes unnoticed, but there are others. Unlike a purely physical illness the symptoms of PMT are not easily defined from the way you may feel normally. It wasn't until after the birth of Jane's second child that things became serious.

> 'I suppose I just thought it was me and my personality. I would oscillate between feeling depressed and feeling aggressive. You can feel so depressed that you are on the point of suicide, and the aggression can be to the point of killing somebody. I used to get this immense surge of adrenalin, that gives you so much power that you could easily do somebody an awful lot of harm. Power which you would never normally have unless you found yourself in an extreme situation. In an odd sort of way the same power is there when you are depressed, only then it is channelled into doing yourself harm. You don't care if you hurt yourself, or if you burn yourself; you know you would still hold your hand on something that was burning. There is no rationality in it whatsoever.

Jane with her husband, John

Nothing was done for years because I would deny that there was anything the matter. I couldn't handle the thought that I was at fault, so far as I was concerned everybody else and everything else was at fault . . . but it wasn't me. I denied it, and denied it . . . and that stopped me getting help for a long time.'

Another reason why it is easy to ignore the fact that something is the matter is that the symptoms only last for a few days, or at worst for a couple of weeks, and when they are not there you can forget about them.

'Of course it was only like that half the time, and as soon as you come out of it, into your good phase, it never seems that it was that bad. You think, "Why is everybody making such a fuss?" Your self-protective mechanism comes into play, and stops you looking at it honestly, and squarely. You think up all sorts of reasons, all sorts of excuses, anything but admit there is something the matter with you. Perhaps the reason is that the obvious alternative is that there is something wrong with your personality . . . and you will do anything to avoid that conclusion.'

However, probably the most common reason for not being aware of PMT is a prejudice that lurks behind that age-old taboo of menstruation. A prejudice that is summed up in the belief that this is after all the woman's lot.

'Of course it wasn't that I'd never noticed. I'd suffered for years and years. But because it isn't widely accepted as a problem you find yourself in the old situation of, "Pull yourself together, woman." It is not only everyone else, you tell yourself as well that there's nothing you can do, that it's all part and parcel of being a woman, and you should be prepared to accept second-quality life. So you go along with it . . . but it doesn't take it away.'

Jane's problems became worse after her children were born

Without a label, without an illness with which to explain her behaviour away, Jane became cut off from friends and family.

'I just felt it was hopeless, I just felt totally isolated. Despite John, my husband, who was very understanding, I really felt I was going out of my mind. I felt there was nowhere I could turn, nobody to turn to. It wasn't the sort of thing that people talked about; instead you were just categorized as that sort of personality. Either you were miserable, and people would say,

"She's a miserable so-and-so," or you were bad tempered. In both cases you were somebody to be avoided. By women just as much as men.'

It was John who finally forced Jane to do something about it, but the first indication of what might be the matter came when Jane decided to come off the pill.

'Now, looking back I can see that the pill made me ten times worse. When I actually came off, I felt incredibly alive, whereas on the pill I was in a kind of depressive state, where I didn't really know what was going on. I tried all sorts of different pills but it wasn't until I came off them altogether that I made any real improvement. In fact that enabled me to think about the problem more clearly. Because until you feel there is something wrong, you can't even think of doing anything to put it right.'

As soon as Jane recognized there might be a problem she started to notice a number of physical symptoms which until then she had been either unaware of, or had thought were unimportant and just to be expected.

'The first thing is that everything would be too much effort. In fact getting up is the first hurdle of the day. Especially since I tended to sleep very badly with PMT, and I'd get a lot of vivid nightmares. So I'd wake up exhausted and fight with myself to drag myself out of bed. All your movements are slow; you feel clumsy and inefficient. But your mind feels slow as well as your body. I would think, "I should know the answer to that," but it just wouldn't be there. It was like there was a block . . . sometimes I'd have to concentrate just to find out what it was that I was talking about. It was really quite frightening.'

Gradually Jane started to note down her symptoms, and she began to realize that they came on a regular basis. Not that realizing necessarily made it any easier.

'You feel you can't go on. You know that you've been shouting and you know that it is going to return. It's going to come back again in a couple of weeks. It is not as if you might be instantly better and that you would never feel depressed again. Instead you've got this certainty that it's going to keep coming, and keep coming. It wears you down after years and years, it really wears you down.

It didn't really have a pattern to it; I just knew it wasn't right, but then when you've lived with it for so long, you are no longer sure what's right and what's wrong. It certainly wasn't as if it would always be worse on Day 12 or something. It could be at any time in the two-week span before my period – any time after ovulation. It seemed almost completely random . . . it wasn't as if I'd even start depressed and become aggressive, there was no pattern like that, no particular order. So I wasn't sure; perhaps I was imagining it, perhaps it was just me. You lose touch with reality. You lose touch with the quality of life that other people have. After years there is no you left . . . you eat, sleep, and breathe it, and you really believe that is you, that is what you are.'

Besides feeling exhausted and clumsy there were many other symptoms which over the years Jane had become so accustomed to that she simply took them for granted.

'My stomach and my breasts would get incredibly sore and sensitive. So much so that I couldn't even wear an apron or hug the children because it was painful. Your ankles ache if you stand for any length of time. Your fingers hurt and your joints swell up. Fluid would collect in the sinuses at the top of my head. If I got up quickly, everything would spin round and I would get very dizzy. At the same time all sorts of throat and ear problems would get worse . . . but for me one of the worst things was spots that I used to get under my skin. As a teenager I'd always had greasy skin – everyone told me I would grow out of it. But I never did. It used to depress me incredibly. You feel you're unattractive and that everybody is looking at the nasty marks on your face. It's horrid. Your confidence is at zero anyway; it used to just about finish me off.'

Jane often found that her physical symptoms made her emotional problems much worse. Since it is not the sort of thing that is discussed openly – in fact it is surrounded by an element of secrecy – Jane rarely asked for any time off from her secretarial job.

'I would make all sorts of typing errors. I couldn't think quickly enough to catch my hands as I normally could. I would miss out words, and make stupid mistakes. I used to have to make mounts for pictures, and somehow I would manage to cut them the wrong way round. Anyway, it all makes the situation worse because you are lacking in self-confidence in the first place. You're proving to yourself that you are second-rate. It runs so deep and it's linked to so many things. When you have this low opinion of yourself, other people start to have a low opinion of you as well. Society is directed towards people who project themselves in a good way. The others get pushed by the wayside. And of course that just makes things worse. Your self-confidence falls to absolutely nothing.

People say to you, "Pull yourself together," but it doesn't make any difference. The weight of feeling is so powerful that you can't do anything except give in to it. There's nothing you can do about it. That's very difficult for other people to understand; they just think you are not trying. And that's the sad part, because . . . it just makes you despair. Somehow you've tried to combat it, month after month. But there is no way you can escape it. It is then that you start thinking that not being around is more attractive than having to fight . . . always having to fight.'

Jane had given up going to the doctor. She had tried but she hadn't got anywhere. Either it was ignored, or it was to be expected, or if treatment was given it didn't do much good.

'Because of the bloatedness, and build-up of fluid, I had been given diuretics, but sometimes they make you feel worse. Instead of any improvement the loss of fluid seems to aggravate your general emotional and mental state.'

Diuretics result in a loss of fluid because they act on the kidneys to increase the output of urine. Alcohol, tea, coffee are all mild non-medical diuretics. However, in addition to fluid the body loses some salts, mainly sodium and potassium, and this may have been the cause of Jane's deteriorating emotional state. John eventually managed to persuade Jane to see the doctor again.

'This time I was lucky. I got a new, young, lady doctor. She was nice and sympathetic, and what's more she knew about PMT. So I started taking a course of hormone treatment – it's synthetic progesterone actually. But it didn't really work. We tried others and it still didn't work. Even so, it would have been ten times worse if she had been like my previous doctors, who hadn't been prepared to listen, let alone try.'

Since it was fairly clear the treatment was not working, Jane's doctor made an appointment for her to see a specialist. Although the new treatment the specialist prescribed used the same type of hormone it was in a different form and the dose was altered. The improvement was obvious.

'The effect was immediate . . . although, it wasn't constant. But it was an enormous relief to realize that at least something worked. You are only meant to take the progesterone up until a few days before your period – a bit like the pill – but I was so afraid to stop taking it that I began to take it almost all the time. I was dependent on it for my sanity; I didn't dare stop taking it, even if it was only to risk those couple of days. Still I've got over that now.

Another thing that is important is your diet. The specialist had told me that, but I didn't take any notice, and I just learned from bitter experience – the hard way. At the weekend, because I'd lie in, I didn't eat regularly. I started taking the most enormous amount of progesterone because I couldn't understand why it wasn't working . . . I really started to panic. But it was just because I wasn't eating properly. I found out that you have to eat little and often, and protein rather than carbohydrates.'

One of the problems of PMT is that although the symptoms are very debilitating they are also rather vague and general. Furthermore, they are the sort of symptoms that everyone has from time to time. Jane was fortunate in having a sympathetic doctor, but looking back she recognizes what she should have done before.

'The only ammunition that you have got is the regularity with which the symptoms occur. Otherwise the doctor can always turn round and say, "Everybody gets depressed, everybody gets bad nerves, everybody gets sore throats," and, of course, it's true. So the only thing you can fight with is the regularity and recurrence of your symptoms, the fact that you have two weeks of feeling absolutely terrible, of feeling depressed and aggressive, of having all sorts of nasty physical things go wrong with you, and feeling absolutely drained and awful. It is only the regularity that makes it PMT, and all you can do is to keep a record, and see your doctor armed with it.'

Jane's symptoms are only an extreme form of the sort of thing that millions of women suffer from. To say that all of those women are ill would be ludicrous, but surely it should be possible for doctors to recognize that they can treat something without it becoming an illness? For if Jane is in any way typical, the improvement in the quality of life can be profound.

'I used to feel like Jekyll and Hyde. As if I was possessed by an alien spirit that was destroying me. There was no way that I could get rid of it, it just would go on and on destroying me. Now, I feel so much better, I feel like a human being again. My skin has improved marvellously . . . I still get bad days . . . but the main thing is that I feel in control, instead of feeling that somebody or something else is in control of me. I suppose I feel that *my* life has returned . . . I am no longer somebody else, I have become me.'

What you can do

Gynaecological difficulties can be unpleasant enough in their own right, but they can become more upsetting than necessary, for three reasons. Since most doctors are men, some women find their problems hard to explain and discuss, and dislike being examined. There are also still a few doctors who will not take the problems seriously and dismiss them as 'women's troubles'. Furthermore, some women think that to suffer painful periods, for example, does not make them 'ill', and that therefore they do not 'deserve' treatment. But attitudes are changing; menstruation is no longer something that can never be talked about, and you can obtain treatment if you want it.

Menstrual problems The onset of menstruation is marked by changes in the body's hormone balance. What doctors call either 'primary' or 'spasmodic dysmenorrhoea' usually appears suddenly as period pains on the first day of the period, with five-minute spasms of pain every twenty minutes for a day or two. Some people claim that extra exercise or relaxation help, but the evidence is inconclusive, and the simplest remedy is probably to curl up round a hot-water bottle and take some pain-killers. Your doctor may be able to help, perhaps with hormone treatment.

'Secondary', or 'congestive dysmenorrhoea', brings a continuous, dull pain that lasts for several days both before and during the period, and is made worse by smoking. Again your doctor may be able to help with hormone treatment.

Periods sometimes stop altogether. This condition is called amenorrhoea and the most common cause is pregnancy, but it can be brought on by a severe emotional upset, by too great a loss of weight, or by the side-effects of drugs (including the pill). If you are suffering from amenorrhoea it is wise to see your doctor. However, if you are worried that you are pregnant and do not want to go to your family doctor you can be tested at a family planning clinic, through a Brook Centre (*see* page 60), or through a women's centre (contact WIRES, 0742 755290). Telephone the Samaritans if you need immediate support. The British Pregnancy Advisory Service (see your telephone directory, or contact the head office at Austy Manor, Wootton Wawen, Solihull, West Midlands B95 6DA; tel: 05642 3225) can probably provide the help and advice you need. (*See also* page 20.)

When menstruation slows down and stops at the menopause, which is caused by another hormone change, a deficit of oestrogen, you may experience symptoms ranging from hot flushes to irritability and vaginal dryness. Hot flushes are often made worse by tea, coffee, and spicey foods, and by sleeping under too many bedclothes. Your doctor may be able to help by giving you oestrogen. The Family Planning Information Service, or one of the organizations above, can tell you where there is a local menopause clinic.

To help you through any of these difficulties, and especially at the menopause, you might like to consider trying alternative medicine. There is a helpful discussion in Angela Phillips and Jill Rakusen, *Our Bodies Ourselves* (*see* page 124), and further information on page 148.

♀	NOV	DEC	JAN	FEB	MAR	APR
1						
2						
3						
4						
5				H		
6				H		
7			B	H&T		
8			H&B	H&T		
9			H&B	P		
10		H&T	H&T	P		
11		H	P	P		
12		H	P	P		
13		T	P			
14	H	T	P			
15	H&B	P				
16	H&T	P				
17	H&T	P				
18	H	P				
19	P					
20	P					
21	P					
22	P					
23						
24						
25						
26						
27						
28						
29						
30						
31						

Pre-menstrual tension (PMT) The symptoms of PMT are not specific, therefore the best way to find out whether they could be caused by this is to keep a record of them and the dates on which they occur – either on a chart like the one shown above, or on a calendar, or in a diary. Write, for example, B for bloatedness, H for headache, T for tension, and P for period, and within three months you will know. If roughly the same symptoms occur regularly at the same interval before your periods, then you are almost certainly suffering from PMT.

Just to know what causes the symptoms can help, and you can also take preventative measures. In particular eat well and regularly, and make sure you have some protein at least three times a day, and preferably four. This can be difficult when you do not feel like getting up in the morning, and you may hate the thought of eating if you are bloated and overweight, especially if you are on a diet; but if you don't eat enough, if you skip breakfast, for example, your blood sugar level may drop and your symptoms could become worse. Many women put on several pounds before their periods but this is caused by fluid retention; the weight will disappear when your period starts.

You can if you like try either relaxation and breathing exercises (the same type as are recommended for pregnancy) or vigorous exercise such as brisk walking, jogging, swimming, or squash. Many women claim that exercise alone keeps their problems at bay.

For the great majority of women these simple measures are enough, but if they are not, there are other treatments – such as taking extra Vitamin B6 for about ten days before your period starts, or from three days before you expect the symptoms. Vitamin B6 (pyridoxine) occurs naturally in liver and other meats, eggs, milk, cereal, and wholemeal bread; or you can buy it in tablet form at a chemist or healthfood shop – possibly 30–50 milligrams a day, following the instructions on the bottle. For a free leaflet on pyridoxine treatment write with a stamped, addressed envelope to the PMT Clinic, Department of Gynaecology, St Thomas's Hospital, Lambeth Palace Road, London SE1.

Plan your life as far as possible so that you avoid entertaining, interviews, examinations, or important decisions during the pre-menstrual days. Talk about your problems, if possible, with your partner, your family, and your friends; you will all find them easier to cope with if you know what to expect.

You might like to contact a PMT support group such as Understanding Women; *see* organizations listed below.

PMT – Professional help If your own measures are not effective, your family doctor may be able to help. If you read one of the books below you will be in a better position to discuss your symptoms and your treatment. Beware of accepting only a prescription for tranquillizers, which will not solve the problem, although they may make the symptoms more bearable. Family doctors can usually give you progestogens (synthetic progesterone) to try and restore the hormone balance, but dosage and timing are critical, and it may be that you

Once you recognize the problem you can try treating yourself; if that fails do not be afraid to ask your doctor for help

need the natural hormone progesterone, which cannot be taken by mouth. It is worth discussing your treatment, and if it does not work at first, do not give up.

There are specialist PMT clinics at the Chelsea Hospital for Women, at St Thomas's Hospital, and at University College Hospital, in London, and at the Royal Hallamshire Hospital in Sheffield. To find out whether there is a treatment centre in your area contact a family planning clinic, the Family Planning Information Service (27 Mortimer Street, London W1N 7RJ; tel: 01-636 7866), the Citizens Advice Bureau (*see* page 218), Marriage Guidance (*see* page 218), or WIRES (0742 755290).

Do not feel guilty or embarrassed about going to the doctor when perhaps you do not feel you are ill. The important thing is that you can obtain treatment to improve the quality of your life. And do not be tempted, as many women have been, to ask for a hysterectomy in the hope that it will relieve your PMT; on the contrary, it may well make matters worse.

Talking to doctors You may find it difficult to talk about menstruation, especially with a male doctor, but you are unlikely to receive the best possible treatment unless you have an open relationship involving trust and sympathy. There is advice on how to approach your doctor on pages 188–9 and 200, and in *Talking To Your Doctor* (*see* below). Family planning clinics (listed in your telephone directory under the District or Area Health Authority) have more women doctors; you can always go there, and you may be treated more sympathetically. For information on how to change your doctor *see* page 189.

Organizations and books You should be able to borrow all the books below from your library, or buy them from a good bookshop, but if you have any difficulty either go to one of the shops listed on page 59 or contact Sisterwrite, 190 Upper Street, London N1; tel; 01-226 9782.

Understanding Women (6 Hillside Cottages, Leverstock Green, Hemel Hempstead, Hertfordshire) is a voluntary self-help group that offers support to PMT sufferers. Write with a stamped, addressed envelope.

There are women's centres in many towns, and Well Woman Centres in some. To find out about your area either ask at the family planning clinic or contact the women's information service WIRES (P.O. Box 162, Sheffield S1 1UD; tel: 0742 755290) or A Woman's Place (48 William IV Street, London WC2; tel: 01-836 6081). A further useful source of information is *The Spare Rib Diary* (obtainable from *Spare Rib*, 27 Clerkenwell Close, London EC1R 0AT) which has an excellent section on women's health, with useful advice and an extensive list of contacts for further information. Their monthly magazine is also helpful.

- The BUPA Health Promotion Centre (Battlebridge House, 300 Grays Inn Road, London WC1X 8DU) has booklets on PMT and the menopause.
- A free leaflet on the change of life is issued by the Health Education Council, 78 New Oxford Street, London WC1.
- Women's Health Concern (16 Seymour Street, London W1H 5WB; tel: 01-486 8653) has rather expensive booklets on *Premenstrual Syndrome and Period Pains*, *The Menopause*, and *Post-Natal Depression*.
- Mrs Annette Smith, Stepping Stones, 22 Harlech Walk, Throston Grange, Hartlepool, Cleveland TS26 0TN; tel: 0429 36941.
- For information on urinary infections see Angela Kilmartin's book *Understanding Cystitis* (Heinemann, 1973) or contact the U & I Club at 9E Compton Road, London N1 2AP; tel: 01-359 0403.
- Katharina Dalton, *Once A Month* (Fontana paperback, 1978) is a sympathetic and comprehensive account of menstrual problems and their treatment.

- Judy Lever, *PMT – The Unrecognized Illness* (Noonan Hurst, 1979) is an exceptionally clear guide to understanding and also to coping with the problem.
- Peter Saunders is a gynaecologist, and his *Womanwise* (Robert Hale, 1981) is a slightly medical view of gynaecology for every woman.
- Lynda Birke and Katy Gardner, *Why Suffer?* (Virago, 1980) is a handbook about periods and their problems.
- Ruth Thomson, *Have You Started Yet?* (Heinemann, 1980, and Pan, 1980) is an informative guide about the start of menstruation.
- Janice Delaney, Mary Jane Lupton and Emily Toth, *The Curse* (Dutton, 1976, and Mentor Books, New English Library, 1977) is a historical account of the mythology that surrounds menstruation.
- Penelope Shuttle and Peter Redgrove, *The Wise Wound* (Victor Gollancz, 1978, and Penguin, 1980) is a curious book on the psychology of menstruation.
- Angela Phillips and Jill Rakusen, *Our Bodies Ourselves* (Allen Lane, 1978, and Penguin, 1978) is a comprehensive guide to women's health, with sections on feelings, attitudes of doctors, and possibilities for self-help. It does not have much about PMT but there is an excellent chapter on the menopause. Very practical on what to do when you have problems, and on the relative merits of various types of treatment.
- Carolyn Faulder, *Talking to Your Doctor* (Virago, 1978) is a short, direct guide to what women need to know and say when they visit their doctors with gynaeological problems.
- Sheila Ernst and Lucy Goodison, *In Our Own Hands* (The Women's Press, 1981) is about self-help therapy, consciousness-raising, and encounter groups.
- Wendy Cooper, *No Change* (Arrow, 1976) describes the effects of the menopause, and how hormone treatment can help at this time.

You and society

10. Facing unemployment
A job provides more than a salary

11. Mental illness
Can starving yourself to death be rational?

12. The odd ones out
For those who are different, *we* are *their* problem

13. Obsessed with food
Eat as much as you want . . . but only when you're hungry

10. Facing unemployment

Losing a job is more than losing your pay packet, for it is the loss of your place in society. Most of us complain about our work at some time or other – the people we have to work with, the routine of the job, the boredom of the task – but it is those very things we complain about that provide the framework for our lives. Without having a task to complete, without having colleagues to say 'good morning' to, you have to decide what you are going to do; if you are going to meet anybody you have to go out and meet them. Nothing happens by chance any more. You have to make all the choices.

Anybody who is unemployed for a considerable length of time is forced to ask themselves, 'What am I doing?', 'What do I want to do?', 'What is my purpose?'. We can all ask these questions when we are working, but we do not really have to face up to them. We think that if we were not at work we could be doing all sorts of things instead – as if we could have a permanent holiday. But holidays only feel like holidays if you have been working. Of course, losing a job can bring real financial hardship, but above all it is a destroyer of self-esteem.

There are three recognizable stages of unemployment. The first is a period of great shock. During this phase people feel very depressed, but it does not last very long, usually a matter of a few weeks. This is followed by a phase of optimism – a feeling that another job will come along, and meanwhile you can enjoy the free time. This period can last from a few months to a year, but it is gradually replaced by a more pessimistic outlook, and finally by a fatalistic feeling that you have got to accept that you really are unemployed.

There is little doubt that unemployment can cause a deterioration in your health, although there is much controversy over the extent of the problem. The ill health is caused by the increase of stress and anxiety, and unemployment is one of the most stressful experiences you will ever have to face. But the primary effect of being made redundant is to force you to ask very basic questions about yourself and what you are doing. It is not something that is easy to cope with, but for some time to come it is something that many of us will have to face.

Time on your hands

Liz is someone who really knows what redundancy means. She trained as an occupational psychologist and worked as a redundancy counsellor. While

Liz

working both with the employer and with the members of staff made redundant she came to understand the patterns of response that people go through in facing unemployment.

> 'The first reaction to being told unexpectedly that you are being made redundant is shock depression. You feel that you've been rejected by your company . . . you joined them in good faith and you've just been thrown out . . . you feel incredibly expendable.
>
> After the initial period of shock you begin to think that things are all right – this is particularly true of people with professional or executive jobs. You feel that you've got the contacts or you know how to find a job, and you set about following up the possibilities. You start being offered interviews and if you are rejected there is always another possibility in the pipeline.
>
> But when you've been out of work for a very long time you're sort of out of practice with working, and you begin to just accept the fact that you're unemployed – unemployment starts to become your occupation. That's when the real rot sets in. It becomes very difficult to be enthusiastic about any new lead, because you've accepted your position and you think, "Oh well, nothing's going to happen, nothing's going to change – I'm not going to get the job." It even becomes difficult to generate sufficient optimism to apply.'

Liz's role in the firm was not confined to redundancy counselling; she also advised companies about the selection of personnel, their training procedures, and their interviewing techniques. Liz herself had been successful and much enjoyed her work. So when one afternoon she was handed a note from her boss while advising two colleagues on how to deal with a client's staff, there was no reason for her to feel apprehensive. The note just said, 'See me at four tomorrow.' But the abruptness of the note irritated her.

> 'There was no explanation why, no please, no nothing, just see him. I was annoyed about that – I had other things to do. So I phoned his secretary and said, "What's this all about?" She said she didn't know – not even whether it was important. So I went back to my meeting fuming.'

There was no reason for Liz to think any more about the matter until the appointment the following day.

> 'I had decided that he probably wanted me to do some research so I went in with my notebook ready. He was standing up by the window, and he just said, "Liz . . . I've got some bad news for you. I'm going to have to make you redundant." And I . . . it just blew me apart. I couldn't quite believe it – he was silhouetted against the window, and I was looking at him, and I just didn't respond at all.'

What made it worse was that six months previously business had been particularly bad and Liz had specifically asked whether there were going to be any redundancies. She was told that there were not, and that even if there were she would not be one of them.

> 'I was so shattered I don't remember saying very much. My boss was saying that, of course, they would do everything they could to help me get a new job, but there was polite advice that if I took them to an industrial tribunal all that goodwill would be withdrawn.
>
> The first reaction from everybody at work was astonishment. They were really shocked and terribly upset . . . they were very supportive. But they were all busy that evening so I went home and phoned my boyfriend Bill – he was flabbergasted too. Still he just said, "Typical bloody company, I never did approve of the job anyway." He was very shocked and upset – after all I was the major breadwinner, earning twice as much as he was. That evening we talked about it continuously – it was rotten really because it was Bill's birthday and we didn't go out at all.'

One of the first things Liz tried to do was to find out why she had been sacked. But nobody would tell her. She considered taking her case to the industrial tribunal but the problem with the Employment Protection Act is that you can do yourself much more harm by fighting the case than by accepting things quietly.

> 'I heard from one of the managers that they were getting very worried about a tribunal because they didn't think it was worth dredging up all sorts of stuff because of my future career. And that's what's so awful, because if you are bothered about your career you can just forget going to an industrial tribunal; just absolutely forget it. You can be thrown out for

> unfair reasons but if you do anything about it, you will lose a reference, and from then on any future employer can ring them up, and they can tell any story they like.'

Liz knew all about the effects of unemployment, but it did not help her during the first few weeks.

> 'I never stopped talking about it. I cried, I couldn't sleep – all that sort of thing. The following day I went into my office to clear out my stuff and I just couldn't believe that I was no longer an employee, that I was no longer part of it. It was all going on around me – something that yesterday I was part of, something I was concerned about, and now I wasn't. It all seemed so accidental. Why me? What had I done? Sometimes I think of the people I used to work with – I know their problems, I know what they will be worrying about, I know all of this and yet it is no longer mine; I no longer have my place there.'

One of the first things to deal with if you are unemployed is your depression. Liz was supposed to know the answers.

> 'If somebody is redundant and has been unemployed for a certain length of time, you talk to them, you say, "This is your situation, there's no point in looking at all the reasons, there's no point in thinking about the bad points. You must look at what you can do – build on the positive things." You tell people that they must be active, they must apply for jobs, and you tell them how to do a good interview. So . . . I'd gone through all this with other people and then suddenly it happens to me. I knew the theory, so I phoned up all sorts of contacts and I revamped my curriculum vitae. The trouble was that I knew what I should be doing and I felt guilty if I started to get depressed because I knew that in the end I was responsible for myself – and no one else could help.
>
> I've a little bit more understanding now. You say pull yourself out of it, look for the positive side, but it's very difficult to do that when you are on your own for ten hours a day. You can look on the positive side for a while but then the time seems to wear you down, and when you begin to feel sorry for yourself you can't stop it; it just overcomes you.'

By working, we meet people, we talk to them, not because they are friends but because you both happen to have the same reason for being in that place at that time. Without that casual contact life can become more intense than we would like.

> 'The one thing you really miss is people contact; that's the most important thing for me I think. You can go out and walk down the street, talk to people in shops, but it's not the same. You need to meet people that you have something in common with . . . people who know you, and know how you are different from the way you were yesterday and the way you will be tomorrow. The difficulty with being unemployed is that nothing just happens

Enthusiastic telephoning of her contacts helped Liz to fill time and boost her optimism

to you – you don't bump into someone in the corridor. Instead you have to go and see them; everything has to be arranged; you have to have a reason; you have to have the will . . . and when you're unemployed and depressed that's just what is lacking.'

The real difficulty is that unemployment saps your enthusiasm for anything. Suddenly you are a free agent – you can do anything at all . . . but that is just what makes it so difficult. Because you have no constraints, because there are no deadlines, gradually there seems to be less and less point in doing anything. Half of the battle is to force yourself to do something, but even for Liz, who was aware of this, it was a battle she did not always win.

> 'I'd spend a lot of time phoning people up and arranging interviews, and that's why I suppose I didn't get depressed for three or four weeks. But then I would see people and they would say they liked me but in the present circumstances, with the recession and so on, there was no way they could give me work. And then I started to get a bit depressed because I knew I would have to kill time, and I'm not very good at killing time. There were masses of things in the house that were building up that I should have been able to do – like building shelves and so on . . . I'd even bought all the shelving for it – but I still haven't done it.
>
> One thing that really hit me is that when you're actually in employment you're moaning all the time – you've got to get up, and you've got this problem, and so on and so forth. All the hassles of your employment and all the hassles of your boss harassing you all the time. But then when you haven't got all that you really miss it. You think you'd miss it like a hole in the head but actually you don't.
>
> Bill's friends would come round in the evening and they'd be talking about their work and they'd be moaning and groaning about going to work and I'd think, "Yeah, I can sleep in all tomorrow – what a bore. Who shall I see at lunch? Well I don't know." You miss the routine . . . you miss the routine desperately.'

The most obvious point about work is that you are rewarded not only financially, but also by completing a task, by achieving a goal, by others who thank you, or congratulate you, on occasion perhaps even promote you. When you are unemployed you lose all of that – you are setting your own goals, and congratulating yourself, and that is something that few of us find we can do for very long.

One way of dealing with the freedom is to impose a routine; to turn your day into a day of work.

> 'What I have had to do is take my work life into my home life. I make a list of everything I've got to do each day – it doesn't matter what they are, I still make a list. And I know that when I get up at nine o'clock I've got to finish those things – and if I do finish them I've achieved something; I can feel that I have done something that day and that I haven't just wasted it.'

After five months out of work Liz decided to start her own business. There are many who will persevere for longer without finding a job, and for most the financial aspect of unemployment is more important. Although the financial distress caused by unemployment can be devastating it is often the psychological pressures that are the most difficult to deal with – because unemployment forces you to examine yourself, to give goals to yourself, and to judge yourself.

You may know – as Liz did – what to do, but in the final resort there is still no one else who can solve your problems. Trying to be as positive as possible, adopting a regular routine, giving yourself tasks – this is all sound advice, advice that Liz once gave to people who came to her as a counsellor – but in the end it is what you make of it; no more, no less.

> 'There were times when I would think, it's all very well knowing about what I should be doing, but I don't feel like doing it. But when I got really depressed I would think about other people that I had met who are not only unemployed, but who have other problems as well, like being disabled or whatever; and I would know that they are in a much worse position than I am to get a job. And when I thought that, it made me feel very guilty, because I realized that there were things I could be doing and wasn't, things that made everything easier for me that I was ignoring . . . and I suppose I realized that what I had to do was to look forward – to set myself a goal, and then to achieve it.'

What you can do

Anyone who is going to be made redundant is entitled to a reasonable amount of time off with pay, during working hours, to look for another job, or to make arrangements for training for future employment. Visit your Citizens Advice Bureau (CAB) or Citizens Rights Office if your employer makes any difficulty over this.

When you actually lose your job there are two things that you must think about: money, and the future. You might also like to make sure that the way you lost your job was fair.

Unfairly dismissed? You can be made redundant only if your job has ceased to exist. You are entitled to a letter giving you written reasons for your redundancy, and to a redundancy payment if you have worked for the company for at least two years. If you find out that someone else has been given your job, or that although the company claimed a 'last in, first out' policy someone who joined later than you has not been made redundant, then you can go to an industrial tribunal and claim unfair dismissal. If your case is upheld you could demand your job back.

The problem about going to an industrial tribunal is that it might ruin your future career: the company will immediately note you down as a trouble-maker and may inform your prospective employers. If you still want to do this consult the shop steward of your union, or one of the organizations or the books listed at the end of this chapter. Alternatively, you can go direct to a solicitor, but he will charge you money, and may not be an expert in this branch of the law.

If you are wrongfully dismissed and have not been given your notice or holiday pay, you can sue the company for breach of contract by going through the county court.

Redundancy money When you are made redundant you are entitled to a lump sum (cash and tax-free) which is calculated on your age and length of service. If you are made redundant but no money is paid to you or if you disagree with the amount, you can go to an industrial tribunal to appeal; *see* page 137 or talk to the CAB.

Money – and how to sign on When you lose your job you have three possible sources of money: redundancy money, unemployment benefit (UB or the dole), and supplementary benefit (SB).

The first thing to do is to sign on for *unemployment benefit*, even if you think you will get another job quickly, because you will be credited with National Insurance contributions for each week you are registered. If you cannot sign on within a few days, write to the manager of the UB office saying you wish to claim benefit immediately.

In order to qualify for UB you must have paid enough National Insurance contributions. (The complicated detailed rules are set out in the Department of Health and Social Security (DHSS) leaflet NI35.) You must also be fit, available, and looking for work, which means that you must have signed on for suitable work at the Jobcentre; so go there first. Find your nearest Jobcentre by asking at the post office or looking in the telephone directory either under 'Jobcentre', or 'Manpower Services Commission'. They are generally open from 9 a.m. to 5 p.m., Monday to Friday, but the benefit office is open only from 9 a.m. to 12 and from 2 p.m. to 3.30 or 4 p.m.; so don't leave it too late.

When you visit the Jobcentre ask to register for work, and state which type of work your require. You will then have to see a Vacancies Officer, who will ask you questions, tell you whether he has any suitable vacancies, and register you as looking for work. He will give you a docket and send you to the Claims Section or UB Office – ask where it is.

You sign on for the dole at the UB office and provided you fulfil the basic conditions you are entitled to this as a right.

Ask for a form B1, which you will need if you wish to claim *supplementary benefit*; it is worth doing this even if you do not think you are eligible. (*See also* below.)

UB is paid weekly by giro sent to your home address; it takes ten to fourteen days to sort out. If you are in financial trouble before that you may be able to claim SB, or other help – *see* below. The money you

Signing on is depressing and demoralizing

receive is not taxable, and need not be declared to the Inland Revenue. You are still eligible for Family Allowance.

UB is calculated according to a basic rate which depends on how long you have been working. To find out how much you should be paid consult one of the books or agencies listed at the end of this chapter, or ask for form NI12. You are not entitled to UB if you are under 16, over retiring age, or self-employed unless you have made Class 1 contributions. The CAB or Citizens Rights Office will advise you about this, or if you disagree with the verdict of the UB office. They will also help you with SB and put you in touch with other relevant services and organizations.

Supplementary benefit (SB) It is almost always worth applying for SB; complete form B1 and deliver it or post it to the SB office (find the address in the telephone directory under 'Health and Social Security, Department of' – or from a post office). Telephone the office and arrange an interview. If you need money urgently visit the office personally and ask to be seen immediately. Or you can ask someone to visit you at home.

It is most important to be on time for your interview. If you are not you may have to wait a very long time, and it could delay payment. (If you are unavoidably held up, telephone in advance and explain.) You should take with you your rent book or mortgage repayments book, your child benefit book, and other evidence of your circumstances. You will need to know your National Insurance number, and your income tax number; you may also need P45 or P60 tax forms, bank statements, and your letter of redundancy or dismissal. Women should take evidence of maintenance payments from present or previous husbands or partners.

SB can be paid quickly – within those first two weeks before the UB arrives – and for this reason you should apply early. You will not be paid anything for the first week if you were given a week's wages or for the first month if you were given a month's. But if you received nothing you should be sent the first SB payment within a week. If you have no money ask for an emergency payment. This will probably be an interim payment; an officer may call at your home later to check on your circumstances. If you left work voluntarily, or were fired for misconduct, you will be given a reduced rate of SB.

SB should ensure that everyone has a certain minimum income. In order to assess you the SB office will ask you about all your sources of income and your necessary expenditure. Some people who apply make false claims and you will therefore be asked a large number of questions. If the office find that you are eligible, then you may be helped with your rent, rates and other expenses and also essential items such as children's clothes.

If you disagree with your assessment telephone the office and query it; but it might be advisable first to consult the CAB or the Claimants' Union (CU) who will tell you whether you have a reasonable case, and what to say.

Other financial help Even if you are not entitled to SB you may be able to get rebate for your rent or rates. Apply to the rebate section of your local authority housing department (see address in the telephone directory under e.g. 'Leeds City Council'), or go to the CAB who will arrange for the application form to be sent to your home.

If you are in financial trouble it is worth writing to your mortgage company to ask whether you may pay the interest only for a period, postponing capital repayments, and also to the Gas and Electricity boards to explain the situation; they will generally defer disconnection while the immediate problems are being resolved, and may help by arranging a weekly repayment scheme. You may also get free dental treatment, prescriptions, and school meals for your children.

Plans for the future The first question you will be asked when you sign on at the Jobcentre is what sort of job you are looking for. You are likely to be in a state of shock, after losing your last job, and lacking self-esteem. Do not fall into the trap of asking for a job way below your skills or qualifications. You are more likely to be offered something if you aim low, but you would probably find the job terrible, and you might have to take it or have your dole suspended.

It is demoralizing on the dole and can sometimes be intimidating. Do not let it get you down. If your interview begins to feel like an interrogation, wait a second or two before you answer each question. Smile, be firm, and keep your temper. Ask some questions yourself to avoid staying on the receiving end. Do not be pushed into accepting any job that is going.

The best way to look for a job is to try everything you can think of. You should look regularly at the cards in the Jobcentre, and apply quickly for any job that is suitable. On the whole the positions which are advertised there will be those that are most difficult to fill. You can also try private employment agencies, which will probably claim to be able to work wonders; but beware of accepting temporary industrial work. You are liable to find the job is most unpleasant and lasts only a week. During that time you may be on an hour's notice, and at the end of it you will have to go back and sign on again; you may even get your dole suspended for a couple of weeks.

There are three main ways of looking for a job in addition to using agencies. First, look at the advertisements in the newspapers. Secondly, telephone all the local firms who might have something to suit you. When unemployment is high they may not need to advertise, and telephoning them is the best way of catching a vacancy. Thirdly, ask friends and relatives to look out for you. It may be embarrassing to ask them but it is a surprisingly effective way of getting back to work. When the Tress Engineering plant on Tyneside closed in 1978 over half the redundant men who later found work did so through informal contacts.

You may consider investing redundancy money in a small business and setting up on your own. You might like to subscribe to the *Business Ideas Letter*, a monthly information sheet about ideas for small businesses; write for information to the Institute of Small Business, 13 Golden Square, London W1. Godfrey Golzen's *Working for Yourself* (Kogan Page, 1975) has advice on how to start, form a company, handle tax, and look for opportunities. Contact The National Federation of Self-Employed and Small Businesses (32 St Anne's Road West, Lytham St Anne's, Lancashire FY8 1NY; tel: 0253 720911) who will send you free helpful leaflets and invite you to become a member. If you decide to go ahead you should talk to the CAB; it will give you accounting advice free. Later, the Department of Industry's Small Firms Service may be helpful.

Self-discipline and self-esteem After a few weeks on the dole you will find that the worst enemies are boredom and apathy. It will help to develop any hobbies that have interested you. Avoid buying papers and magazines; go to the library and read them there. While you are there, ask about evening classes.

The first month can be like a holiday, but after that you may feel things are going downhill. There is a real danger that people out of work, especially men in their fifties, just let themselves go; they get up late, don't bother to shave, don't wear clean and tidy clothes, and drink too much. This makes it much harder to get moving again if any opening does materialize and ruins your chances of getting a job if you do get an interview. Do not let this happen to you.

Use the time to consider and replan your future. Do you really want to go back to the work you were doing? Is this the time for a new start? You may be able to get on a government re-training scheme such as TOPS (details are available from the CAB or Jobcentre). This is no guarantee of a new job but it will occupy you, and may convince a prospective employer that you are keen to return to work.

There is one type of employment that you can always find, and that is voluntary work. Hospitals need drivers to transport patients; agencies such as the CAB need staff. Many people who have been unemployed for any length of time find that voluntary work is stimulating and enjoyable, and provides a real sense of achievement. If you are interested, ask at the CAB, or go to the Volunteer Bureau at the local Council for Voluntary Service (see under 'Volunteer' or e.g. 'Leeds Council' in your telephone directory). They keep an index of employers who need volunteers, and provide a counselling service to suggest what sort of work will suit you. For more information see Elizabeth Gundry, *Sparing Time* – the *Observer* Guide to Helping others (Allen and Unwin, 1981).

Organizations and books The CAB (*see* page 218) will provide help at all stages. It does not aim to give a counselling service, but it will help you sort out problems over benefits and appeals, and give practical advice about your financial difficulties. It will also provide free and confidential advice on financial and legal matters connected with unemployment.

The Claimants' Union believes in a fair deal for everyone claiming benefits. It may be able to provide someone to represent you in appeals over your benefits. The head office is at Dame Colet House, Ben Johnson Street, London E1; tel: 01-790 9070; it will put you in touch with a local office.

The Citizens Rights Office runs a regular telephone information service about benefits, and will advise you about your rights. It may also be able to represent you in appeals. It is run by the Child Poverty Action Group (1 Macklin Street, Drury Lane, London WC2B 5NH) which has branches all over the country.

There may be a local advice and information centre in your area; ask at the library, post office, or Social Services office, or look in your local newspaper.

Your union may help in a dispute with your ex-employer. Talk to your shop steward or union representative. Another source of free legal advice and assistance for industrial tribunals or benefit disputes is a Law Centre. If there is one in your area (see the telephone directory under 'Law'), you should be able to talk to a lawyer there. Otherwise ask the CAB about the Green Form scheme, which is operated by most solicitors to enable advice to be given cheaply.

Peter Laurie, *On the Dole* (Kogan Page paperback, 1976) is exceptionally helpful on the practical details of survival on the dole: how to get benefits, what you are entitled to, how to appeal, and how to plan for the future. Although slightly out of date, it provides exactly the information you need.

Dismissal, Redundancy, and Job-hunting (Consumers' Association) covers the legal aspects of redundancy and unfair dismissal, and provides advice on the practical and personal problems of being unemployed.

11. Mental illness

Insane, incoherent gibberings interrupted by wild outbursts of manic intensity – this is the sort of picture that we conjure up when we think of madness. However, the overflowing mental hospitals and homes throughout the world are filled with people who have almost nothing in common with this archetypal image. Once we used to protect ourselves from the mentally ill by locking them away in prisons – asylums for the insane. Today we give them a bed in a hospital ward. A staggering one in nine will be admitted to an institution for mental illness at some point in their lives. Almost all of us will know a friend or relative who has been, or is now being, treated.

Mental illness, our polite, modern, 'medicalized' phrase for madness, is a relative term. There is a norm of behaviour, a norm of thought; if you step too far outside you can be called mentally ill, but there can be no rigid definition of abnormal behaviour because circumstances are all important.

On the battlefield it is considered perfectly sane to kill someone you have never met before; in the confines of your home it is not. Mental illness therefore is all to do with breaking the rules, and since there are no agreed universal rules of social behaviour it will always be possible to argue whether someone is, or is not, mentally ill. It would be comfortingly simple if society's unspoken rules were in some sense rational, but we only have to think back to the battlefield to realize that is far from the case. To a considerable extent growing up is a learning of these unstated rules. If as an adult you ignore them and behave in a child-like way you are quite likely to be thought of as mentally ill, even though we would not think the same of a child behaving in precisely the same manner. Being seen as mentally ill depends not only on other people's ideas of correct behaviour but on our own position in society. To behave like the Queen when you are the Queen is expected, to behave like the Queen when you are not is to be called mad. Children alone can play at being kings and queens, as an adult we musk take our places and abide by society's rules as they apply to us – rules which are of course no more than convention.

Mental illness should not be compared with mental handicap. While the mentally handicapped are of subnormal intelligence, the mentally ill suffer no such impairment of ability. Quite the reverse; they may be highly intelligent. The vast majority of mental illness is not illness in the normal sense of the term – usually there is no apparent physical cause and there is no recognized clear definition of symptoms. However by calling it an illness we give the impression that it is the sort of thing which might have a cure, and which can be dealt with by doctors, and in hospitals. If mental illness is to do with going beyond the bounds of accepted behaviour, in what sense is the thief or murderer not mentally ill? And why should we call a social problem an illness? The most obvious answer is that unlike thieves or murderers whose actions are premeditated, the mentally ill are unable to change their own behaviour; they may well in fact seek help. Although this answer goes some way to explaining why we call it mental *illness* it does not detract from the underlying problem that often the issue is at root a social and not a personal one. Once we realize this it is no longer surprising that it is often the relatives, rather than the person concerned, that actually call in the doctors. When the grandmother, or husband, or daughter is *called* mentally ill it can come as a great relief to the rest of the family. No longer is it just their problem. Treatment is on its way: someone else will sort it all out. The cause of the anxiety, the cause of the depression can then be forgotten about. If we call it an illness, we can think of it as an illness; a few pills and it will be cured. Unfortunately it is hardly ever dealt with so easily.

What we have to decide in any particular case is whether calling the person mentally ill is going to do any good. The danger is that in thinking of someone as mentally ill we see it as the person's own private problem. We are able to separate ourselves; it no longer has anything to do with us. Of course there are occasions when there is no alternative, but the extent of our mental institutions and the relative impotence of the treatment is testimony to the very limited use of categorizing someone as being mentally ill. Calling someone mentally ill is too often a means by which we avoid our responsibility for their behaviour. It becomes a complete explanation of why they are behaving as they are – they are simply ill; but it is an explanation that usually tells you nothing as it gives you no idea of the cause and also no idea of how it might be solved.

The problems can start in the home, and often, apart from psychotic illness, any real solution is likely to be found there also.

Losing control

Anorexia nervosa is popularly seen as the slimmer's disease. Most commonly, it affects girls in their early and late teens and more recently those in their early twenties. Although it seems like an extreme form of slimming, sometimes with a refusal to eat anything even to the point of starvation, the analogy is a confusing one because the anorexic unlike the slimmer has no *desire* to eat.

Sheila was sixteen before any problem developed. Her parents had saved up to send her away to a boarding school so that she could have a better chance in life than either of them had been given. She was a very bright child and had just completed her O-levels, but was rather unhappy away at school.

> 'I had great difficulty in fitting in. It was all right when I was thirteen, fourteen, fifteen, but after that I began to feel I really wasn't like the others. Most of all I felt pushed into doing things I didn't want to do, and that my

Sheila

good qualities were being overlooked. My parents desperately wanted me to succeed academically and the school concentrated on good exam results . . . like most anorexics I was a good little girl and I tried to live up to everyone's expectations and do what they wanted, but I knew somewhere that it wasn't really what *I* wanted. I felt beleaguered from all sides, I felt I had no control over my whole life, that was the key thing, I felt I had no control.'

Sheila was caught by a contradiction in her emotions. On the one hand, she wanted to please her parents and fulfil their dreams, and on the other she didn't really want those dreams for herself. There was no way out. Either she hurt her parents or she continued to do something in which she had no interest. As a result, one lunchtime, she rebelled. At the time, even if it had been noticed, it would have seemed a trivial gesture, but really it was a desperate act born out of a situation for which Sheila could find no solution.

'I simply got away with eating hardly anything . . . They were strict about food at school – you had to eat everything – and by avoiding eating I found the one way I could to rebel. My body was the one area of my life that was still mine, that I still had control over . . . it belonged to me and I had the power to decide what I would do with it.'

For quite a while no one at the school realized anything was the matter.

'I asked for small helpings and then I used to smear it all out round the plate and put my knife and fork over it so that nobody would notice. I would also eat very, very slowly so that it looked as if I was eating a lot. I used to miss all the meals like breakfast and tea where there were no teachers around. I began to feel this was something I was really good at, something that I could do well, that was for me and not for anyone else.'

Paradoxically although anorexics are obsessed with avoiding food their motivation may have nothing to do with food at all. Sheila did not start out disliking food; instead avoiding it was a bit like a game, a goal to be achieved.

> 'At school, meals were an important part of the day. People would think about what they were going to eat, and however boring it was it broke up the monotony of the institutional day. I turned it all upside down: I looked forward to the meals too, but to see what I could get away with . . . each meal was an opportunity for me to show myself what I could do, another chance to convince myself that I was in control of my life.'

Unlike anorexia, slimming is centred around food, you want it and you try to avoid eating it. Ironically, because of the stress on being slim, Sheila actually found herself being congratulated on losing weight.

> 'Suddenly I had found something that I was good at, that was mine, and moreover people kept telling me how much better I looked. So it is very difficult to get through to people that I didn't become anorexic because I wanted to be slim, or because I was slimming. Losing weight was almost a by-product of the task that I had set myself. As soon as it started to become successful it rapidly took on a momentum of itself. All I knew was that I must eat less and less.'

The school regularly weighed all the pupils, three times a term in fact, so it was not long before Sheila's weight loss began to attract some concern.

> 'I was given special food: milk at every meal, malt and ovaltine. I couldn't bear any of it, so I used to get rid of it by passing it on to somebody else, or by throwing the milk down the loo. Gradually more and more of my energies were spent in working out how not to eat . . . it was like studying for an exam, only instead of concentrating on the books I was concentrating on eating as little as possible.
>
> The more successful I was the better I felt. For the first time I began to feel superior to everyone else, because I thought of myself as being terribly well-disciplined. Other people were messy, untidy, and weak-willed in comparison to me. At the same time I became obsessively tidy and up until then I had always been pretty scruffy.'

For parents of an anorexic the question they most persistently ask is why should their daughter, or occasionally their son, do such an apparently irrational thing as deny themselves food? Sheila has no doubt about the prime cause.

> 'It was a basic feeling of inferiority that led me to it in the first place. Once I began I found the delights of power I suppose . . . power over myself more than power over other people. I always thought of it as a perfectly logical type of behaviour: a response to the situation I was in. I felt pushed into a position with my back against the wall, and I had to lash out in order to say who I was, otherwise I thought I would just go under. It was a hunger

> strike – an act of rebellion. The only means of attack was my own body. When you have nothing else left in the world you still have your body and you can still use that as a weapon. You can still use it to say to people, "This is what I am, this is what I am saying."'

A number of so-called mental illnesses have this characteristic in that people try to assert themselves in what they feel is an impossible position. There is no orderly way they have of dealing with the situation they find themselves in, and so they turn to the only alternative left, which is to break the rules in some way. This can take many forms, from someone attempting suicide or having a nervous breakdown, to those suffering from symptoms associated with serious mental illness like schizophrenia. The irony of this behaviour is that it often results in the person having even less control. Instead of drawing attention to their predicament, people around them assume that they have simply gone crazy and effectively stop thinking about them as a person at all. As a result they try to break the rules more and more outrageously and become even further estranged from those close to them. In Sheila's case her parents tried to ignore the problem and strangely this did less harm than you might expect.

> 'It wasn't so much of a challenge at home because I wasn't being forced to eat. I could avoid eating so easily that there was less incentive to do so. My parents hardly seemed to notice. My father said nothing at all except to tell me that I looked thin, or that I looked awful. My mother just said how silly I was being and pretended that I was on a slimming diet, which really angered me because if I was simply slimming it was no longer a protest.'

One of the symptoms of anorexia is that the person seems to stop growing up. Girls stop having periods, not because of avoiding food but because of the emotional stress. Some psychiatrists have suggested as a result that anorexia is centrally linked to problems with the person's sexuality.

> 'I didn't have a boyfriend while I was anorexic and I had never had a boyfriend before that . . . sex was something I didn't feel I was ready for. I didn't feel able to deal with sex or child-bearing or anything connected with being a woman. It was all much too frightening. None of that was ever consciously connected with my not eating, but looking back in hindsight I can see that it probably was. Partly I think it is because when you are a child you know who you are, you're a child. You've got a niche, you know what you have to do, and what you mustn't do. Children behave in certain ways, have certain privileges, certain restrictions, but once you have become an adolescent, you have to start thinking about what it is to be an adult, what it is to be like a man or a woman. As a girl you are faced with a choice. There is you the attractive woman, who should be thinking about getting married and having children, and there is you, the person who is meant to succeed on the same level as boys, with exams and a career. I think for some girls these pressures can become intolerable.'

Most teenagers of Sheila's age although apprehensive enjoy the process of developing into an adult. Sheila's feelings, however, could not have been more divergent.

> 'I felt it was all a terrible imposition.When my periods stopped that was my first great triumph. I was so pleased . . . I was actually beginning to reverse the process of growing up . . . I had achieved this fantastic control. Perhaps growing up is part of losing control, your body is suddenly doing all these things and you can't do anything about it.'

Over a period of two years Sheila steadily lost weight. First it was down to eight stone, then seven, and then six. The longer it went on, and the less Sheila ate, the more irrational it apparently became, but it was an irrationality based on a relentless logic, a logic that had originated in Sheila's attempt to avoid the pressures facing her.

> 'One of the many strange paradoxes about anorexia is that you're full of energy and you leap around all over the place in a manic kind of way. You are driven to this because if you start flagging you would have to admit that something was wrong; instead, you have to tell yourself that not only are you not ill and fading away, but that actually you are in much better shape than you ever were before. It is for that reason that, as an anorexic, you can look at yourself in the mirror and see yourself as being beautiful, but to anybody else you look like something out of a concentration camp.
>
> To start with I did feel hungry, although I told myself that I didn't, but in the end I got to the stage where I really couldn't tell if I felt hungry or not. My will had been so strong in overcoming my hunger that eventually I didn't have to pretend any more, I didn't have to exercise any self-control, I simply didn't feel hungry.'

By the time Sheila had reached six stone it was obvious to anyone that she was very ill. Long ago people had stopped saying how nice she looked, but by then Sheila was so immersed in her own world that she could explain away anything to herself.

> 'When people told me that I looked awful I thought they were just jealous, or that it was rubbish and that I was using different criteria to them. Then, when people told me I was going to die I didn't believe them either. I told them, and myself, that I felt healthy and strong . . . and I did of course. I almost started to believe that I had transcended death, that I had become immortal, that it couldn't possibly happen to me because I was so in control of my body that it couldn't possibly die, it couldn't be just switched off. By then it was all self-delusion . . . and yet it had started so reasonably.'

As in other mental illnesses, the easiest thing is to decide the person has gone crazy. The underlying problem that brought it about can be forgotten, instead we can feel content in saying that they should pull themselves together, that they should stop being so silly. Far from being silly the behaviour is often a recognition that they cannot escape their situation by sticking to the rules, so they will break them. Although it is not true of all mental illness, in many cases the behaviour will probably only stop when either the circumstances have changed or the person realizes that it is not going to work – that breaking the rules will not solve the problem any more than sticking to them. The worry is that in the momentum of the game the person becomes unable to see that it is not working. For Sheila the crisis came when she was at home in the summer holidays. She simply stopped eating altogether.

> 'At school I used to weigh myself all the time to check that I hadn't gained even an extra half pound, but at home there weren't any weighing machines. I began to get worried because I didn't know what was going on, and I was so terrified that I would go up to eight stone that I gave up food completely.
>
> Then one day I walked four-and-a-half miles into the nearest town to weigh myself on special scales that they had at the railway station. I remember I got on the scales and I weighed five-and-a-half stone. It was a real shock . . . I'd lost half a stone instead of gaining two. I suppose at that point I realized that I wasn't aware of what was happening.
>
> I still felt pleased that I had done better than I had hoped but for the first time there was an uneasy feeling as well. I was the clever girl who passed all her exams but this wasn't very clever was it?
>
> Gradually I started to admit to myself that I was apart from everybody else . . . people had started to regard me as a freak . . . it was as though there was a thick glass wall between me and the rest of the world. I suppose I realized that I was back where I started before I became anorexic, I was back feeling isolated and hopeless. In a way I was admitting that my strategy was out of control. It simply wasn't working any more, I was losing that feeling of being on top of things. I didn't admit it consciously, but somewhere it was beginning to get to me.'

The vital turning-point came just a few days later when Sheila was talking to her mother.

> 'She offered me a plum . . . but she did it in such a way . . . polishing it, and making it look like something beautiful, and talking about how nice it looked and what a wonderful summer we were having, that I took it. I held it up to my mouth and I could smell it . . . it smelled of food and I felt afraid. I hesitated, and my mother looked at me. I didn't want to hurt her so . . . I started to eat. I could hardly bear to have it in my mouth, I felt suffocated by it. I couldn't face eating anything by this time, it was so strange swallowing. Yet, because my mother was still standing there I did.
>
> I was thinking that there must be something wrong with me if this beautiful object makes me feel sick. When I had finished, instead of feeling as I expected I would, totally bloated and overfed, I felt all right. I realized I had been wrong.'

Sheila did not recover immediately, but the spell was broken. The game had been lost; there was no need to fight so hard to avoid eating in future.

> 'I sort of realized that nothing terrible would happen to me if I did eat, but I still felt that I'd been tricked and that I'd lost control over myself. I was terribly disappointed. I had failed.'

Fortunately Sheila had recognized that her strategy was failing, for the sad truth is that successful anorexics die. Last year a frightening number of people literally starved themselves to death. However all was not over for Sheila. Like many others she got over her anorexia only to return to it when similar circumstances arose, when once again she felt she had no control over her life.

> 'Anorexia isn't a mental illness; it is a way of coping with life. Perhaps it would be more accurate to say that it is a kind of hunger strike. It is a protest. A protest undertaken by somebody in a position of hopelessness and helplessness . . . but it's dangerous, you can't maintain control in the way that you think you can.
>
> I often ask myself what I would do if one of my own daughters became anorexic. It is very difficult, but I think the important thing is not to focus on food too much. Instead you have to try and get at the underlying conflicts. If you try and force the anorexic to eat, whether at home or in hospital, you are probably going to fail, because the anorexic is going to be much more determined than you. You will get more and more worried, and that will only fuel the problem, it will only go to show how successful and how much in control she is.'

With any mental illness, easy though it is to say, 'Get to the root of the problem', it is always going to be difficult to do, and sometimes impossible. Even if we can find out what the conflict is there will probably be no straightforward solution; if there was, the person would not have been driven to such bizarre behaviour in the first place. However, there is nothing we can do unless we try to understand what is going on, and calling something a mental illness is an admission that we do not understand at all. Certainly Sheila's anorexia could only rather oddly be called an illness.

> 'Looking back it was in a sense not being at home in the world, not knowing my place. It was my only way out, the only fixed point that I could hold on to. I suppose it is the same with many things that are called mental illness, they are really a means for living. The unconscious finds a way out when the conscious person can't.'

What you can do

Sheila believes that most anorexics resist strongly any attempt to treat their symptoms – to force them to eat more and that the best approach is to try and understand anorexia, to recognize that it represents a protest against overwhelming social pressure, and to try and tackle that pressure.

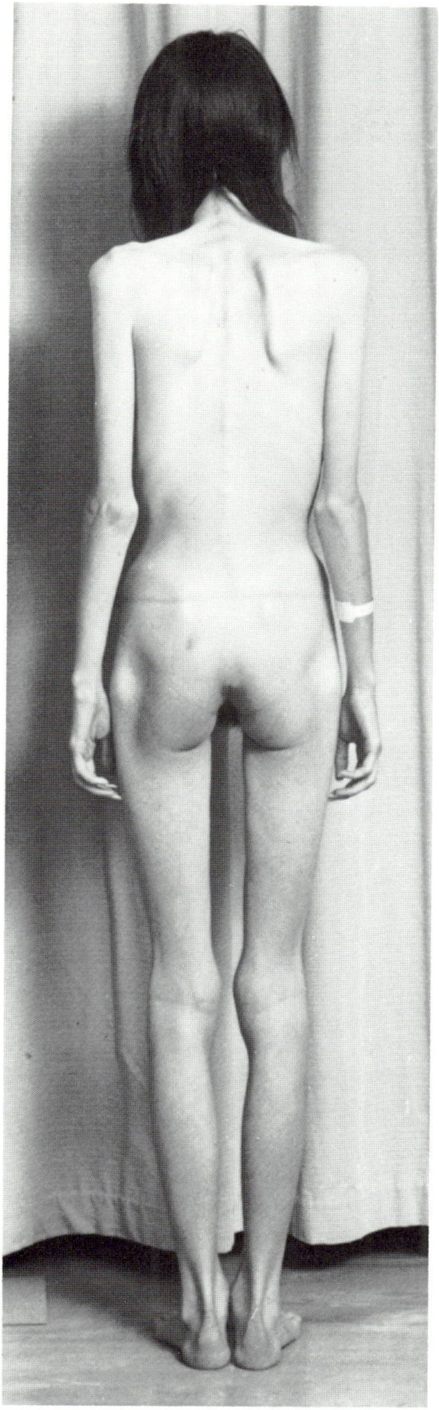

Anorexia nervosa

- Anorexic Aid (The Priory Centre, 11 Priory Road, High Wycombe, Bucks) is run by ex-anorexics, and aims to provide, through a network of voluntary self-help groups, support and advice for anorexics, their families, and their friends. Write with a stamped, addressed envelope for information and a reading list.
- Sheila MacLeod's own book *The Art of Starvation* (Virago, 1981) describes her experience in detail.
- Hilde Bruch, *Eating Disorders: Obesity, Anorexia Nervosa, and the Person Within* (Routledge and Kegan Paul, 1974) and her shorter book, *The Golden Cage* (Open Books, 1978) provide useful insight.
- Peter Dally, Joan Gomez, and A. J. Isaacs, *Anorexia Nervosa* (Heinemann, 1979) is more medical.
- R. L. Palmer, *Anorexia Nervosa* (Penguin, 1980) is a guide for patients and their families.

Types of mental illness One of the drawbacks of the medicalization of antisocial behaviour is that people who break the rules are given frightening labels: mentally ill, schizophrenic, psychopathic, or anorexic. Unfortunately the conditions are in many cases not well understood: nor is the treatment always convincingly effective. In the end there seem to be three broad classes of mental disturbance: personality disorders, psychosis and neurosis. There is more information on page 77; for further details you should consult either *The Whole Mind Book*, or *First Aid in Mental Health* (*see below*).

Mere eccentricity is unlikely to be harmful, but when someone's behaviour becomes so irrational that it is impossible to cope with, or is dangerous, then that person needs help. And no one should be allowed to become so unhappy as to be suicidal.

Treatment In an emergency, telephone your doctor, or the Samaritans, or the Social Services. If you cannot persuade someone who is clearly in trouble to seek help, then contact one of these organizations yourself, or telephone MIND, the National Association for Mental Health – (*see* page 219) and ask for their advice. They aim to provide assistance for all types of people with mental handicap or illness and are there to help.

If you go to your doctor he may give you pills to reduce your anxiety, and although drugs are not the magic bullets they were thought to be in the 1950s they can help you to improve your mood, to alleviate stress, to make you feel better, and with luck to give you enough stability and confidence to tackle the problems at the root of your disturbance. But drugs alone are unlikely to cure you.

Your doctor may refer you to a psychiatrist – *see* pages 85–7 for more details. The psychiatrist is also likely to prescribe you with drugs.

If you are going to cure the problem, you have to concentrate on the underlying causes. To do this you have to find someone to talk to; you have to seek social treatment. Your doctor may be able to refer you to a psychotherapist – a doctor, a social worker, or a psychologist who can help you by encouraging you to talk through your problems and focus on what is important. This is the type of treatment that helped Pat (*see* page 32) and Mary (*see* page 69). Or you may find a sympathetic and helpful social worker, as Anne did (*see* page 84); you can always go direct to the Social Services (*see* page 87). You may find, however, that given a chance your partner, friend, or relative can be just as helpful as a professional person. Or you can try Marriage Guidance (*see* page 218 for further information).

If none of these ideas seems to work, you can go to MIND (*see* page 219). They may be able to put you in touch with a helpful professional therapist, or with a group therapy meeting. They may also be able to suggest alternative types of treatment, such as hypnotherapy or yoga. Non-orthodox treatment certainly works for some people, and you might like to try it. For information on what is available, look at *The Whole Mind Book* (*see below*) or one of the following:

- Andrew Stanway, *Alternative Medicine: A Guide to Natural Therapies* (Macdonald and Jane's, 1979). This is a selective and attractive guide, written by a medical doctor.
- Malcolm Hulke, *The Encyclopedia of Alternative Medicine and Self Help* (Rider, 1978). This book is unselective and variable, but has at the end an excellent directory, where among other things you will find a list of associations and societies, which may well be the best method of discovering how to obtain a particular type of treatment.

Mental hospitals Although there are no longer asylums in this country, and although some general hospitals now have 'psychiatric units' which are supposed to be more pleasant, the fact remains that mental hospitals are depressing places. If you become a patient, responsibility for your problems is taken away, and this may be a great relief, but there is a danger that you will become 'institutionalized', and even less able to cope when you come out. In the majority of hospitals there is occupational therapy, group therapy, or psychotherapy, but one of the worst problems is that for much of the time there is nothing to do, and surrounded by other unhappy people you may well feel useless and increasingly depressed.

If you are unlucky you will receive little medical attention apart from drugs, and you may find it very difficult to attract the attention of a doctor long enough to discuss your condition. 'Informal' or voluntary patients have the right to refuse any treatment, from drugs to surgery; but if you want to do this you should be careful, and try discussing this first, otherwise the staff may threaten you with compulsory detention.

In severe cases people can be compulsorily detained

Ninety per cent of the people in ordinary mental hospitals are admitted as voluntary patients, and can leave when they want. Their rights are the same as those of any other hospital patients (*see* pages 188–9). Following the Mental Health Act of 1959 you can be detained compulsorily 'on a section' under one of these circumstances:

- Under Section 136, for seventy-two hours in a 'place of safety' by a police officer if you are suffering from a mental disorder in a public place.
- Under Section 29, in emergency only, for seventy-two hours in a hospital after application by any relative or by a social worker and medical recommendation by one doctor.
- Under Section 25, for twenty-eight days in hospital for observation, after application by your nearest relative or a mental welfare officer, and two medical recommendations – by the family doctor and a psychiatrist.
- Under Section 26, for one year in hospital, after recommendations from two medical sources, and with the permission of your nearest relative.

If you have been compulsorily detained and you want to be discharged, you or your nearest relative can apply first to the District or Area Health Authority and, if they refuse, to a Mental Health Tribunal.

For details of the rights of patients, of compulsory detention, and of how to appeal, see one of these books:

- Larry Gostin, *Patients' Rights Handbook* (MIND, 1981).
- Gerry and Carol Stimson, *Health Rights Handbook* (Penguin, 1980).
- *First Aid In Mental Health* (*see below*).

Or you can contact MIND, or the Citizens Advice Bureau (*see* pages 218–219), or the Patients Association (11 Dartmouth Street, London SW1H 9BN; tel: 01-222 4992).

People coming out of mental hospitals can find life particularly difficult; it is important that they should receive support and help. Social workers can provide this, alternatively you can contact MIND, or Marriage Guidance, or the Mental

MIND can help people discharged from mental hospitals by providing support and help at day centres

After-Care Association (Eagle House, 110 Jermyn Street, London SW1Y 6HB; tel: 01-839 5953), who aim to provide hostels, homes, and holidays for the mentally ill, or the Richmond Fellowship (8 Addison Road, London W14 8DL; tel: 01-603 7373), an organization that tries to find family type homes for disturbed people after discharge from hospital.

Other organizations that may be able to help:

- Age Concern, Bernard Sunley House, 60 Pitcairn Road, Mitcham, Surrey; tel: 01-640 5431.
- Al-Anon Family Groups (61 Great Dover Street, London SE1; tel: 01-403 0888) provide advice and support for the families of alcoholics.
- Alcoholics Anonymous (P.O. Box 514, 11 Redcliffe Gardens, London SW10; tel: 01-352 9779) is for alcoholics who want to stop drinking.
- Anorexic Aid, National Headquarters, The Priory Centre, 11 Priory Road, High Wycombe, Buckinghamshire. (*See also* page 147 for more detailed information about this society.)
- Gamblers Anonymous, 17–23 Blantyre Street, Cheyne Walk, London SW10; tel: 01-352 3060 or 01-368 0316.
- Institute of Family Therapy, Mary Ward House, 5 Tavistock Place, London WC1; tel: 01-388 3872.
- Institute of Social Psychiatry, 115–121 Newington Causeway, London SE1; tel: 01-407 2311.
- Mental Health Advice Service, 19 Handen Road, London SE12; tel: 01-318 1330.
- National Schizophrenic Fellowship (78–79 Victoria Road, Surbiton, Surrey KT6 4NS; tel: 01-390 3651) offers information, advice and support to schizophrenics and their relatives, and publishes helpful leaflets.
- The Schizophrenic Association of Great Britain, Tyr Twr, Llanfair Hall, Caernarvon, Gwynedd, North Wales; tel: 0248 670379.

Books The MIND Bookshop (155–157 Woodhouse Lane, Leeds LS2 3EF; tel: 0532 30918) can supply all MIND publications, and will advise on others. *See also* the note about bookshops on page 59.

- Silvano Aristi, *Understanding and Helping the Schizophrenic* (Penguin, 1981) is a clear and helpful guide for family and friends.
- Tom Crabtree, *An A-Z of Children's Emotional Problems* (Hamish Hamilton, 1981) is a useful reference book for worried parents.
- Muir Gray and Heather McKenzie, *Taking Care of Your Elderly Relative* (Allen and Unwin, 1980) is very practical.
- Joy Melville, *First Aid in Mental Health* (Allen and Unwin, 1980) is an excellent account of the most common types of mental illness, the symptoms, the possible treatments, and the roles of the medical professionals, with details of hospital admission and patients' rights. There is a useful list of self-help organizations.
- Thomas S. Szasz is a non-believer in mental illness, and argues his case in *The Myth of Mental Illness* (Secker and Warburg, 1967; Granada, 1972), and in *The Manufacture of Madness* (Routledge and Kegan Paul, 1971; Granada, 1973).
- Denise Winn, *The Whole Mind Book* (Fontana, 1980) is an A-Z of theories, therapies, and facts, from Abreaction, Acupuncture, and Addiction, to Yoga and Zen.
- Philip G. Zimbardo, *Shyness* (Pan, 1981) tells you what it is and what to do about it.

For books on depression *see* page 87; for books and tapes on anxiety and phobias *see* page 110.

12. The odd ones out

There is enormous pressure in society to conform. If you do not conform you are ignored, avoided, or abused. Even relatively minor matters like the clothes you wear are sufficient to generate much antagonism if you cross the limits of conformity – and you do not have to wear a Roman toga or dress in the clothes of the opposite sex to cross those limits. If your clothes are slightly too garish, or too faded, slightly too smart or too casual, others may take offence, and as a result react to you differently. But conformity is not only to do with our clothes, our accents, or our opinions, it is also to do with our physical attributes.

Our society is organized for the fit and healthy and if in any way you diverge from that the problems multiply. If you are handicapped, little is designed with your difficulties in mind; all too often there is no room for wheelchairs, there is no alternative to the stairs, and almost every door is a problem. But the practical, physical difficulties that you face are only one aspect of being different from the norm. What is more unpleasant is being set apart from others. As a result of the handicap or disability you no longer go to the same events or places as everybody else; inevitably you find yourself mixing with others in a similar position. You become estranged from the rest of the community – through no fault of your own, and without any deliberate plan on the part of everyone else. Simply because of your physical handicap you become separated from the activities and concerns of those who were perhaps once your friends.

In addition to this understandable, if unfortunate, division that is generated, there is a more profound and certainly more damaging gulf that can be formed. For no apparent reason the physical handicap becomes a barrier not only in the obvious practical ways, but in a more comprehensive and insidious fashion. Suddenly you are no longer regarded as being fully human in some intangible sense. Rather than people starting a conversation with you and treating you as an equal – as someone who has had useful experience, or has a particular aptitude – you are treated in a rather patronizing way . . . if you are spoken to at all. And that is just it, you are more likely to be avoided; a meeting with you is an embarrassment rather than something that might be interesting or enjoyable. You no longer conform to what is regarded as being normal and as a result you are avoided and cut off.

You do not have to differ very far from the norm for this isolating process to take place. Experiments in the streets of New York have shown that passers-by avoid, by stepping to one side, anyone who 'isn't quite right'. It might be that they are dishevelled, or rather unattractive. We know that happens on the street; how much more does it happen at a party, or in an office?

It makes little difference how you diverge from the norm – what matters is that you are unusual. Whether you have a disfiguring facial birthmark, or have lost a limb, or have a speech impediment, the sort of responses you receive will have many things in common. People will either actively try to ensure that they do not have to talk to you, or when they do they will do so reluctantly. They are likely to talk down to you, almost as if you do not have the same sort of experiences as they have – and with many physical disabilities it is common for them to assume that you are stupid as well. Anyone who is deaf will be aware of that. And, even if you are being treated as a normal human being, there is still almost always an area of embarrassment; you may talk about everything else rather than the obvious topic of conversation, namely whatever it is that makes you different, which will somehow be avoided.

The story that follows is about two people who have spent their lives facing these seemingly intractable problems. Few of us will ever have to experience a situation as difficult as theirs, but a substantial number of us will go through similar sorts of problems at some time – even if it is just having a broken leg. All of us, however, are responsible for the way we treat those who are not quite typical. The odd ones out cannot solve their problems without the rest of us solving them too.

Walk tall

> 'I think it's most difficult in childhood. I just wished I was normal . . . and I'd wonder, you know, "Why, why do they laugh at me?" That's what really hurt . . . when people laughed. They'd point me out as the one that was different. It did – it hurt.
>
> Children can be very cruel . . . if I went into a street where they didn't know me, they'd say nasty things, and call me names. "Let's bash him up," that was the most likely reaction . . . just because I wasn't like them . . . I was never like them.'

Childhood can be difficult when you are not quite the same as everyone else

Arthur and Penny

Until Arthur was eight years old he was not really aware that anything was wrong.

'My parents had told me what was the matter but it didn't really mean anything – I certainly didn't give a damn in my early childhood – but as the years went by I gradually began to realize how for me everything was going to be different.'

Arthur suffers from achondroplasia – to most of us he would be more simply a dwarf. There are a number of different causes of dwarfism, from malnutrition and emotional deprivation to a lack of growth hormone or abnormalities in the development of the foetus. In Arthur's case the cause is a bone disorder which results in the growth of long bones being retarded. Achondroplastics, unlike other types of dwarf, tend to have a relatively normal-sized head and trunk but short legs and arms and have a perfectly normal intelligence.

Arthur's parents were not dwarfs, but they never treated him differently from the rest of the family. He certainly was not protected from the harshness of other people's spite. As a result he learned the hard way.

'I was taught to stand up for myself – not that it was always easy. If people laughed at me, I was told to laugh back at them – it was them that was being silly. Well, it was easy enough to say, but when there's a bunch of other kids and they're saying, "Hasn't he got a big face? Isn't he tiny? Let's go and kick him in," it's rather more difficult! The only defence I had then was to pitch in and do what I could – either that or get on my bike and peddle like mad.

But my parents were right not to shield me – otherwise when you are left on your own, and a time will come when you are left on your own, that's it . . . you can't fend for yourself at all. It's not easy but gradually I began to realize that nothing's going to change, so why bother about it – just get out there and show them what you're made of.'

As he grew older Arthur's problems changed. No longer was he teased or bullied, instead he was excluded. As a child he could play with the other children in the street but as a teenager he could not go to the same parties and he could not flirt with the same girls.

'My mother realized that I had to meet people like myself. Right from an early age she had written off to a circus so that I could meet other little people. Through my childhood and my teenage years I kept in touch with little people in different areas of showbiz; so it wasn't surprising that when I was seventeen years old I joined the circus myself.'

While Arthur was at the circus he met Penny for the first time.

'It's not easy finding a girlfriend if you're a dwarf. I did have a little girlfriend before I met Penny, but nothing came of it. I remember in the first few minutes of talking to Penny I was wondering whether she might be saying to herself, "Oh God, I don't want to talk to him. What will he say? What will he do?" I thought she was worried that I might make her problems worse by highlighting them – that talking to her I'd show her up to the other people.'

Penny had been much more sheltered than Arthur and meeting him is an experience she will never forget.

'I didn't really want to go to the circus; I wasn't much interested, but my sister insisted. She bought me a ticket, and said, "You're going." When we got there we were shown to our seats and there was this dwarf man. I just looked at him aghast, I was amazed. I thought, "My God, he's like me . . . he's just like me." I'd never seen anyone, you know . . . never. I just stared at him. Shocked. I was embarrassed because I knew people were looking at him, and then they'd look at me, and . . . well, I was like him – I was so embarrassed.

Then he spoke . . . and I thought, "My God, he speaks too." I'd thought I was the only one in the world. I didn't believe there was anyone else, particularly a man. All my life I hadn't seen any – only on television – and I'd heard that dwarfs were unfriendly and would bite your head off, so I was a bit frightened in a way. Anyway, he spoke and he seemed kind and considerate, and then I was even more embarrassed because then I thought, "Here's someone wanting to know about me."'

There was no way Penny was going to be able to concentrate on the show. All she could think about was what she was going to say when she met him afterwards, and more than that, how she was going to react to him. Suddenly,

Soon after they met Penny joined Arthur at the circus

she could see how other people reacted to her. They were afraid of her, as she was afraid of him.

> 'I was worried to death. Was he going to mind if I looked at him? I didn't enjoy the show at all, I could only think about what was going to happen. Finally, I'd decided that he would run off and not want to speak to me – that he'd try to keep out of the way. But he didn't.'

Arthur did not have the same doubts.

> 'I realized she was embarrassed, so I decided I had to do something about it. After all, I thought she was very nice . . . you know. So at the end of the show, I went over and asked her to come outside . . . and I chatted her up a bit. I asked her what she liked doing, and how she was getting on. And perhaps we could see each other again . . . to think about it – and write to me.'

Until then Penny's only real life had been in the Church; at least there she had been able to find friends and company. But now . . .

> 'I went home . . . oh, I was happy, I was so happy. Here was somebody like me, somebody I could talk to about my problems, somebody who could help me. From that day, the church lark just went out of my head. I went shopping, and I thought, "Well, Arthur said, keep your chin up and walk tall," – and I did.
>
> Arthur's last words had been, "Leave it a couple of months, and write." I could only leave it a week. I wrote . . . and I was longing for a letter to come back. It was marvellous, someone taking an interest in me, interested in what I had to say. Not for pity . . . but because they wanted to know. It had never really happened before . . . I realized I had never even really been spoken to before – not properly.'

Arthur and Penny wrote to each other: they wrote about everything, the things they liked doing and the things they didn't like doing. Through letters they shared the things they could not share with anyone else. Then one weekend when the circus had returned near to Penny's home, Arthur invited her out.

> 'I couldn't wait. There was nothing else that interested me . . . nothing else that could interest me. I just wanted to go . . . to go and see Arthur, and speak to Arthur. I was fifteen . . . and it was my first . . .
>
> I got to Arthur and I saw the show, and the day after we went walking together. He asked me if I would go out with him. And I said, "Yes." And I held his hand and I felt proud to hold his hand, and go down the street – I wanted everybody to see. I'd got a boyfriend – I'd got a fella. And from that day to this it has never bothered me that I am little.'

Eighteen months later Arthur and Penny were married. Not quite the normal reception – an elephant's back for transport, and circus clowns for company.

Transport of delight

Meeting Arthur not only changed Penny's life, but it changed her attitude *to* life. Until then Penny had little self-esteem . . .

'I always used to feel embarrassed when I went out with my friends: I thought they'd asked me along out of pity. Especially when I was fourteen, fifteen, my friends started getting boyfriends . . . we used to go out to discos; there'd be a group of us, and my mates would all be dancing with blokes, and I'd be the one left in the corner to guard the handbags. I ignored it a lot of the time but when I was on my own I would think about it, and it hurt. I thought, "Well, why do I bother? Why do I bother going to these dances?" The blokes would only come back and sit with me for a bit and have a laugh, and I'd get the feeling that I was forcing them to sit by me. It was just that feeling that no one really wanted you around, they might pretend, but really I was just in the way.'

Since Penny and Arthur's first meeting life has been very different.

'Now if we go to a dance with another couple, Arthur will ask the wife to dance, and I'll overcome the husband's embarrassment by asking him to dance too. Once you've broken the ice it's all right from then on. The answer is to forget that everybody's looking at you, and to treat yourself as a person. In a way I blame myself for not having a more "couldn't-care-less" attitude when I was younger. You have to go out and accept life as it is, and accept you as you are. It is very simple; nothing on earth is going to change you. Either you accept it or you suffer.'

However, even if you accept it, everything is not always plain sailing. Arthur and Penny decided they wanted to have a family and although the circus was great fun it did not provide the stability and security they needed. So Arthur took a course in electronics and began looking for a job.

> 'It's not easy finding a job if you're short. People take one look at you and think, "No, you can't do it," and that's it. They assume you're stupid . . . they talk to you as if you were a child and use short sentences. I suppose it's the same whether you're blind, or you're small, or in a wheelchair, somehow you're different – and then you are automatically dim-witted. It's not only when you go for a job, it happens to you everywhere. It can be really frustrating – you can be sitting with somebody and someone else comes into the room. They automatically talk to the other person and not to you. It's almost as if you don't exist, or you're not capable of answering. It can really destroy you that – and it gets you mad, because you feel like saying, "Oi, what the bloody hell's wrong with talking to me?"'

When Arthur was offered a job he soon proved his worth. Penny had similar difficulties when she applied to be a computer operator.

> 'I insisted that I was given a chance and eventually they agreed to a month's trial. I went along and showed what I could do and at the end of the month my boss said, "I didn't believe you could do a thing. But I had to be fair and give you a trial . . . and I'm very glad I did."'

When you are different from the norm your problems are not primarily of open discrimination, they are of a more gentle all-pervading nature. You meet prejudice in every contact, in all of your day-to-day meetings and chance events.

> 'In many ways we're victimized. A lot of people think, "Oh, don't worry about them – they're little." We're shunned aside, anybody with anything wrong with them is shunned. I remember once I was in hospital for a cyst and I overheard them say, "She's only a dwarf, we'll take her down to theatre, open her up and see what we can find." I thought, "My God, what are they going to do with me – I'll wake up and they will have taken my insides out, you know just because I'm a dwarf." It was absolutely horrifying.'

Just going to the shops can be difficult.

> 'Being small it can be difficult getting stuff off high shelves in supermarkets – they always put everything you don't want at the bottom – but people can be so unpleasant. You'll be in a queue to pay and someone will reach their arm over your head – they know you're a woman, but they treat you as a kid, and try and shove you out. You have to be direct – look round and say, "Excuse me, there is a queue." Usually they look down with embarrassment, and go all red. But you have to show them that you're not going to be trodden on.'

The real problems are not in the supermarket but in other people's prejudices

Behind all the discrimination and prejudice there is the unsaid fear of the unknown. These people look different and so it is assumed that they are not quite like you, they do not have the same feelings, the same aspirations, the same desires. This underlying uncertainty can make us all very callous.

> 'I don't know why people do it – it is as if they just want to forget about us, to pretend that we're just not there. If they'd only step back and think that I am a person, I am a human being – I'm a woman and a mother. People have the most extraordinary ideas: they think we live in some special house with special furniture, but we don't; we live in a normal house in a normal area. Sometimes I think people believe we should just be all locked away so we can't cause any trouble.

People think we've got a little bed – they think we sleep in a little tiny bed . . . I've had people come up to me and ask me. Even sex, you know, I think people believe we have a different sex life to other people . . . but we don't; it's quite ordinary I assure you.'

Our suspicion, disregard, and lack of consideration for those not quite like us is passed on from one generation to the next. The prejudices of the parents are visited on the children.

'We were out in the street one day and a child tugged at her mother's clothes: "Mummy, Mummy, what are those little people? Why are they little?" And the mother grabbed the child and said, "Come away, they're freaks." When that happens it hurts, because you know the child is going to go away thinking they mustn't approach a little person . . . they're evil.'

Adults learn to control their reactions. Children are more outspoken and have to be taught to ignore the obvious comments that embarrass parents by drawing attention to something they would rather not face.

'People try to avoid us rather than face talking to us. Last week a boy looked round and said to his mother, "There's a little lady", and the woman walloped him. I saw her a few hours later and she said to me that she was very, very sorry for what her son did. She was so embarrassed, so sorry. I said, "It's all right, but really I'd rather you explained to your son." I'd rather people come up to me and find out what is wrong, rather than think the wrong thing or ignore it.'

Often our reticence in talking to people like Arthur and Penny is based on a concern for them. But that concern can also be an excuse for not coming to terms with the embarrassment that we feel. And it is not only embarrassment, it is a feeling that they are something apart from us, something different, something we have nothing in common with. Perhaps we have these feelings as a safety valve for our own insecurity, to avoid the thought that we could be like that; so we separate them from us and pretend to ourselves that they are of another world. But they are not.

'If only people would realize that we are like them. We are people too. But instead they put up great barriers . . . we spend our lives breaking down those barriers. We don't get spoken to, so you have to start the conversation, it doesn't matter what it's about, just start talking and show them that you are capable of intelligent conversation. It helps if you make a joke; somehow they don't expect you to be able to talk at all, let alone tell a joke.'

By leading a normal life and taking their full place in the community, Arthur and Penny have converted their once shy neighbours into good friends.

'Friends have said to me, "Penny, when I first met you I was so embarrassed I didn't know what to say. I don't know why, it seems so riciculous now." Again and again, you've got to go out, and keep achieving things . . .

Although isolation can be a serious problem for dwarf children, it will never be one for Nicola, their adopted daughter.

keep proving yourself. Every time you try to get a job you have to prove yourself. It's tough . . . but then life's a challenge.'

Penny would probably never have gained her self-confidence without Arthur's example, and Arthur would probably never have been so assured without his parents and their determination that he should be treated normally and learn to look after himself. For those like Penny and Arthur the world is not so much a hostile, but an alien place. It is built by, and made for, people different from themselves. People who are not different in themselves – people who share the same humanity, but people who are different physically. The rest of us should face the fact that it is only a minor difference; in every other way – in the emotions they have, the things they worry about, and the thoughts that excite them – they are no different from us. Arthur would like us to stop building a world without thinking about them, but above all he is determined to show us he can and will manage despite our thoughtlessness.

'I have a disabled sticker on my car, but I feel we shouldn't really need it. Shopping areas should be built in such a way that the problems don't arise. Since they do, I'll make use of the sticker. But I don't consider myself disabled. The difficulties in our lives show that we are disabled to some degree, but I like to think I can get by in my own way. It might take me a bit longer . . . it might take me a bit more effort, but I can do it. There may be more problems, and more obstacles, but I like to show people . . . show people that I can do it.'

What you can do

When you meet someone who is different do not put up barriers; instead, start to break them down. Any unusual feature, whether it is a squint or a wheelchair, is embarrassing both to you and to the other person but do not think therefore you are meeting someone who is less interesting or less intelligent than you are.

Start a conversation; talk about the weather or the news. If you are going to be talking for more than a minute or two, ask directly about the problem. You cannot pretend you have not noticed a terrible scar, or a missing hand. It is embarrassing to think about it, but it is even worse, and probably rude, to pretend that you have not realized that anything is 'wrong'.

The other person knows what it is like to live with the problem; he has thought and probably worried about it, and has determined to face the world with it; he will probably be glad of the chance to tell you how it happened and what it means. What is more, once you know the basic story you have cleared the air, removed the barriers between you, and no longer have to worry about embarrassing one another.

Aim for quiet sympathy; avoid pity. Dick Francis put this well in his thriller *Odds Against* in a conversation between two disfigured people who agreed that pity is easy to give but embarrassing to receive. The hero with the crippled hand says to the girl with the burned face: 'Sympathy is discreet and pity is tactless . . . It was sympathetic of you to feel sorry that I can't cut up my own food, and tactless to say so.'

The easiest and most common trap to fall into is the assumption that anyone with a visible problem is mentally subnormal. The very worst thing you can do is to ask a companion, 'Does he take sugar?' Talk directly, and ignore the difficulty; try to behave as you would with anyone else.

It may be obvious that someone in a wheelchair cannot open a heavy swing door, or reach a high shelf in the supermarket; by all means offer to help, but do so politely – don't insist on helping. Many blind people have been maddened by being forcibly helped across roads that they never wanted to cross in the first place.

There is no better way of overcoming your embarrassment than by working with handicapped people. If you would like to do this, contact your local Council for Voluntary Service (see the telephone directory under e.g. 'Leeds Council' or 'Volunteer'), or look at the *Observer* Guide to Helping Others – Elizabeth Gundry, *Sparing Time* (Allen and Unwin paperback, 1981).

If you yourself have an unusual feature that sets you apart, you have to come to terms with it. This is often easy when the symptom is 'medical' and temporary; when you have a black eye, or your arm in a sling, you can usually joke about it. When the problem is permanent, however, you have to learn to live with it, and that means making plans, and setting yourself goals. Be realistic about this but do not accept despair. Don't try to lock yourself away; you can lead a full and active life if you decide to do so, but you do have to take that decision.

You also have to decide whether you are going to let your difficulty control your life, or whether you are going to ignore it. You can hide eczema on your ankles, but not on your hands. With a squint, are you going to wear dark glasses all day? If you do, you may feel more secure, but you are also isolating yourself, putting up another barrier between yourself and everyone else, as though one were not enough. What you need to do is get into society, not find another way to cut yourself off. Take off the dark glasses, and face the world.

Remember that the people you meet are embarrassed, and do not know what to say. They are not trying to make it difficult for you; they are just genuinely ignorant. It is therefore up to you to make things easier for them. Besides, you have more experience; you have lived with the problem. So break the ice; start talking. As soon as you can talk about it, do so: 'Don't worry about my leg; it's just rather a bore.' Or 'My face looks bad, doesn't it? It used to worry me too; but at least it doesn't hurt.'

You may think that to talk about it is not only embarrassing and difficult but also disgusting or boring or selfish. You are probably wrong; most people will be interested to hear about your difficulties, and more important than that, once you have shared your feelings you have broken down a great barrier; you will suddenly be a normal person again, and at least one more friend will no longer see you as a freak.

Professional help You may find your disability very hard to come to terms with; the world may seem impossibly bleak. You could well find professional counselling helpful; you can obtain this through your doctor, or you can seek non-medical help. One possibility is Marriage Guidance (*see* page 218) or a local family counselling service – ask at the Citizens Advice Bureau (CAB). Another possibility is MIND (*see* page 219). If you are desperate to talk to someone, telephone the Samaritans. All of these organizations will listen sympathetically to your difficulties, and see what they can do to help. They may be able to help you unravel some of the problems yourself; and put you in touch with organizations or people like yourself.

Your doctor may be able to give you practical help. There could be medical ways to reduce your problem, perhaps by plastic surgery for burns, or by hormone treatment for children of short stature. Discuss it with your doctor. If you think your doctor is unhelpful, *see* pages 189 and 200.

If you are classified as disabled you may resent the label, but one way to get your own back is to 'cash in'. You may be entitled to all sorts of benefits and assistance that no one has bothered to tell you about. *Sickness benefit* is a weekly payment to those who are usually employed or self-employed but cannot work because of

Forget about the wheelchair; treat him as a person.

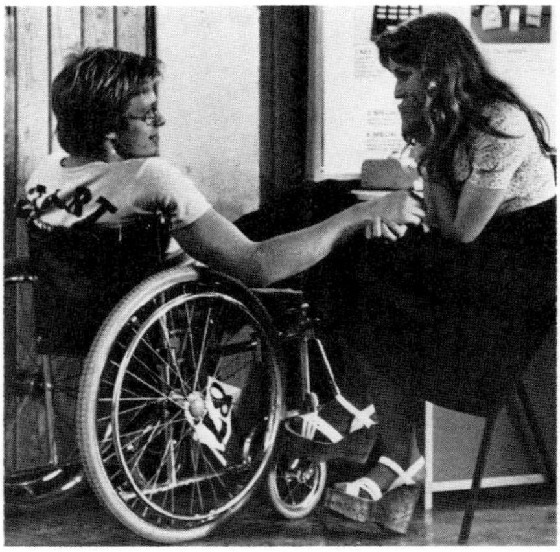

illness or disablement. *Invalidity benefit* takes over from this after six months. The *invalid care allowance* is a taxable weekly payment to men and single women who cannot go out to work as they have to look after a disabled relative. The *attendance allowance* is a weekly payment for disabled people who need continual supervision. The *industrial injury benefit* is a weekly payment for employees who cannot work because of an accident at work. The *industrial disablement benefit* is a pension or lump sum payable to the victim of an industrial accident when injury benefit stops. The *mobility allowance* is a taxable weekly payment for disabled people. For full details see the Department of Health and Social Security (DHSS) leaflet HB1, go to the CAB or the post office and ask, or look at Phyllis Willmott's *Consumer's Guide to the British Social Services* (Penguin, 1978), or at Dr James Bevan's *Your Family Doctor* (Mitchell Beazley, 1980).

Self-help organizations One of the most useful sources of help is an association or self-help group set up by people with a particular problem to support and help others who share the same problem. The Patients Association (11 Dartmouth Street, London SW1H 9BN; tel: 01-222 4992) will do their best to put you in touch with someone who can help you. They publish not only a leaflet on how to use the lesser-known services and concessions of the Health Service, but also a book *Self-Help and the Patient*, with a substantial list of organizations.

If you think that one of the groups listed below could perhaps help you, telephone them, or write with a stamped, addressed envelope, and ask what sort of services they actually provide. No one is going to bring about an instant miracle, but you may well find a group that you can become part of, and be proud to be a member. If you cannot find what you want here, try the index at the back of the book.

- Association for All Speech-Impaired Children, 347 Central Markets, Smithfield, London EC1A 9HN; tel: 01-236 3632/6487.
- Association for Research into Restricted Growth (ARRG) (3 West Croft, West End, Clevedon, Avon) publishes a layman's guide to restricted growth, and is concerned with the welfare of all who are unusually short. Alternatively, if you would like to contact Penny and Arthur Dean, whose story you have just read, write to us (the authors) and we will pass your letter on; they would be happy to try and help anyone with the same sort of problems they have faced.
- Break (100 First Avenue, Bush Hill Park, Enfield, Middlesex; tel: 01-366 0253), provides holidays for deprived, disturbed, and handicapped children.
- Breakthrough Trust Deaf/Hearing Group (Charles W. Gillett Centre, Selly Oak Colleges, Birmingham B29 6LE; tel: 021-472 6447) promotes social and self-help ventures for deaf children and adults.
- British Association for the Hard of Hearing, 6 Great James Street, London WC1 3DA; tel: 01-405 5182.
- British Deaf Association, 38 Victoria Place, Carlisle CA1 1HU; tel: 0228 20188.
- British Dyslexia Association, 4 Hobart Place, London SW1 0HU; tel: 01-235 8111.
- Disability Alliance (21 Star Street, London W2 1QB; tel: 01-402 7026) publishes guides to income benefits, aids, and services.
- Disabled Living Foundation (346 Kensington High Street, London W14 8NS; tel: 01-602 2491) runs an information service which aims to answer any enquiry associated with daily living problems of disabled people with the exception of purely medical matters.
- Disablement Income Group (Attlee House, Toynbee Hall, 28 Commercial Street, London E1 6LR; tel: 01-247 2128/6877) has a number of local branches,

provides an advisory service, and publishes a guide to services and information for disabled people.

- Kids (16 Strutton Ground, London SW1P 2HP; tel: 01-222 1517) gives practical help to children with special needs in their own homes.
- MIND (22 Harley Street, London W1N 2ED; tel: 01-637 0741) or look in your telephone directory. (*See also* page 219.)
- National Bureau for Handicapped Students, 40 Brunswick Square, London WC1N 1AZ; tel: 01-278 3459.
- National Deaf Children's Society, 45 Hereford Road, London W2 5AH; tel: 01-229 9272/6.
- National Eczema Society, Tavistock House North, Tavistock Square, London WC1H 9SR; tel: 01-388 4097.
- Physically Handicapped and Able Bodied, 42 Devonshire Street, London W1N 1LN; tel: 01-637 7475. Their aim is precisely the aim of this chapter: to break down the barriers of fear, ignorance, and prejudice, and to keep the physically handicapped in the community on equal terms.
- Psoriasis Association, 7 Milton Street, Northampton NN2 7JG; tel: 0604 711129.
- Rehabilitation Engineering Movement Advisory Panels (REMAP), Thames House North, Millbank, London SW1P 4QG; tel: 01-834 4444 ext. 412. Each panel consists of a group of qualified engineers who work voluntarily designing and making individual aids for disabled people; these panels have been set up and work throughout the country.
- Royal Association for Disability and Rehabilitation (RADAR), 25 Mortimer Street, London W1N 8AB; tel: 01-637 5400.
- Scottish Paraplegic Association, 3 Cargil Terrace, Edinburgh EH5 3ND; tel: 031-552 8459.
- Spinal Injuries Association, 5 Crowndale Road, London NW1 1TU; tel: 01-388 6840. This is run by paraplegics and tetraplegics and their friends to help individuals meet their own goals, to bring about the best medical care and rehabilitation, and to stimulate scientific research. The Association publishes a quarterly newsletter, books such as *So You're Paralysed . . .* and *Able to Work*. It also has holiday facilities such as caravans and a narrowboat adapted for control from a wheel-chair.
- SPOD (Association For the Sexual and Personal Relationships of the Disabled) c/o RADAR, 25 Mortimer Street, London W1N 8AB.
- Union of the Physically Impaired Against Segregation, Flat 2, St Giles Court, Dane Road, London W13; tel: 01-579 9679.
- Wales Council for the Disabled, Llys Ifor, Crescent Road, Caerphilly, Mid-Glamorgan CF8 1XL; tel: 0222 869224.
- Wider Horizons (Ghyll Cottage, Ings, Kendal, Cumbria LA8 9PU) promotes wider interests among the physically handicapped by means of correspondence and also by publishing a bi-monthly magazine for disabled people.

Books Paul Brickhill, *Reach for the Sky* (Collins, 1954; Fontana paperback, 1957) tells the story of Douglas Bader, the pilot who refused to accept defeat even when he lost both legs in an air crash.

Kristine Gibbs, a young social worker, was struck down by two major brain haemorrhages. Her life was saved by surgery and luck, but when she woke up she found herself paralysed and unable to speak. In her book, *Only One Way Up* (Darton, Longman, and Todd, 1981), she explains what it means to have to learn to do everything again.

Further information about holidays, services, and rights for disabled people can be obtained from Ann Darnborough and Derek Kinrade, *Directory for the Disabled* (Woodhead Faulkner, 1980) and from the *Disability Rights Handbook*, available from the Disability Alliance, 21 Star Street, London W2 1QB.

13. Obsessed with food

Many people in the West have at some point attempted to lose weight by dieting. Numerous women spend their lives going on and off diets. But slimming is more than an international pastime for the affluent nations, it is a giant industry. Low-calorie versions of everything from bread to fizzy drinks are sold in supermarkets. Almost everyone is in on the act – from articles in glossy magazines, to the television ads. We are in a world where to be slim is to be beautiful, and where to stay slim means eating the right food.

There is no doubt that there are medical as well as cosmetic reasons for being slim, and most people now realize that being considerably overweight is a health risk. Surprisingly, the statistics show that the dangers are greater for men than women – at least before the menopause – and are increased if other factors such as stress and smoking are also present. The main risks are of an increased chance of heart disease as a result of the narrowing of the arteries, and the possibility of developing diabetes in later life. A greater recognition of these health risks has given renewed impetus to our concerns about being overweight. At its most blunt: the fatter you are the shorter your life expectancy.

The cause of being overweight is in the vast majority of cases only too obvious – eating too much. Occasionally there is a physical problem, but for almost all of us it is an apparently simple matter of eating less food. Some of us can eat more than others and still not put on weight due to variations in our metabolism – but mostly if we are overweight we should eat less. This simple matter is, however, often an endless and intractable problem.

Despite the enormous amount of literature and interminable articles on the subject the mechanics of putting on weight are frighteningly straightforward. Food is energy, and if we take in more food, and therefore more energy, than we need, the excess is converted into fat. Calories are simply a way of measuring energy – a low-calorie food is automatically a low-energy one. By reducing the calorie intake you are reducing the energy intake and therefore you are less likely to exceed the amount your body requires, and so less likely to put on weight. The only major way that this simple account is made more complex is that gain or loss of body fluid can be responsible for quite considerable changes in weight. The loss of weight in the first few weeks of a diet may be primarily due to this loss of body fluid – and often once the diet is stopped this weight will be immediately regained.

Since the gain and loss of weight is so straightforward there should, in principle, be no real difficulty in losing weight. That, however, is precisely the reverse of most people's experience. Many weight problems are not simply the cause of accidentally taking in slightly too many calories each day – if that were the case there would be no trouble in making the reduction. The problem, and any solution, goes deeper, to the cause of overeating in the first place. If weight is to be lost on a long-term basis a change is required in the attitude to food and eating habits as a whole, rather than a constant and permanent totting up of calories.

The underlying reasons for eating too much are very diverse, but if you solve them, you will have solved your weight problem for good. You will also automatically find your correct weight, which may be more or less than the norm as listed in standard weight tables. Slimming pills and diets can work, but for the great majority of people they only work temporarily. Once the diet is over the weight goes on again. As there are no simple methods of losing weight the slimming business is full of miracle solutions and drastic cures. Exercise machines and health farms, slimming clubs and wonder non-fattening foods abound; even operations for removing fat are available. One thing is certain, if there is an answer it is less likely to be in the unusual, and more likely to be found close to home – in yourself.

Only when you're hungry

Clair was twelve when she first went on a diet. Far from being a sign of defeat, this was a great day.

> 'I was delighted; going on a diet was like becoming a woman. It was a real bond with my mother – we were dieting together. As the others dug into their ice cream and cake there we would be sighing away. It was my mother who started being worried about my weight, not me. I think she worried that she had been a fat adolescent and she didn't want her daughter to be, because if you were a fat adolescent you didn't have dates, you didn't fit into the nice clothes – you were ostracized from the best people.'

It is a relatively modern phenomenon to think that to be slim is to be attractive, but knowing that once upon a time you would have been the right weight is no consolation when the other girls in the class are the ones that get asked out.

> 'I really started to care about my weight when Twiggy hit the scene. Suddenly she was everywhere and with her millions of other boy-like girls with no hips. Skinny girls instantly became popular – and I didn't.
>
> My main feeling was, "What's the matter with me? Why am I not like that?" . . . so I periodically went on diets, not to any great effect.'

Clair had already begun a vicious circle. A circle in which her weight and her boyfriends were intimately connected. The first time she went on a really serious diet was when she was sixteen.

Clair

'It was all to do with Charles. Not that he ever knew. He hadn't shown any interest in me, but I thought, "Well, he doesn't love me at twelve stone but maybe . . . maybe at nine stone . . ." So I dieted like a crazy person – I even remember fainting at school because I wasn't eating enough. I'd make all sorts of cakes and things for the family, and I'd watch them eat and I'd think, "Aren't I good, and aren't they bad." I went on for months and months – I lost about forty pounds – it was a wonderful feeling. I could see it all, when I met Charles that summer he was going to be bowled over, he was just going to say, "Wow." It wasn't to be . . . Charles didn't like me any better at nine stone than he did at twelve; instead he went off and snogged on the beach with my best friend Betsy.'

Without Charles the pounds crept on again. Perhaps it was just safer being fat . . . there was an excuse for not having a boyfriend, and also there was no point in slimming any more.

'I would make up all sorts of reasons for eating – I needed the energy, it was good for me . . . but while I was cramming in the carbohydrates really I felt terrible. I suppose . . . the main thing, the thing at the root of it all, was that I didn't have a boyfriend. I wanted a boyfriend so much. At sixteen, it was all I wanted . . . to hold hands and snog on the beach. But I wasn't – so I ate another bowl of cereal instead.'

From that time Clair was always concerned about her weight. Whether on a diet or bingeing after it, food was never just simply something to eat . . . it was instead something perhaps to be guilty about, or greedy about, or sometimes

But boys didn't seem to like Clair any better when she was thin

even something to be self-satisfied about, but never just something to eat. In the end dieting became a way of life.

> 'I went to college and lived in a flat with three other girls, and basically we were all constantly on diets. I tried every diet under the sun, and believe me there are a lot of diets. I tried the protein and water diet. I tried the protein and fat diet. I tried the grapefruit and egg diet. I've tried them all. They're awful . . . awful. And none of them work. I mean they worked – I lost the weight, but as soon as I came off the diet the weight crept on. And not only the weight crept on, but more weight crept on. It was a really desperate situation.
>
> I remember I went on one diet and I got so tired of it that I went round thinking . . . thinking what would be the most disgraceful thing to eat . . . finally, I opened seven bottles of milk and drank the top inch off each one. It wasn't the only time – I've eaten two jars of peanut butter, and even once an entire jar of Coffeemate.'

It never seemed to get any easier. As a teenager at school not having a boyfriend had been bad enough, but the problem never went away – if anything it got worse.

> 'You don't see fat girls with boyfriends do you? So there was the diet. But then I'd lose a few stone and there'd still be no boyfriend and I'd think, "My God, now I'm slim and I still haven't got a boyfriend. What's the matter with me? Maybe it's my personality or something." I'd put the

weight back on to avoid having to answer that. You see, a boyfriend is all there is, more important than good grades, or your future, more important than anything. You can't ignore it – it's so important.

In a way I suppose fat was a good excuse. It is like that for many women, they may have problems with their marriage, or the kids are causing trouble, or they can't pay the rent . . . but as long as you're fat you're okay, because you could be slim, and then it would all be different. The husband would come right, the kids would turn into golden angels, and there would be money for everybody . . . everything would be fine. But when you get slim it doesn't happen. The same old problems are there, and more immovable than ever. So you get fat again.'

When Clair left university she was twelve-and-a-half-stone – not massively overweight but far enough from her ideal nine stone for everyone to notice. There was no whirlwind solution, but three things happened in her life that made all the difference: a man, a job, and a book.

'It wasn't that I'd never had a relationship before, but I met a nice man who liked my body. Usually I got into bed and pulled up the covers and just hoped they wouldn't notice . . . I liked it a lot when someone actually said, "Oooh, nice!"

Then in my new job I found somebody who wanted me, somebody who thought I was good at what I was doing, and that was a great help too. At the same time I read a book which told me some amazing things about myself, and one thing in particular – that I didn't eat because I was hungry . . . in fact that I was never hungry.

From that point I tried to eat exactly what I wanted. I tried to eat only when I was hungry. It sounds easy, but when you eat compulsively as I did, you have forgotten how to feel hungry . . . you don't know how to recognize it at all.'

Hunger quite simply is the way the body tells us that we need food, the energy source that keeps us going. If it wasn't for hunger we might almost starve to death and not notice. But just because hunger is the sign that we need food, we don't feel hungry *unless* we need food. If you don't eat until you are hungry you cannot put on weight. Over the years Clair has found ways of rediscovering how to feel hunger, thus discovering how to lose weight.

'When I was a schoolgirl, I'd come home ravenous, and my mother would say, "Two hours till supper – don't eat anything now." But I did of course, I stuffed myself with digestive biscuits and pieces of cake, and then at supper time I wouldn't be hungry but I'd stuff myself again. I had to try and unlearn all that . . . to eat whatever I wanted – cream cakes, the lot – but only as long as I was hungry.

It's really odd – I think the first step is realizing that you like food, that you like particular types of food. You don't just want any old bread, you want white bread – but what type of white bread? French bread? Hot or cold? And toasted? And then the butter, what sort of butter? It is ironic, but choosing just the right food is the beginning, because you stop eating any old junk that just happens to be lying around the kitchen. You start eating food because you want the food, and not because it's something to do, and makes you feel better.

As soon as I wanted particular foods – it didn't matter what they were, it could be hot chips with salt and vinegar – I was on the way to feeling hungry.'

We all change our eating habits because of our emotional state – some people stop eating if they are depressed or anxious, others just eat more. If you recognize that you are eating because of your feelings it does not necessarily make it any easier to stop, but it does mean that you can concentrate on the cause rather than the effect.

'If I find myself looking in the fridge at three o'clock in the morning and wanting to eat everything in it – the chocolate mousse and the left-overs from dinner – I'd say to myself, "Hang on a sec., what's this all about? Am I upset because I've just had a fight with my boyfriend or my parents? Why am I eating, why?" You can't always solve it, and even if you can, maybe there's nothing you can do about it, and perhaps you are going to eat the chocolate mousse because it's going to make you feel a lot better, but at least you can try and sort it out, at least you've got some idea of what's going on.'

Clair finally threw away her diet sheets and her calorie charts . . . and she lost weight – not that her boyfriend noticed. Two years later Clair had been so successful that she decided to set up a group to help other women like herself who wished to lose weight.

'I think the majority of women who come along are compulsive eaters, who eat for all sorts of emotional reasons which have nothing to do with physical hunger. A lot of them find that if they don't eat, and they don't cram down piece after piece of toast with butter and jam, they start to feel all sorts of tension and anger that makes them very scared.'

One way that Clair tries to get the women in the group to lose weight is to recognize their underlying emotional needs through imaginary fantasies.

'You imagine that you are at a party and all of a sudden you get fatter and fatter, and then you get thin – as thin as you ever wanted to be. When I tried this fantasy on myself I found that as a fat person I was great big jolly Clair. I could go and hug all my friends, men and women. Everybody loved me, and more than that I was like a presence at a party, I was someone everybody wanted to know. As a thin person I imagined that if I even talked to a man his girlfriend would get jealous. And I felt cold – cold physically as well, somehow I was cut off from everyone. If a man approached he would seem to get very close, and to be threatening.

The Spare Tyre Theatre Company that Clair became involved in

I realized from this fantasy that I was using fat as a positive thing – it gave me some presence, and it helped me avoid tensions and anxieties with men.

Another fantasy we do begins with a trip to the supermarket and you have an unlimited amount of money and you go round and get exactly what you want. You get all the cheeses, and breads, and fruitcakes that you feel like – but you have to be specific about the type and the brand. Then you come home and fill up the kitchen with it all. How do you feel about having all that food around? Most people who are worried about their weight try to keep food out of the way, so they won't be tempted. But that just makes you want it all the more. Fill the place with biscuits or chocolates so that you know you can't eat them all. Once they are no longer scarce you are more likely to eat them when you actually feel like a biscuit, rather than stuffing yourself with the odd one that is lying around.'

Once Clair had learned to eat only when she was hungry, not only did she lose weight, but weight ceased to be something she even thought about.

'I used to weigh myself at least once a week – in fact I felt I should be weighing myself more, but I couldn't stand having to do it more often. I thought that if I was the right weight I'd weigh myself every day with no trouble. But now I don't bother – there's no need. I eat when I want to and as much as I want to, my weight will look after itself.'

Clair is no longer overweight, but she has not discovered a wonder cure – there is no wonder cure. For all the slimming aids and low-calorie foods, we are no closer now to a miracle diet than we were fifty years ago before they all existed. Apart from a handful of rare exceptions, our weight is determined by how much we eat, and our own bodies will tell us when we need to eat and when we don't better than any chart or formula. Clair was fortunate: a change in the circumstances of her life, which made her feel happier with herself, made it easier for her to shift back to eating for nourishment rather than for emotional support. If her emotional problems had remained the whole process would have been much tougher.

Not everyone who is overweight is eating for these underlying reasons, but for a very large number of people, and particularly women, food is a way out. Until the problems are confronted the diet sheet will remain. It is hardly surprising that 95 per cent of those who go on a diet put the weight back on again when they come off it. For most of us the truth of Clair's story is that if we are to lose weight we must change our eating habits, and if we are to change our eating habits we must learn to eat when we need and want food and not for any other reason. None of that is very straightforward; a diet that worked would be much easier but the evidence is that it will not. The alternative may be difficult, but the rewards can be very great as Clair discovered.

> 'I used to think that like so many women, I would be on a diet for life. That I would be for ever hiding the chocolate bars, surreptiously treating myself and feeling guilty. I look back now and I realize how miserable I was during those years about my weight and my eating. I never enjoyed food then. Never. Either restraining myself, or stuffing myself – but no pleasure, no appreciation.
>
> Now, I can eat anything and I love it. If I want a Mars bar I have it, if I want some cheesecake I eat it. I don't have to think about it anymore . . . I can just enjoy it.'

What you can do

The trouble with our society is that food is so plentiful that we almost always have the opportunity of eating more than we really need, and we don't get rid of the extra; instead we store it as fat, which means that many of us go about our lives carrying a thick, heavy blanket of adipose tissue.

Weight The more fat you carry about, the more work your muscles and therefore your heart must do every time you walk upstairs, or stand up, or even breathe. As a result, fat people are more likely to have arthritis and other joint problems and also circulation problems. American insurance companies, after noticing the connection between excess weight and early death, drew up a table of 'ideal' weights, which statistically give you the best chance of living to a ripe old age, depending on your sex, height, and frame. (For the full table see for example *The Facts of Food* page 124.) Because the table is complicated, doctors have produced a formula that works for both men and women. You have no need to worry about your weight provided that your weight in kilograms divided by the square of your height in metres is between 20 and 25.

Either the table or the formula will give you some idea of what you should weigh, but neither contains any magical truth, and your ideal weight may well lie outside the range they suggest.

Diets There are diets in every slimming magazine, in every woman's magazine, in dozens of books, and in many newspapers. If any one of these were effective in the long term then all the rest would disappear. Why is it that they seem to work to begin with? There seem to be three reasons.

- First, any diet is likely to be useful because it imposes rules. Someone who is overweight has lost the self-discipline needed to avoid overeating, and the imposition of outside rules can be helpful – in the short term. But in the long term the effect may be reversed, for when the external discipline is removed – when you come off the diet – you may find it even harder than it was before you dieted not to eat too much.
- Secondly, any new diet is likely to be effective to start with partly because it is interesting and partly because it is new; you are inclined to believe the claims for its effectiveness. But next week there will be another new diet. Does that mean that your old one is no good any more?
- Thirdly, any diet becomes boring. This has a double advantage. You grow bored of what you are supposed to eat, and so you eat less of it. Also you know precisely what you have to eat at every meal (especially with rigidly prescribed diets), and so you never have to think about what you are going to eat next, which automatically removes some preoccupation with food. But because the diet is boring you are more likely to cheat, by nibbling at snacks, or to break it totally and go back to 'real food'.

If you try dieting you will probably find that one diet will work only for a week or two, after which you will have to change. Change to another diet if you want – treat it as a game; it may even be a reasonable way of trying out different types of food. You are unlikely, however, to find that the pounds just 'melt away' with a diet.

If you really want to restrict your calorie intake cut out sugar. Cut down on alcoholic or fizzy drinks. Cut out fried foods, and don't eat butter or margarine on your bread. Do not regard these changes as a diet; just adapt your eating habits a little.

You might like to look at Jill Wordsworth's *The Diet Revolution* (Gollancz, 1976) or at *Which? Way to Slim* (Consumers' Association).

Clubs Some people who believe in diets but lack the self-discipline to stick to them find that joining a club is the answer to their problem. In essence these clubs are a type of group therapy, where the members meet, discuss their problems, and set targets for the week ahead. Weight Watchers meet once a week, and each meeting starts with a weigh-in. The members of each group are kind, friendly, and understanding – and very positive in what you may or may not do. They aim to provide the discipline that you need in your eating habits. There is a high success rate among members, many of whom get down to their ideal weight and stay there. If you would like to get in touch with Weight Watchers or a similar organization look in your local newspaper for the times and places of meetings, or write to the head office: Weight Watchers, 635–637 Ajax Avenue, Slough, Buckinghamshire SL1 4DB; tel: 0753 70711.

Your eating is controlled by these clubs, and if you leave you suddenly have to cope on your own, without instructions or support; you may find this harder when you are thin than when you were fat, and when you are thin you do not appear to need help. You may even gain more weight than you lost in the first place.

Exercise The Greek philosopher Socrates stayed thin by dancing every morning. The more exercise you take the more calories you burn, thus exercise will help you lose weight or stay slim; but do not expect the effects to be dramatic. Fifteen minutes' fast walking will burn perhaps 10 grams of fat; so to lose 1 kilogram you would have to walk all day, or play squash for several hours. Regular exercise will help keep you fit and your muscles working, and it will have a slow but cumulative effect on your weight. But it is not the whole answer, and if you eat anything 'for energy' when you are taking exercise, or have a drink afterwards, you may well be consuming more calories than you are burning up.

Special exercise routines and machines, like diets, can sound wonderful when new, but they too can become boring; if you lack the will to eat less you are unlikely to keep up a regular exercise programme, however scientific it may be.

Medical methods Slimming pills work either by suppressing your appetite, or by making you feel full. They also may be effective to begin with, but in the long term they just represent another form of external discipline. Their effect may be temporary, and when you come off the pills you may find control even more difficult than before. If you don't come off you could become dependent on them.

If you go to your doctor, telling yourself that your overeating is an illness, you may be given a diet sheet, or you may be referred to a specialist organization or a self-help group, of which there are now several. If you are grossly overweight your doctor may judge that there is a real medical risk, and may suggest referring you to a specialist for more drastic treatment: some people have fat removed surgically; some have an operation to by-pass some of the intestine so that the food they eat cannot all be digested; some even elect to have their jaws wired together so that they cannot eat solid food for a period of several weeks or even months. These are the most drastic forms of medical intervention, of medical control of your weight. Again the problem is that this is external. In particular doctors have found that patients who lose a great deal of weight while their jaws are wired frequently put much of it back on again in the following months when the wires are removed. An elegant solution to this particular problem was reached by a London specialist who noticed that a model wore a gold chain soldered round her waist as a reminder not to eat too much – she felt its pressure very quickly if she indulged, and quickly cut down. So he tried welding a piece of nylon string round the waists of patients who had had their jaws wired, and found they were then able to keep to a lower weight. You might even like to try this idea yourself; wear a tight belt.

Stop worrying If you really want to get thinner and stay thinner you cannot rely on discipline from an outside agency; you have to take control of yourself. For ideas on the psychology of diets, exercise, and self-control see Hilde Bruch's excellent if academic book *Eating Disorders: Obesity, Anorexia Nervosa, and the Person Within* (Routledge and Kegan Paul, 1973).

The book that helped to change Clair's life is Susie Orbach's *Fat is a Feminist Issue* (Paddington Press, 1978, and Hamlyn, 1979) which is a self-help guide for compulsive eaters. After Clair read it she learned not to be obsessed with food, or with her weight, and in particular to eat what she wanted, but only when she was hungry. And that is the best way to take control, to reach your ideal weight, and stay there. Every time you reach for food, just ask yourself, 'Am I really hungry?'.

You and your doctor

14. Giving your consent
The unwanted operation

15. The whole truth
Keeping someone in the dark, or just the easy way out?

16. Before and after treatment
How the real trauma can be the way you are cared for

FORM IV NON-THERAPEUTIC STERILIZATION

CONSENT BY PATIENT

....Hospital.

I.. of..

....

hereby consent to undergo the operation of..

....

the nature and effect of which have been explained to me by Dr/Mr..

I have been told that the intention of the operation is to render me sterile and incapable of further parenthood. I understand that it may not be possible later to reverse the effect of this operation.

I also consent to the administration of a general, local or other anaesthetic.

*No assurance has been given to me that the operation will be performed by any particular surgeon.

Date........................ (*Signed*)........................ (*Patient*)

I confirm that I have explained to the patient the nature and effect of this operation.

Date........................ (*Signed*)........................ (*Medical Practitioner*)

AGREEMENT BY HUSBAND

This part of the form should be completed only if the patient is living with her husband.

I.. of..

....

the husband of..

hereby agree to the operation of.. the nature and effect of being carried out on my wife, the nature and effect of which have been explained to me by Dr/Mr..

Date........................ (*Signed*)........................ (*Husband*)

I confirm that I have explained to the patient's husband the nature and effect of this operation.

Date........................ (*Signed*)........................ (*Medical Practitioner*)

*This sentence should be deleted in the case of the private patient.

14. Giving your consent

Your health is your own concern. You are the one who decides whether to go to a doctor, and whether to accept his advice. If you are ill you have the right to know what treatment is being suggested, and what its effects are; if you are not satisfied with the answers you can always refuse it. No one can insist that you have any particular treatment. As an adult there are only two exceptions to this: when you are unconscious, or when you are mentally ill and compulsorily detained under the Mental Health Act. Consent must then be obtained from your nearest relative or legal guardian.

When you call on your doctor you effectively agree to treatment by going along to see him in the first place; by rolling up your sleeve you accept the injection; in most cases, therefore, consent is implicit. Operations, however, are different. They are irreversible assaults on your body and before any operation can start you have to give the doctor your agreement in writing.

Written consent to an operation usually only involves your signature on a hospital form that has been filled out with the details of the operation in question. The consent form is designed to protect both you and the doctor. You are entitled to know about the nature and effect of the operation, and by signing the form you state that this has been explained to you, and that you consent to the operation. The doctor by his signature confirms that he has explained the nature and effects of the operation to you. If you are unsure about any aspect of the operation you must ask the doctor before you sign.

This sounds straightforward and works well in most cases. Unfortunately it is not always quite so simple – you may feel intimidated by the doctor, you do not understand the words he is using, he seems pressured for time, and feeling ill you may not be up to an argument.

The cases of Sylvia and Carole that follow are happily not typical but they do indicate how things can go wrong. Sadly statistics show that these are not just isolated cases. For most types of surgery statistical evidence is hard to find, but in the case of sterilization there is circumstantial, though worrying, evidence that women are being persuaded to have an operation they do not want. The fact is that if you go into hospital for an abortion, you are seven times more likely to be sterilized at the same time on the National Health Service (NHS) than if you are a private patient. Since private patients presumably get what they want, the implication is that NHS patients are being cajoled into undesired operations but the figures are not strictly comparable.

Doctors are trained to make decisions for people who are too ill to make their own. Understandably they are inclined to think that they know better than the patients what is best for them. In most cases they will be right, but in some cases this is not so and it is up to you alone to make sure you are not one of them.

On the dotted line

Each year in Britain there are two-and-a-half-million operations, of which 75,000 are sterilizations. In principle the procedures for obtaining consent should be the same for all operations. If anything, there is a case for more discussion before a sterilization operation, since although it is mechanically relatively straightforward, the operation has lasting effects.

Sylvia and her husband saw a hospital doctor two weeks before her third child was due. They could hardly have expected that there would be discussion of anything except the birth. Her two daughters, Emma and Caroline, had both been delivered by caesarian section, but so far it seemed that their third baby would have a normal delivery.

> 'I'd taken my husband along as a little bit of moral support – I knew there was always the possibility of a caesarian, and I didn't really fancy it. I remember I couldn't really understand the doctor very well because he had a rather strong foreign accent. We were talking about the birth, and all of a

Sylvia was surprised that sterilization was even mentioned

sudden he suggested that I had a caesarian and sterilization at the same time. I was bewildered . . . I couldn't understand why he had suggested it. I certainly didn't like the idea. He said something about having too many caesarians was risky.'

One of the first difficulties she had was finding somebody to talk to, somebody she could understand. Unfortunately, her doctor had recently left, and she felt uneasy about discussing such a personal dilemma with a new doctor. As it turned out, the appointments that Sylvia did make were cancelled; so she did not have the opportunity to discuss the matter further. She did manage to see a doctor at the family planning clinic but all she was told there was that the decision was up to her.

Once she reached hospital, any hopes that sterilization would be forgotten rapidly disappeared.

'The first doctor I saw just assumed that I was expecting to be sterilized. I was terrified to begin with because I don't like hospitals and operations at all, and the hospital was pretty Victorian, and they didn't seem to take care with anyone . . . but I couldn't believe it . . . I didn't know what to say . . . he was so casual about it . . . it was all so arranged.'

Before the operation could take place, however, Sylvia had to sign a consent form. If she did not want to be sterilized, all she had to do was simply not sign the form.

'The first doctor arrived with the consent form in the afternoon. I was concerned about the caesarian, because my first caesarian had been very unpleasant, while the second had been perfectly okay. I just wanted to make sure that this time it wasn't going to be like my first. So I asked about the details of the operation and he just rurned round and said, "If you're going to ask questions and make a fuss and bother about it, you won't have any treatment at all."

Later on, the doctor who was actually going to perform the operation arrived with another form. By this time I was rather frightened of arguing. I began to think that if I started arguing again I would get into trouble and that they would refuse to do the operation. And here was the surgeon who was actually going to do it the next day – I certainly didn't want to get him annoyed.

I asked him why he wanted to sterilize me and he just said they thought it was a good idea. And when I said that I didn't want it, and that was my only objection – I didn't want to be sterilized – he simply held up the form and insisted that I sign . . . Oh, and said that it was ever so easy to reverse anyway.'

Sylvia signed the consent form.

If there had been two consent forms (one for the caesarian and one for the sterilization), if she had not felt under pressure from the doctors, if she had not been worried about what would happen if she did not sign, then there would have been no possibility of her agreeing to be sterilized.

> 'It was just the pressure – a bit of persuasion that you have to have this or else . . . it was a sort of unspoken "or else something terrible is going to happen to you." Nothing specific, nothing that I could argue with, just a feeling that there would be trouble. And then, there are all the doctors, and the consultant, and the nurses, and they're all agreed, and you don't know what's going on. Everyone's waiting for your decision.'

Sylvia's husband, Tim, signed the form too, because his wife had done so. It was a decision that he now regrets very much – a decision he feels they were battered into.

> 'I was disgusted with the way they treated her. They were like gods in little white coats . . . they intimidated us. I couldn't even get to see the consultant afterwards; he just refused to see me.'

Just before giving birth is not the time anybody should be pushed into making a vital decision, for it is a time when the body's hormone changes make it practically impossible to make a calm, considered choice. It's not surprising that there are times when Sylvia blames her husband.

> 'I asked him to come to the hospital because I know that I'm not a very forceful person and that people tend to bully me, and I sort of expected him to stand up to the doctors. I thought, "Well, they may be able to bully me, but they won't be able to bully him" . . . but they did.'

Even though they had signed the form, Sylvia still did not really believe that she would be sterilized; somehow she felt they would only do it if it was really necessary . . . and afterwards she just hoped they hadn't, and perhaps didn't want to find out.

> 'Two or three days later when the baby was all right it first dawned on me that they really might have sterilized me, but it wasn't until about a week later that somebody actually admitted that it had happened. Even then, it wasn't until six weeks later when I went back for a post-natal appointment and actually saw my notes that it seemed real . . . terribly real. It really hit me. You could hardly say that the bottom drops out of your world, but it feels like that . . . it feels as if you're stomach's sunk right down and everything's just fallen apart. I ended up in my bedroom crying my eyes out. The doctor gave me some pills, but I wasn't eating anything, and everything seemed automatic, as if it was a dream. I wanted it to be a dream. I couldn't face it being real, I couldn't face the fact that I had been sterilized . . . but I had.'

Two and a half years later Sylvia had another operation – this time to reverse the process. She does not yet know whether it has worked but it has a much smaller chance of success than she was promised.

Carole had no idea that the birth of her third child would bring such sadness

It might be said that although Sylvia was bullied into signing her form, it was nevertheless her decision. She could and should have opposed it if she felt strongly enough. Ironically many women have difficulty in obtaining sterilizations they want, and furthermore, many doctors do not support the idea of sterilization with caesarian section. However, Sylvia's experience is not just an isolated example; if anything Carole's case is more alarming because in effect she was never consulted at all.

Carole, like Sylvia, had two children, but her births had been uncomplicated and both babies were born at home. When her third baby was due, however, she went into hospital for the birth to be induced.

She found herself in a ward with three other expectant mothers. They were all given the same induction treatment but in her case something went wrong. One by one, as the day wore on, the others left the ward to have their babies until eventually she was left alone. Around her there seemed to be growing concern. Doctors came and went. Through a haze of drugs Carole began to lose any idea of what was happening to her.

> 'Everything got quieter and quieter, and really I wasn't aware of what was going on. I wasn't aware of anyone talking, or any noise. People seemed to be milling in and out for examinations. I don't remember much, but I do remember an air cylinder hitting the bed as it was wheeled in, and being given the mask . . . to inhale the gas. It was just a dazed state – like waking up from a dream. I didn't realize this was my life, my body, or what was going on . . . it didn't even dawn on me whether the baby had been born or not.'

Then Carole remembers a figure appearing at the foot of the bed.

> 'It looked as if she was wearing a mask with earrings at the corners of her mouth – in fact I think she was just wearing a lot of make-up. Then she asked would I agree to a little operation. All I could think of was that I wanted the baby born alive – so I agreed. I was never told what the operation was for, someone helped me to sit up and they took the mask out of my hand. A pen was placed in my fingers, but it just fell straight through. It was put back in my hand and my fingers were held round the pen so that I could write my name and address. I don't remember seeing the paper . . . that's about all I can remember. I didn't even wear glasses – I'm blind as a bat without them, but it just didn't occur to me . . . I just did exactly as I was told.'

The signature on the consent form for the operation, of course, did not look much like Carole's normal signature, and the address was mis-spelled. But the operation went ahead: the baby was delivered by caesarian section and Carole was sterilized at the same time.

Carole did not see her baby for three days. She was too drugged most of the time to know what was going on and the staff were not as friendly as they might have been.

> 'I kept asking the staff if I could see the baby. No one told me what was happening. But the sister said, "No; you're not a paying patient; you don't get VIP treatment here. You'll have the baby when I'm ready." In the end I was in tears – Saturday evening, that was the first time they would let me see him. I was rather upset, and one of the nurses said, "Never mind, love, you'll never have to come in here again." I asked why. The sister turned round and walked out of the ward, and the nurse followed. No explanation. Nothing.
>
> I felt a rush of panic – sterilization was the first thing I thought of. I remember cuddling my baby and being glad that he was alive, but at the same time crying. I expected someone to come and tell me what had happened, but nobody did. I couldn't sleep . . . I was so frightened.'

The next day Carole asked the doctor what had happened to her during the operation.

> 'Calmly, as though it was an everyday occurrence, she said, "Do you mean the sterilization? We do this . . ." and she started doing a drawing on the bedside table. I remember looking at her and looking at the pictures and drifting completely away. I don't know how long I drifted away. From then on my stay in hospital was hell.'

As she recovered Carole began to discover that almost everybody had known whe was going to be sterilized – except her.

> 'I went back to my own doctor, and asked why it wasn't discussed with me, because there had been absolutely no discussion at all. And he said – I

could hardly believe what I heard – he said, "Because it would have frightened you. You get over hatred, but you don't get over fear. It's better to carry it out and let you find out afterwards." It was shocking – this from a doctor that had helped me conceive.'

When she came home, Carole hesitantly tried to tell her husband what had happened . . . and then she realized that he had signed the form as well.

'I couldn't believe that he would have consented to anything like it. One part of me can see how he could consent because you do believe what doctors tell you, but another says that he should have known me better than he did.'

Carole still really blames her husand and their marriage has never been the same since.

'I've never forgiven him. The nightmare still continues – we've come very close to splitting up; nothing is as it used to be. It's a nightmare; there's no other way to describe it.'

Carole has three children and there are many mothers in the same circumstances who would not feel as strongly about being sterilized as she does. But for her, quite simply, children are her life.

'I need children around me . . . I need their company more than they'll ever need me. They give me a reason for living – they are my reason for living. It's sad, but it's not my husband, it's the children.

For Carole her children are her life

It is as if they've taken away my rights. They have left me with no identity at all. I'm no more now than part of the furniture . . . it is as if my life has been taken away . . . when I feel depressed I almost feel I would have preferred them to have left me to die, because somehow it has taken away my rights to be a person.'

Over a number of years, and through the courts, Carole sued the hospital for damages.

She won.

What you can do

Many patients in hospital are comfortable, happy, and satisfied with their treatment. Doctors and nurses are often dedicated and competent, and work hard for the benefit of their patients. But as in all areas of human life things can go wrong, and what you need to know is how to avoid the pitfalls.

First, remember that doctors are human beings, however powerful and knowledgeable they seem to be. They are much more likely to be helpful and kind if you try to treat them as friends.

In hospital When you are going to have an operation, it's important to find out about it. After all, your body is going to be cut up and you are going to have to live with the results for the rest of your life; you must discover what they are likely to be. In particular you should ask your hospital doctor, or the consultant, the nature of the operation and the risks involved.

There is often a problem in communication. The consultant says he is going to perform a mastoidectomy and goes on to tell you how safe it is. He is not trying to confuse you; it's just that to him the word 'mastoidectomy' is as common as the word 'toothpaste', and he forgets that you don't talk all day in medical jargon. So when he uses any word that you do not understand, stop him politely and ask what it means. No operation is so complicated that it cannot be explained to you; do not be afraid to go on asking.

Of course, all sorts of difficulties may arise. There may not be a doctor about when you want one; if so ask the ward sister to arrange for a doctor to see you. You may find you do not like your doctor or that you don't believe that you really need surgery. You can always ask your consultant for a second opinion. Do not do this because you do not fully understand the first; if you do not understand, ask. Get a second opinion only if you really believe that the suggested treatment is misguided.

In the end, it is most important that you do not sign the consent form until you are quite happy about the operation. If when the form arrives you understand the operation but are unhappy about some part of the form, do not feel that you cannot alter it. If necessary cross out the words you do not agree with, or add more words, before you sign. As a last resort you can always discharge yourself from the hospital.

When you are lying alone, feeling ill, in a hospital bed, you may well find it difficult to summon up the energy and enthusiasm to chat cheerfully to consultants. For that reason it is always a good idea to make sure you have a friend with you when you go into hospital and to be able to call someone in when you need moral support. You want someone who knows you and understands your medical condition – your husband, wife, partner, mother, or a good friend. If no one is available, ask your doctor to come in. Any one of these friends can help you get the information you need about the treatment or the operation, and make sure that your wishes are known to the doctors.

In the surgery The question of how to talk to doctors is most pressing when it crops up suddenly in hospital but the same principles also apply in the doctor's surgery. If your doctor suggests any treatment, ask about it – what it is, what it will do, and what side-effects there might be. The person most interested in your illness is you, and you are the one who needs the information and the treatment. Your doctor is the source of both, and should be happy to discuss the situation with you.

Research has shown that the great majority of people who visit their doctors forget most of what they are told by the time they leave the surgery. It may, therefore, be useful to make a list of questions and to write down the doctor's answers. If you are given a prescription ask what it is, how to use it, and how long to take it for. There is no need to be offensive about this – make a friend of your doctor and you have a powerful ally.

How to change your doctor People do fail to agree sometimes, and you may fall out with your doctor. If for any reason you want to change your family doctor there are instructions on your medical card. But basically there are three methods. If you have moved, even to the next house, you can go to a new doctor and ask to be registered. If you haven't, then either ask your doctor to sign the medical card giving consent to change (you do not have to say why you want to change, or who to) or, if you don't want to have to see your doctor, write to your Family Practitioner Committee (FPC) and tell them that you want to change, giving them the new doctor's name. You can obtain the FPC's address from your medical card, from the telephone directory, from the Community Health Council, or from the District or Area Health Authority. Before you do this, however, you should make sure that the new doctor will take you on, or you may be left without a doctor at all.

How to make a complaint If you think you have been badly treated and want to do something about it, be warned that to make a formal complaint against the medical profession is a long, difficult, frustrating business. It is also unlikely to do you much good in the end because eventually it will probably come down to a question of 'clinical judgment' unless you can positively prove that a medical professional was negligent.

For detailed information about how to make a complaint, and for further advice on how to deal with doctors, and on your rights as a parient, you should consult one of the following paperbacks:

- Gerry and Carol Stimson, *Health Rights Handbook* (Prism, 1978, and Penguin, 1980).
- Angela Phillips and Jill Rakusen, *Our Bodies Ourselves* (Allen Lane, 1978, Penguin, 1978) a health book for women.
- Carolyn Faulder, *Talking to Your Doctor* (Virago, 1978), a gynaecological guide for women.

The Patients Association (11 Dartmouth Street, London, SW1H 9 BN; tel: 01-222 4992) produces leaflets on how to change your doctor, on patients' rights, on what you can and cannot insist on, and on going into hospital; for details write with a stamped, addressed envelope.

15. The whole truth

What should a doctor do when he is faced with the awful knowledge that someone has a serious, possibly terminal, illness? It is not easy to tell someone something that will probably cause much distress; furthermore the person may not want to know. Understandably, therefore, a doctor will often tell the relatives first, on the grounds that they know the patient best, and are most likely to know whether he would want to hear about the illness, or would rather not be told. Although almost always well-intentioned, the doctor and the relatives sometimes avoid telling the person because it is such a painful thing to have to do, and they justify this to themselves by saying that it would only make matters worse. There are obviously no hard-and-fast rules, but we should never assume that it is best to hide the truth.

Only very occasionally is the question of telling the truth as dramatic as deciding whether or not to let someone know that they are going to die. More commonly doctors and relatives are in the position of having to decide whether to tell the person the full implications of the illness, or whether they should err on the side of optimism. Further, should a doctor tell you what might develop? If you go to your family doctor with stomach pains and a loss of appetite should you be told all the things which might be wrong with you – some of them very serious? Doctors often argue that they do not tell people such things because patients will only worry. On the other hand not knowing can be even more disturbing. What is clear is that anyone who wants to know should be told, and none of us should use the difficulty of actually telling someone some bad news as an excuse for false optimism or equivocation.

However, perhaps the greatest deceit between doctor and patient is one that both sides encourage and foster. It is the assumption that the doctor always knows what is going on. We all like to feel when we are ill that we can go along to our doctor, that we will be told what is the matter, and be sent away with the magic potion to cure us. Doctors on their side of the fence like to give the impression that they do indeed know what is wrong and that with some treatment the problem can be solved. Sadly, this comforting story is far from reality. It is closest to the case with children who most often are suffering from specific diseases and sometimes those that can be treated, like tonsillitis or a middle ear infection. Perhaps one of the reasons for our belief in doctors is because of their observable effectiveness with children. Adult health is however rather different. Often the symptoms are too vague to lead to any diagnosis.

Common symptoms such as weariness or lack of energy, headaches, indigestion, can be very serious but in the vast majority of cases they disappear without our ever knowing why they were there in the first place. Even if the doctor is able to give a name to your problem it is unlikely that you will be cured by treatment. Drugs can and often do alleviate the symptoms but they rarely cure the disease. Surprising though it sounds, even if you have a nameable illness and there is treatment which can improve your condition, your doctor will still often not know how the illness will develop, how long it will take for you to get better, and apart from the vaguest of answers there may be little suggestion of the cause of the disease.

Medicine pretends that it is a science, but primarily when it does work, it works by trial and error. People have been seen with the problem before; in the past such-and-such a treatment was tried and was partly successful; so we will try it again. Diseases are not as straightforward as we tend to think they are – as if once we have found a name to our problem we have solved it; they do not always fit neatly into their box, or develop as predicted. As a result, with relatively minor complaints, doctors often do not know what is the matter. In more serious cases they probably will have a name but they may still not know the likely outcome.

We have come to believe that doctors can do anything, but until we become more realistic it will be difficult for doctors to tell us the truth – which sometimes will be no more than, 'I don't know'. How much of the truth we wish to be told is going to remain something that will vary between individuals; however, one thing that is certain from the story which follows is that keeping the truth from someone can do great harm, and telling the truth can be much less devastating than we think it is going to be.

Kept in the dark

As a teenager, Barry was one of those people who are exceptionally good at all sports. By the age of twenty he had become a professional table-tennis player, and represented England. His lasting love, however, was golf.

> 'I never took it up professionally . . . I just wanted to play the game. I love being in the countryside, but I can't just wander around; I've got to be going somewhere, getting from A to B. Golf gives me all of those things.
>
> That I need the game to keep me out there has got something to do with the fact that I've got a very strong competitive streak . . . I must win. If I don't win, I don't enjoy it as much. In fact Jeannie, my wife, used to complain that I was impossible when I came back from a table-tennis tournament and I'd lost.'

Barry was in the peak of condition so he noticed immediately when one day during a round of golf he felt a strange feeling in his left leg.

> 'It was sort of . . . a tingling sensation . . . almost impossible to describe. Around my knee. I knew that it was something unusual, something I

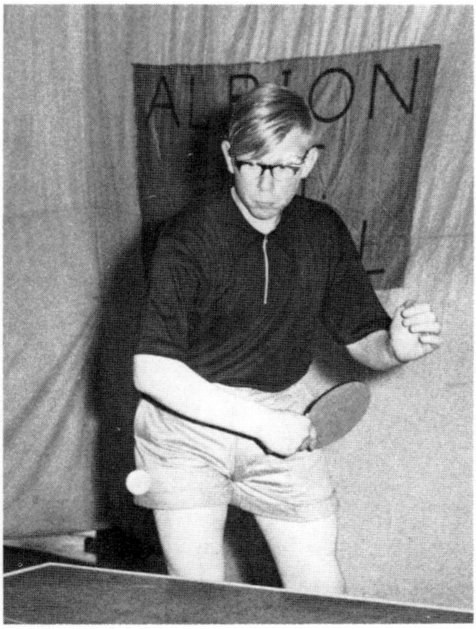

Barry knew at once when something was wrong but Jeannie didn't let her awful secret spoil their wedding day

hadn't felt before. There was obviously something wrong, but I didn't really think anything very much of it at the time. I certainly didn't think it was serious; there was no reason to do so.'

So Barry ignored it. After all it seemed insignificant; it wasn't even painful. Sometimes it would go away for a while, but it always returned, each time with a little more insistence.

'It was strange, my knee seemed to get heavier, slightly as if a tourniquet had been placed around it. It was at this point that I decided that I ought to go and see my doctor. I thought I got on well with my doctor, I had been with him since I was a child, but this visit was hopeless. Well . . . I got nowhere. He kept saying, "It's a ligament or something." That was ridiculous – I knew what a pulled muscle felt like, and it had nothing to do with what was happening to me. I was really annoyed, he was sort of dismissing it, and yet he wasn't . . . somehow, I felt he was being . . . evasive. Yes, that was it, evasive.'

Gradually it got worse, but because there were periods when the sensation vanished altogether, and because it did progress only bit by bit, it was a few months before Barry went to see his doctor again.

'This time I decided I would try and pin him down. But when it came to it, he always had a reply. In fact, it was the same for the next four years, I never could pin him down, I never could. I felt frustrated, and very angry.

He'd been my doctor for years, he was a friend of the family. I thought he was letting me down . . . because somewhere I think I knew . . . I think I realized he knew something more than he was telling me.'

Barry's symptoms started to become rather more disturbing. Whole areas of his body would become numb. Sometimes the whole of his right-hand side would feel dead while the other side was perfectly all right. When these dramatic, frightening things started happening Barry tried to discover what might be going on from textbooks, but without any previous medical knowledge at all he found he just could not get anywhere. On one occasion when he was with his doctor an arrangement was made for Barry to see a neurology specialist.

'My mobility was particularly bad at the time. Anyway, I was examined and the specialist then said, "Well, I'll tell you . . . you're all cured." I couldn't believe it, I was dumbstruck. Eventually I said, "Well, if I'm cured, what's this I feel? What's going on?" I was furious, I got off the couch, and I stormed out. It was so ludicrous saying I was cured, implying that I wanted to be ill.'

Since she was a nurse, Jeannie had her own idea about what Barry's illness might be, right from the beginning.

'The very day Barry came back from his golf, saying his leg felt funny, I thought it's either multiple sclerosis, or muscular dystrophy. But being a student nurse, you imagine every ache and pain is the beginning of something awful, so I dismissed the idea. However, by the time the doctor had seen Barry about three times, I decided to go and see him myself. So, I went in, and said I thought Barry had got either multiple sclerosis or muscular dystrophy, although he was really too old for muscular dystrophy. Anyway, the doctor said that he tended to agree, and that so far Barry was presenting textbook examples of the disease. Because he was a successful sportsman and so good at everything the doctor thought it would be a good thing for us not to tell him – at least until it was confirmed. And so we didn't tell him . . .'

Jeannie was only nineteen. Perhaps if she had been a bit older she would not have been persuaded so easily, but sadly her training as a nurse had taught her to hide things from patients.

'I thought I knew it all, didn't I? If someone is dying under your very nose in hospital, you say to them, "No, you're not dying, my dear." You're not allowed to tell anyone they're dying, and you're not allowed to tell anyone they've got multiple sclerosis either, let alone tell them they *might* have it.

It seemed the best thing to wait for the results, to give us a breathing space before telling him. But then, by the time they'd done all the tests, and they had confirmed that it was MS, our doctor sort of never . . . never got round to telling him.'

The only person who didn't know

Multiple sclerosis is a disease that affects nerve fibres with which you move your muscles. In its most acute form the disease can kill within a couple of years, but more commonly it is prolonged and gradually gets worse over a long period. As yet there is no recognized effective cure although there is much research in this area. Faced with this future it is understandable that we do not want to tell the person the chilling news. However, it is often everyone else that wants to hide from the disease.

> 'It was a funny thing really. I didn't want to tell him, I didn't want him to know, but the truth was I didn't want to know either. I went round trying to forget it, but of course, that was impossible. In a few years I became very old trying to hold it, suppress it, contain it. It got to the stage where it had become my own personal guilty secret. No one must know. I suppose I thought he just couldn't take it, at least I'd got used to the idea that he couldn't take it. Really, I just didn't have the guts to say, "Look, love, sit down, you've got MS." So instead I shrugged my shoulders. I'd learned in hospital. You tell them, "Ask staff nurse," who says, "Ask sister," who says, "Ask the doctor," who doesn't answer. So, I did much the same with Barry; when he said, "I can't feel one entire side of my body," I'd say, "I expect it will pass love, you must remember to mention that to the doctor. Do you want me to phone up and make an appointment?" What I really wanted was for him to stop telling me the symptoms he was experiencing and therefore confirming all the time that he'd got it . . . when I didn't want him to have it. It was a case of ostriches on all sides.'

Four years after the first symptoms, Barry and Jeannie moved, and at the same time changed their doctor. For Barry it was some hope that things might be different.

'It hadn't occurred to me to change my doctor. Our family doctor was our family doctor, you didn't go to another one, that's all there was to it. And, doctors make it pretty obvious that you shouldn't go to another one. Anyway, I got the same response from the new doctor as I had from the old one. A short while later another doctor I saw suggested it was psychosomatic. I began to think maybe it was, maybe I was imagining it all. If I just thought about it differently perhaps it would all go away. But then, I'd think, "It's rubbish, I know what's happening to me, and it certainly isn't in my mind."'

While Barry was living through the illness and the agony of not knowing what was going on, Jeannie was crushed by her unspeakable knowledge.

'I tried, but I couldn't hide from it . . . it was everywhere. In the end I started to feel it was almost my fault. I felt so dreadful, so guilty, so awful about it. I wanted to run away, just to escape for a while. Sometimes I used to say to Barry, "I wish your bloody illness would go away for a week, so that we could have a holiday." What I really wanted was a holiday from knowing . . . when he didn't know. By then, I knew that when he found out he was going to explode at me as well. To start with I was in league with the doctors, but after the first three or four they were in league with me. I used to go along to the doctors first on the pretence of finding out what these new doctors were like . . . and the first thing I'd say was, "I've come to tell you that my husband has got MS and he doesn't know." In the end I was saying, "And I don't want you to tell him either." I don't know why I did it really. I had just got so into the habit of concealing it from him, that by then I was terrified of him finding out. I may have wanted to run away, but there was nowhere that I could run.'

Over the years Barry's symptoms came and went, but each time they came back they were worse. It became far harder for him to walk. The sensations he had in his leg he began to get in his fingers so that he couldn't pick things up properly, and he kept dropping things. Quite often he would get double vision. These are all classic symptoms of the disease.

With Barry's illness getting worse, and being increasingly less able to carry on the job he was doing they agreed to put their savings together and buy a riding stable. The hope was that Jeannie would be able to run it if things got really bad, although of course Barry did not look at it quite like that. As soon as they had moved Barry decided to go and see the doctor . . . without telling Jeannie, and before she had seen the doctor herself.

'I don't know why I went along; instinct I support. I just felt I had to talk to somebody. I remember going in to see him ready for a pitched battle . . . but it didn't happen. I went in and told him what had been going on, and then I just asked him outright what was the matter with me. He looked at me quizzically, and then he puffed on his pipe and said, "Well, old chap, you've got multiple sclerosis."

I burst into tears, but into tears of relief . . . I was so glad that he'd told me. At last somebody had told me something. No longer did I have this nebulous cloud hanging over me. I believe, perhaps wrongly, but I believe that I can cope with anything once I know what's going on. But I can't cope with confusion. I don't think anybody can.'

Barry asked if he was going to die from the disease and the doctor told him that in his case it was definitely not terminal. On his way home Barry oscillated from feeling relief at knowing what was the matter to concern at the seriousness of his state. What were they going to do with the riding stable which they had so recently bought? Telling Jeannie was not going to be that easy either. However, as soon as he arrived he told her he'd been to the doctor.

'I was a bit annoyed because Barry had got there first, and I asked him edgily what the doctor had to say. When he told me my first impulse was to deny it, to say, "No, you can't have it, he must have been mistaken." But actually I couldn't say anything, I was trying to work out what to say.

It was obvious Barry felt very relieved, so I thought, "We'll go along with it today, and see how he feels tomorrow." As though his reaction to being told he had MS was just another symptom. Of course, it wasn't any different the next day, and I continued to pretend it was a great surprise. Barry kept on asking me all sorts of questions about the disease, some of which I couldn't answer, some of which I wouldn't answer.

I remember one day we sat down to discuss the implications and I don't know how, but it just slipped out. I had never meant to tell him that I'd known. And whoops . . . Barry hit the roof. We had the most terrible rows. Barry was so angry with me, and I felt angry with him for being so angry with me. We went around bashing our heads against each other's anger. The trouble was I felt very self-righteous at that stage. He would be yelling at me, and all I felt I had done was to defend him from it, and ignore it for him. I'd spent all those years protecting him, and then he practically thumps me for it. Gradually however I began to tentatively apologize for it.

It was difficult because for years if Barry had said, "Let's do so-and-so," I could reply knowing what he didn't know. I had to readjust to all that . . . I had to let him have his say, I had to let him decide. But despite that we had the most tremendous arguments, the most bitter rows. They wouldn't just go on all evening, they'd simmer all night and flare up the next day fresh as you like. On and on and on. We were both exhausted, but we'd only pause to sleep before we were at each other again.'

Over the next few weeks Barry discovered not only that Jeannie knew, but that his parents knew, his brother knew, and his sister-in-law. And of course all the doctors he had seen knew. It seemed that everyone apart from Barry was in on the secret. It was something that made him very bitter. Past decisions that had been made, he now realized, were based on his illness. Conversations had happened or not happened because they thought it best. While they had huddled together to talk about his future, he had been left in the dark. He felt isolated . . . cheated. It was a deceit he could not really forgive.

> 'I've got intelligent, responsible parents . . . good parents . . . but they didn't tell me. I think it is a parent's duty to tell their child. Okay, I'm not a child any more, but like all parents they still consider me a child . . . and they should have told me. I blamed Jeannie at the time but I got over that. But it is only very recently that I've been able to forgive my parents. I don't harbour it anymore, and they know very well what I feel, but I still think their duty was to tell me. It is my life . . . and no one else's. I am the person with the illness and it is quite wrong that I shouldn't know.'

Slowly the wounds between Barry and Jeannie started to heal, but it didn't make the illness go away. Knowing what was the matter helped Barry a great deal, but fighting the dragon is not easy even when the blindfold has been taken off. The symptoms were still there, still eating away at what Barry could achieve.

> 'The disease itself is like having an intruder in the house. Like living with an intruder. The intruder is everywhere, wherever you go. It's in your bed, it's in the bathroom, it's with you when you go to the pub. The intruder's there all the time. It's there during your sex life, it's there in your moments of relaxation, it's there as you sit in the sun on a lovely summer's day. The intimate and the not so intimate, the personal and the not so personal, it's there all the time. Think of the person you dislike most in your life, and imagine you're tied to them, you can't get away. They go out with you, they work with you, they go to bed with you. Every time you make love, that person has to be there. It wouldn't be very nice, would it? And that's what the illness is like.'

The disease affects Jeannie almost as much but in a different way. Doing the things Barry cannot do, trying to stop him doing too much.

> 'Barry is very stoical, he just says you've got to cast it to one side, and try and get on with normal life. Well, I hate it. I resent it. I'm not noble about it, it's thoroughly unwelcome. Sometimes I wish I could get hold of it and kick it. I don't like having to see Barry struggle all the time, and all the burdens it imposes. I just hate it, that's all there is to it, I hate it.'

Although Barry had been told what his illness was, and his questions about it were answered, it still didn't fully explain all the symptoms that he could get.

> 'I was halfway up the stairs on my way to bed and all of a sudden everything went black. And I was blind. I don't remember what happened after that.'

> 'Well, Barry was saying to me, "I can't see love, I can't see." I'd had a heavy day and to start with I didn't really believe him, but then I realized he actually couldn't see. It frightened me half to death. I had to lead him around

Barry found it hard to forgive Jeannie; he could not forgive everyone

> and sit him on the edge of the bed. I just kept saying, "It's all right my love, you'll be able to see in a minute." Fortunately the next morning Barry could see again.'

Barry in particular felt they should have been told that it could happen.

> 'I think it is terrible that a doctor will withold anything from you. They should tell you absolutely everything they can. If at all, they should tell you hopeful things because you start looking for signs of things getting better, but really they should tell you everything. Everything they do know, and if they don't know something, they should say they don't know. If there are possibilities of other things happening they should tell you – you don't worry about them, but if they do happen at least you know what's going on.'

Looking back Jeannie feels rather similarly.

> 'The first doctor was fifty or sixty, and I was nineteen. He shouldn't have expected me to make myself old because of his chicken-heartedness. It was his job to present Barry with the facts, so that he could live his life within those limited bounds. It was not his job to disguise those facts and let Barry struggle on in a normal world with normal competition without knowing that he was at a disadvantage. He certainly didn't save us any grief by not telling Barry. Instead he gave me ten years of the female disease – guilt. He gave Barry ten years of absolute bewilderment, and

> losing ground that he need never have lost if he had known. All for the sake of some natural grief in the first few weeks. It would have made so much difference if he had told Barry. Our marriage would have been a lot easier. I'd have been a lot easier to live with, and Barry could have made the right decisions.'

The effects of not telling Barry were extreme but they are no different in kind from the thousands of cases every day in surgeries and hospitals throughout the country, where patients are left wondering, 'What is really the matter? Why am I not being told?' Patients are kept in the dark by student nurses like Jeannie who prevaricate, or pass the buck; by incomprehensible prescriptions and pointless unintelligible jargon. Is all this done for the patient's good? Or are doctors afraid of showing how little they know, and how little they can do? Perhaps it is we who are afraid of finding that out. Certainly if there is to be more honesty between doctor and patient, we are going to have to stop believing in the doctor as the all-knowing God, and the doctor is going to have to vacate the position. Barry, for one, is in no doubt that it would be a move in the right direction.

> 'It doesn't just apply to MS, it applies to every disease, every problem. Especially terminal illnesses. I'd want to know if I was going to die. It's your body, and it's your right to know. If you take your car into a garage, you expect to be told the problem, and I think you value your body more than your car. At the moment doctors are doing it totally wrong. Not just with me, but with everybody. Not everyone *has* to be told, but they should be told if they want to be . . . they have a right, we all have a right . . . to know.'

What you can do

Whenever saying too much can cause pain, grief, and worry, the safest course is to say nothing. Children confronted by their parents, and politicians by journalists, know that anything they say may be taken down and used in evidence later. To say anything is a risk. Doctors are often the same with their patients; it's not that they deliberately withhold information in order to keep you ignorant; they may not know exactly what is the matter with you, and they may be concerned that telling you what they *think* will only cause you pain, grief, and worry.

How to talk to your doctor The decision you have to take, when you suspect that you have a serious illness, is how much you want to know. Some people, like Barry, would much prefer to hear the whole truth – to know not only whether the disease is terminal but also all the symptoms that might occur, so that they can be prepared, and so that they can plan ahead. And if the doctor doesn't know the answers, then these people would rather be told that. Others want to know nothing, and would prefer to rely on hope, putting complete trust in the doctor and his medicine. You have to decide whether you belong to one of these groups, or somewhere in between. You might like to talk it over with someone non-medical before you go to the doctor – with your partner, a friend, or perhaps Marriage Guidance (MG) (*see* page 218).

When you have decided, tell your doctor; be honest and you are much more likely to get openness in return. Say to your doctor, 'I'd rather not know what the problem is,' or, 'I want to know everything.' Many people prefer to learn a little at a time; so ask questions until you are satisfied for the moment. You can always go back later for more. But remember that your doctor is not likely to *volunteer* information; you will be given it only if you ask. And in common with everyone else, your doctor is more likely to be helpful if you are friendly – better to ask him if he knows what is wrong than to accuse him of keeping you in the dark.

You may well find it helpful to talk over with someone else how to approach your illness and what to ask your doctor. The best person is your spouse or partner, and it is important that you should make clear to him or her what you really want, if only to avoid falling into the same sort of trap as Barry and Jeannie. Better still, take an ally to the surgery for moral support. If your partner cannot come, and you haven't an obvious friend or relative, you can always go to MG or the Samaritans (*see* pages 217–18). A Samaritan might be able to go with you to the doctor, or to telephone him in advance, making your interview easier.

If you have decided that you want to be told, the first thing to ask is the diagnosis; does the doctor know what your illness is, and if so what is its name? Once you have the name you can always find out more, if you want, from books and other sources (*see* page 98). Next you may want to ask about the prognosis: will it get worse; what symptoms will appear? And so on. The more you know about your illness the better able you will be to discuss it with your doctor or specialist.

Thirdly, you can discuss possible treatment. Your doctor may offer you a prescription, but you don't have to accept that, or any other treatment. You cannot lose by asking what the treatment is meant to do; is it to cure you, to make the symptoms disappear, to reduce the pain, or to prevent the disease from spreading? And are there alternatives?

If your doctor is unhelpful, try another at a family planning clinic (listed under your District or Area Health Authority in the telephone directory) at at a women's health centre (address from WIRES; tel: 0742 755290). Ask your doctor for a second opinion, or you can change your doctor (*see* page 189). For more information consult one of the books below.

Other sources of help One possible source of information is a self-help group set up specifically for people with the same illness. They will be aware of the latest forms of orthodox treatment and where it is available – which your doctor may not – and also of unorthodox treatment, which your doctor is unlikely to tell you about.

Doctors have to be cautious. They must not recommend anything that might cause the patient harm, and they will avoid raising any false hopes. They are unlikely to come forward and tell you; if you want to know the whole truth it's up to you to find out.

Organizations and books For advice on how to handle your doctor *see* the index, or Gerry and Carol Stimson, *Health Rights Handbook* (Prism, 1978, and Penguin, 1980), or Carolyn Faulder, *Talking to Your Doctor* (Virago 1978).

For information about associations such as Action for Research into Multiple Sclerosis look up the illness in the index of this book, or contact the Patients Association, 11 Dartmouth Street, London SW1H 9BN; tel: 01-222 4992, or see Phyllis Willmott, *Consumer's Guide to the British Social Services* (Penguin, 1978).

16. Before and after treatment

We are inclined to think that treatment is all-important, that its success or failure is what determines the course of the disease. But successful treatment is only one facet of overcoming illness. Just as important, and for the person at the time probably more important, is care.

Illness almost always comes as a shock. Of course we expect to have minor ailments such as colds, but apart from that we expect to keep our health. When we are ill we need to have some idea of what is happening – and what is likely to happen.

An operation is the most dramatic treatment you can have. One moment you are ill, and the next you are cured. At least that is how we like to think of it. But it is rarely like that; usually an operation is used in conjunction with other treatment, or it is a temporary solution to a long-term problem. Even when an operation does function as the miracle cure it is still not always the end of the story.

Doctors are trained to choose the treatment most likely to be effective; unfortunately they are not also trained to provide care and understanding for their patients. Nurses, of course, spend their lives caring for those who are ill, but there are many cases where the nurses are not in a position to help. Before the treatment – an operation, radiotherapy, or whatever – you will be concerned to know what is wrong with you, what can be done about it, what likely result there will be. Sadly, these questions are often left unanswered, and as a result worries and doubts are greater and persist longer than they would have done otherwise. The same type of problems can also occur after the treatment. There needs to be thorough follow-up – follow-up that not only deals with residual difficulties, but also spots any further problems as soon as they occur.

In the story that follows, Barbara has an operation for breast cancer. This is the most common cancer in women, and causes more deaths than anything else in the 35–55 age group. It is a typical case in so far as there is a wide range of possible treatment, and much dispute about its effectiveness. Over the past twenty years or so, despite improvements in early diagnosis, surgical techniques and post-operative radiotherapy, the survival rate has remained almost unchanged.

However, partly as a result of increased recognition of the effects of drastic surgery, the once standard procedure of radical mastectomy (the removal of a whole breast and the underlying muscles) has been replaced by attempts to remove as little as possible, although there is controversy about how much has to be removed to be effective, and even of how effective surgery is anyway. But still it is the case that doctors rarely discuss in advance the treatments that are available in order to discover what the woman herself feels. This is even more true after the operation, and many surgeons are themselves ignorant about the replacement breasts that can be provided.

Discovering that you have breast cancer and dealing with the effect of the treatment is clearly an extremely harrowing experience. The questions of care, understanding, and consideration that it raises are the same as those that are faced by anybody who is ill and has to undergo major treatment – for it is the way you are cared for and consulted, both before and after the treatment, that will determine how easy it is for you to come to terms with your illness.

People not patients

Barbara was not looking for a lump, and when she found it, like many women, she did not want to believe it was there.

> 'I was lying in bed – maybe I had a scratch or something, and I just found this lump in my breast. It was a little pebbly sort of lump, like the stone of an apricot or a peach. It was fairly obvious but I asked my husband to confirm it because really I hoped I was imagining it.'

The fear of finding a lump in her breast not only often stops a woman checking for one, even when she suspects there is something the matter, but also makes her avoid seeing a doctor for some months – months that could be vital. Barbara, however, sensibly saw her doctor the next morning.

> 'It turned out that yes, there was something. But, five years previously, I had a cyst in the same breast which had proved no problem, so I went along to the specialist without too many qualms.'

The specialist confirmed that it was probably just another cyst, but that Barbara should have a mammogram – a breast X-ray – to make quite sure.

> 'The mammogram was really quite hilarious. They get hold of your breast and take it to this machine, and then lay it flat on a little platform and squash it like a pancake – first diagonally and then vertically. I began to get a bit worried, though, because they went away and then came back to do some more. Then the same thing happened again.
>
> It took ten days for the results to come through, and all the time I was getting more nervous. It was odd, because my husband and I are very close, but I started to feel alone, absolutely alone – even when I was lying in bed in his arms.'

The thought of what might be can be worse than anything else. Your imagination plays with the anxiety of not knowing – even the most awful things are possible; it doesn't matter that there isn't evidence for your fears; they just breed on your underlying uncertainty that makes anything feasible.

'It was strange. It was already November, but I began to think, "Am I going to see Christmas? Will I see the kids grow up?" The tension of waiting for the results just got worse and worse . . .'

When Barbara eventually saw the specialist she was told that they had found some calcification in her breast and that she would have to go into hospital to have it looked at.

'I was told virtually nothing – just, "We want you in hospital for a check-up. Good afternoon." But I might as well have been told, "You've got cancer," for all the difference it would have made.

Those days before I went into hospital were murder. I was watching my fears come true – I'd been taken over, it was just happening to me, it was no longer under my control. I couldn't sleep, I had to take all sorts of pills, and all the time there was this growing, awful feeling of being alone. I wondered what would happen to the children: should I get their clothes for next summer in advance? I suppose . . . I suppose I'd decided that I was going to die.

I don't think we talked a lot . . . silent comfort really. We discussed how much we should tell the children, and I let the school know that I would be in hospital – it was all very practical. I told Gordon how I felt, as if I was alone, even though I knew I wasn't . . . but then there wasn't much he could do, was there? I just had to try and keep my mind on something else . . . the trouble was . . . I couldn't.'

By the time Barbara went into hospital she was in quite a state; this had not been helped by being told on the day she was due to go in that there was no bed available. That was sorted out but still no one had said what was wrong with her, or what was going to happen.

'After a number of tests two nurses came along with a spotlight to shave my breast, removing every tiny hair. I'd signed a consent form, but still nobody said, "You're going to have your breast off" . . . it was assumed that I realized that. I don't think it was that they meant to keep me ignorant, but it was easier to assume I knew what was going on. I was hoping that it was just going to be a lump and they wouldn't have to take off the breast . . . but more than that I was hoping that I would survive the surgery. I even wrote a little letter to my husband and children in case I never came back from the theatre. Looking back it was all rather irrational, but there is nobody there to talk to, no one who knows what you are going through, and it's funny, it is almost as if nobody really wants to know – as if you aren't really any different from anyone else.'

Barbara hardly slept the night before the operation despite a sleeping pill. Early the next morning she was taken down to the theatre.

'I climbed on to the trolley and I was quite with it all the way. There were people waiting in the ante-room. The last thing I remember is somebody

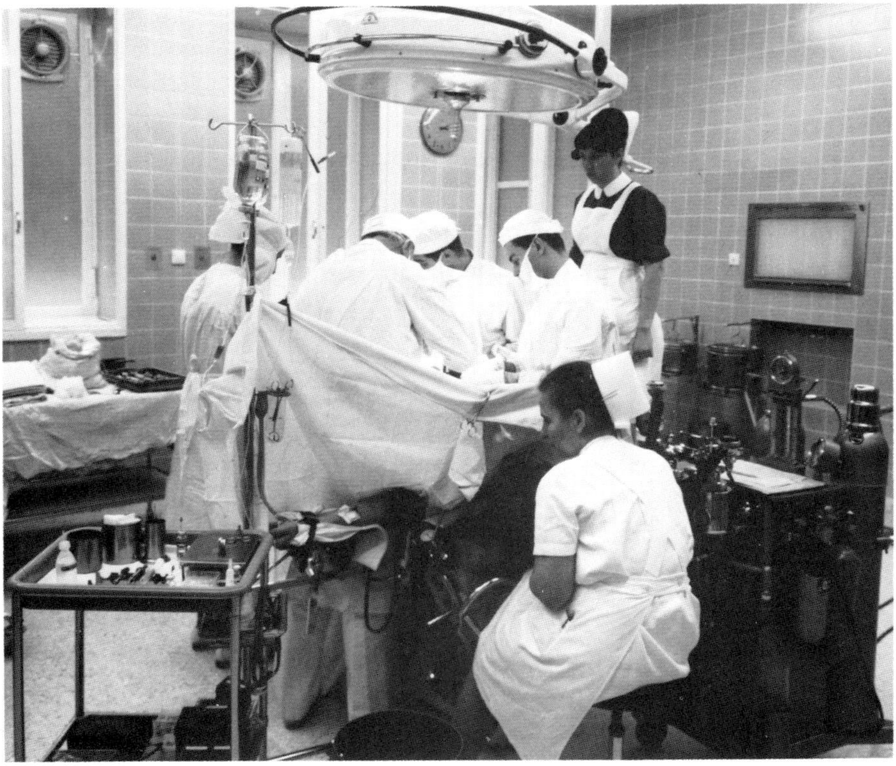

asking me if I was worried, and I replied, "Worried about what you might find." Then I was asleep.'

Barbara's fears that she would not survive the operation were totally unjustified; it is only in exceptional circumstances that there is any danger from the operation itself. However, during the operation Barbara's breast was removed.

'I wasn't in agony when I woke up, but I was on a very narrow trolley which was rather painful. When I got back to the ward I asked if my breast was off – and I was told. In a way I was relieved that everything was over: if that was it, well that was it – it was over, and I was back in the ward. At that stage I wasn't worrying, just hoping that everything would be all right from now on.'

Five days later, after an examination of some of the tissue taken during the operation, they also found cancer in the lymph glands under Barbara's arm. As a result further treatment in the form of radiotherapy, which attempts to kill the cells by the use of powerful X-rays, was found necessary.

'I was lucky. I didn't feel sick as a result of the treatment – it only made me feel tired, although it did make me dreadfully burned. But then, that was it,

I was discharged, and there was no further advice really. There was no information about a replacement breast or anything. The sister did show me one actually – someone coming in for another operation had brought theirs in – but apart from that there was nothing.'

Just as Barbara had been given very little advice before the operation, so there was also almost no advice afterwards. How would she feel about having only one breast? What could she do about it? What sort of artificial replacements – known as prostheses – were available, and what difference would they make to her?

Normally the routine would be that Barbara would wait until an appointment with the surgeon, who would decide whether her skin was sufficiently healed to allow a prosthesis, and then give her a prescription. With this prescription she could then have visited the appliance officer in the hospital, who would show her the alternative prostheses available. Once she had decided, the type of prosthesis would be written on a prescription and she could then go to a shop to have it fitted. In principle, there is no obvious reason why this system should not provide an effective service for those women who have to face the disturbing experience of coming to terms with an artificial breast. Unfortunately it is not always like that, as Barbara discovered from someone in hospital with her who had already gone through the whole process.

'This lady told me that when she went to see the appliance woman she just looked at a few prostheses that were laid on a desk in front of her. They weren't her size so she wasn't able to try them in a bra – she could only feel them. As a result she imagined that the only one she could cope with would be the lightest one – which is one filled with little acrylic balls. Well, I didn't think much of the idea of just going in and seeing them laid out on a slab, like fish.'

The radiotherapy treatment knocks you out quite a bit, but as soon as Barbara felt up to it, she determined to do all she could to find out about the possible alternatives.

'If you are willing to pay for them privately there is a choice of a dozen or more; on the National Health there were only a few. The cheapest are a nylon covering over little acrylic balls – they are shaped a bit like a bosom but you've sort of to push them into shape. Then there are some you blow up like a balloon – you just hope an ardent flag seller doesn't stick a pin in too hard. In an aeroplane, I believe, they explode. Others are filled with oil, but to me the best ones are silicone-gel filled, because you can wash them like skin; there's no problem, you can even go bathing in them.'

Armed with the knowledge of what was available and which prosthesis she wanted, Barbara waited for the next appointment with her surgeon.

'I'm not being critical when I say that the surgeon wasn't helpful, it was just that I don't think he was bothered one way or the other; his job was

A wide range of prostheses is available – from the 'seed bag' (top left) to the silicone forms (seen in the lower part of the photograph)

over, and what happened to me from there on didn't really come into it. As far as the prosthesis was concerned it wasn't important what I got, and he wrote out a prescription for the one I asked for, and that was that – I'd been dealt with.

With this prescription saying "Silicone prosthesis" I went to see the appliance lady, and sure enough, out came all three of her favourite ones, the cheapest, filled with little glass balls, and crunchy. All sorts of ridiculous arguments were trotted out, like how the silicone prostheses were very heavy and that during the first year or two a lighter one would be better, and when I said I would be swimming a lot, suddenly the silicone ones didn't dry instantly and wouldn't be any good. But I stuck out, and eventually I got what I wanted, but not without being told that I did realize that in having such an expensive one I would never be allowed another one ever.'

Although it would have been a great help to Barbara to have had some good advice about an artificial breast, perhaps what was most difficult was simply having to come to terms with losing a breast.

'It's not the hospital staff's fault. They just feel that the job's over when you've been treated and you're recovered.

What you need is some sort of counselling. I certainly found that talking to somebody else who'd had a breast off was a tremendous relief. Just to talk to somebody who'd gone through the same sort of thing – even if you don't talk about boobs, just to talk to someone who you feel knows what it's all about. Hearing her tell me how she'd felt awful for ages, you'd think it would make you feel worse, but it didn't. I started feeling, "Well I'm doing all right; I don't feel as bad as she did." But more than that, it breaks the feeling of isolation.

I went on feeling alone after the operation. I talked to my husband about it . . . it's very odd, I think it's to do with having to cope with it yourself – there's nobody else that can go through it for you. Usually if you're not managing with something, you can be helped – someone can give you a hand – but it's not like that, no matter how much they want to there's nothing they can really do. That's why it's so good to talk to somebody and know you are not the only person who's been in this position.'

Despite finding someone to talk to, the inevitable trauma that follows losing a breast was not something Barbara could fully avoid. In fact it was not until she had returned home from hospital that it overcame her.

'It was the first night at home . . . getting undressed, and putting a nightie on, I burst into tears. Suddenly, I felt deformed . . . yes, deformed. It was as though I was absolutely horrible, and this was it for life. For life . . . that's what drummed into my head. I just couldn't bear looking like this forever.'

Barbara had seen the scars in hospital, but because hospital is not home, because it is a different world, it is sometimes easier to accept things there than it is back in your own surroundings with your family.

'In my ward the dressings had been done every day. In fact, on the first day after my operation I had said to the nurse, "Don't change the dressings today, I don't want . . . I don't want to look at it today, I can't cope today."

Barbara on holiday with her family

> But by the second day it wasn't too bad. It's such a funny environment; you're not really yourself in hospital – it's almost essential to get you through the experience. But then the first night at home, it really hits you.'

One of the most basic fears that any woman faces after a mastectomy is that they will no longer be attractive to men, or worse, that men will feel revulsion. Fortunately that fear is usually unfounded.

> 'The only worry my husband ever had was that I would come out all right. He didn't care whether I returned with one breast or no breasts as long as I came out, that was all that mattered.
>
> I hadn't got such a wonderful bosom to start with, so my feelings weren't anything to do with not being attractive. Strangely, I think people who have amputations of any sort have similar thoughts. Maybe the crunch of it is that an outer part of you, a part that is visible, has gone – somehow, in some obvious way, you're not quite the same as you used to be . . . but at the same time you feel just the same, you haven't changed, and yet the way you appear has. There's a part of you missing, and you feel it should be there, and if it's not there you're deformed, you're not as you should be.
>
> Sometimes, even now, if I get out of the bath and see myself, I think, "Oh God, how awful you look." But it has never mattered to Gordon, and certainly it never altered our sex life in any way.'

During the months after the operation Barbara was visited by many of her friends. All of them meant well, but there were times when they could be rather thoughtless.

> 'I was told the most horrific stories, people who had their breasts off and then died, or cases of people who thought they just had a lump and then it turned out they were dying of cancer. And the number of people who came to see me that knew of somebody that had one off and then six months later they had to go and have the other off . . . People have no idea what misery they can cause.'

However, most of the friends that came to visit her expected the operation to have been much worse than it was.

> 'Some of them almost thanked me for showing them the scar. One girl in particular said that if she found a lump she had always thought she wouldn't tell anybody because she couldn't bear the thought of looking so awful. When I showed her my scar, she completely changed her mind.'

Barbara's determination to find out things for herself, and the continual support she received from her husband, have made a terrible experience into something manageable. For many women without those advantages, the uncertainty before the operation and the lack of concern afterwards are sufficient to make it all just too much to handle. We should never underestimate the fears before treatment, and the effects of it afterwards.

> 'Looking back, I think the consultant could at least have spent five minutes with me explaining what he thought was necessary, and what the options were. I got about a dozen words.
>
> I mean, you don't always have to have your breast off, and I think you should know that – you would feel better afterwards if you were given a bit more idea of the options. And I also think that it's quite ridiculous that you have to fight, just to get the right prosthesis for yourself. But above all, I suppose, what you need is someone to talk to before and after the operation, someone who can act as a counsellor – ideally someone who has also been through it. Someone who can provide you with the support and understanding that you need. Someone who is aware of your unspoken fears. I'd love to do such a job; I only wish someone had done that for me.'

What you can do

Barbara's comment on reading this chapter was, 'Oh, dear! Don't I sound a misery?!' This demonstrates the point that the majority of women do experience an emotional low after mastectomy, and highlights the value of counselling by mastectomees who have come through this trying time. Barbara today is happy and well and actively involved in mastectomy counselling.

Breast cancer and mastectomy are such emotive subjects that many women find them hard to discuss or even think about calmly. The most important thing is to be realistic; shying away in alarm is not going to do you any good, whether or not you develop the disease.

There is advice about how to handle your doctor on page 200, on whether to discuss your illness and your treatment on page 95, and on preparation for going into hospital on page 96.

Prevention The cause of breast cancer is not yet well enough understood for there to be any sure way of avoiding it. Statistics show that you are less likely to get it if you have a child while you are young (below twenty-five), and there is some evidence that breast-feeding may inhibit a later attack. There is also considerable geographical variation (Japanese women have much less breast cancer), which may be something to do with food, or life-styles. Even in this country 93 per cent of women will never contract the disease.

Detection This is where realism is so important. Finding a lump in your breast is a terrifying experience, and research has shown that 70 per cent of women who find lumps delay going to the doctor because they are so frightened of cancer. But there are two vital reasons for going to a doctor at once. First, three out of four lumps turn out to be harmless, and can be easily and often invisibly removed. This is the most likely outcome, and yet most women still suffer agonies worrying about what will happen, and do not go to be checked out.

Secondly, if it is cancer, your chances of survival are much better if action is taken promptly. So the longer you leave it the more you worry, and the worse are your chances if it does turn out to be cancer.

Examine your breasts once a month for changes in size or shape of either breast or nipple, for discharge, puckered skin, or rash, and for lumps. Look at them by sitting or standing in front of a mirror, first with your arms by your sides, then with your hands above your head. Explore for lumps by pressing gently with your fingers flat, searching gradually round the whole breast, using your right hand on your left breast and vice versa, holding your free hand first by your side and then above your head. Concentrate on changes, or differences between your breasts. See a doctor at once if you find anything unusual. For full details of how to examine yourself, see one of the books listed below, or write with a stamped, addressed envelope for a free leaflet from the Mastectomy Association (*see* address below), the Women's National Cancer Control Campaign (1 South Audley Street, London W1), or BUPA Medical Centre Ltd, Webb House, 210 Pentonville Road, London N1.

You may not want to go to your family doctor, either because he is a man, or because you do not want to tell anyone you know. You can always try the family planning clinic (look in your telephone directory under the District or Area Health Authority). The doctors there are often women, and are usually sympathetic towards women. Or telephone the Mastectomy Association (*see* below), who can give you a wide range of advice in complete confidence.

When you do see a doctor, the most likely thing to happen is that you will be told it is harmless; but if the doctor does not know, and cannot do any necessary tests, you will be referred to a hospital for a biopsy. You should get into hospital within a week. The normal procedure is to ask you to consent to a biopsy and if necessary mastectomy, under the same anaesthetic, since the biopsy can be done within a few minutes once the surgeon can get at the lump. What is more, mastectomy is likely to be the best course if you have cancer, and most women would rather not be woken up just to be told they need a mastectomy. You do not have to agree to this; you can always insist on having a biopsy only, if you would rather discuss the situation again afterwards.

If you do consent to both operations you will wake up to find either that everything is fine, or that you have lost a breast; and it is because of this possibility that you should, before you go into hospital, start facing the idea of life with only one breast.

Will I be only half a woman? No, you won't. No one will think any the less of you with only one breast. Husbands, boyfriends, children – very few are put off; very few will reject you. Breasts have acquired enormous importance to sexuality, to body-image, and to self-esteem, and to have one removed can feel like losing half your life. But it is not like this for other people. Men in particular are not turned off by a missing breast, although they may be badly upset by your excessive worrying about it.

Action Do not sit around feeling miserable, waiting for things to happen. If you have a lump, and you suspect breast cancer, then the faster you move the more choices you have. First of all, find out more about the disease, either from one of the books listed below or from your family planning clinic or Marriage Guidance (MG) (*see* page 218). The advantage of finding out is that you will then be able to *discuss* treatment with your doctor, instead of just taking it lying down. There may be a specialist breast clinic to which you can be referred, instead of the local hospital.

The most common treatment for breast cancer is 'simple mastectomy' which means removal of the whole breast and no more, but there is no general agreement for this treatment among the doctors and surgeons of the world, or indeed this country. In some cases the surgeon may suggest 'radical mastectomy', which is much more severe, or lumpectomy – the removal of just the lump. Or there may be the possibility of non-surgical treatment, by drugs or X-rays. These are likely to be unpleasant, but might be better than removal of the breast.

Some doctors, perhaps because they know what an emotive subject mastectomy is, tend not to discuss the possibilities with the patient; they do what they think is best, and do not want to cause any more painful feelings than you already have. But if you are forearmed with information you can talk sensibly to your doctor about the disease and the treatment. You will certainly save yourself uncertainty, and you may by discussion find a more acceptable form of treatment than the one your doctor would have suggested in the first place.

Take a friend along when you go to see the doctor. You will need support, before, during and after the interview; your husband, boyfriend, daughter, or colleague can provide you with confidence and determination. Then you will have a better chance of finding out what you want to know, and remembering what you are told.

If you want to change your doctor *see* page 189.

Going into hospital *See* page 96.

After mastectomy You will feel sore for a week or more. You will have a large dressing and probably one or more drainage tubes, which will be removed after a few days. You will be able to go home after ten or twelve days. Your scar will be unpleasant to look at when it is fresh, but will settle down to a faint line, not at all repulsive.

Immediately after the operation you may well feel euphoric, because at least it is over, and the uncertainty is gone. But within a few days you are likely to feel again all the depressing anxiety about having lost your breast. This is the time when you should talk about how you feel. You need support badly; talk to your husband or boyfriend, or even better to another mastectomy patient, one who has been through the problems and has learned how to handle them. A few hospitals have mastectomy counsellors; this is when you need one.

Contact the Mastectomy Association, if you have not already done so; they will provide you with advice and support. They can arrange for you to meet someone else who has had a mastectomy if you want.

You may need further treatment, either drugs or X-rays (radiotherapy) after the operation. The point of this is to try and prevent spread or recurrence of the cancer. During this period you are likely to feel tired and ill. Rest when you need to, but try and take some gentle exercise, and return to your normal lifestyle as soon as you can.

If your life does not soon return to normal *see* Chapter 7 – 'Serious Illness'.

You can get a prosthesis on the National Health. Talk to the hospital mastectomy counsellor if there is one; otherwise the normal procedure is for the surgeon to refer you to the hospital appliance officer, who should show you a selection of prostheses to choose from.

Some women prefer not to wear a prosthesis at all, but unless your other breast is very small this is likely to make you feel lop-sided, and may result in backache. The hospital should provide you with a light 'temporary' breast form, and you may find that this is convenient in the weeks after the operation, while your scar settles down. Wearing it will give you time to find out what else is available. The Mastectomy Association also produce these 'Cumfies' in case you cannot get them from the hospital, or want extra ones.

Ask your doctor, your surgeon, or your appliance officer, where you can go to see a full range of prostheses, and try them on. If you have difficulty, the Mastectomy Association can tell you about suppliers in your area; they will also send you details of all the available types of prosthesis, and which you can get on the National Health.

The cheapest and worst prothesis is the shapeless 'seed bag', which is still routinely prescribed in a few hospitals. Slightly better is one made of foam with a filling of granules. This type has a reasonable shape, but suffers from two disadvantages: first, it will be lighter than your natural breast so that although it may look reasonable when you are standing up it will have the wrong shape when you are lying down or bending forward – and you will feel lop-sided. Secondly, it will get wet when you swim; then it will be heavier than your other breast, and will sag and leak water.

Fluid-filled prostheses are comfortable and popular, although there is the slight danger that they can be punctured.

The most satisfactory types are made of silicone. When you first pick one up it may feel heavy. But it will match the weight of your natural breast; it will sag a little when it should; it will move with you like your other breast; and when you have been swimming it will dry just like your skin. Some are provided with nipples, which will allow you to look really feminine when your confidence returns.

All prostheses are held in place by bras or swimsuits. These do not have to be special mastectomy clothes; you will probably be able to modify your own bras by sewing in pockets or ribbons to hold the prosthesis in place, and you can certainly find excellent ones at any shop you normally use. You will need a good bra or swimsuit, and in particular one that does not ride up when you raise your arms, or come away at the top when you lean forward; but there is no need to worry about being conspicuous. You will probably find that no one notices, even when you go into a shop to try on new dresses; in fact a good prosthesis is incredibly hard to detect under even the laciest bra.

A false breast is hard to detect even in a bikini

If you prefer you can buy the special mastectomy bras and swimsuits, with the build-in modifications. Many of these are attractive and feminine; the only problem is that they are expensive.

Take your time; find a prosthesis (and also a bra) that you are really happy with. Then go to your surgeon and ask him to write you a prescription for that particular one.

Reconstructions and implants It may be possible for you to have a new breast built up under your own skin. This will depend on the type of operation you have in the first place, and perhaps on your surgeon. The best thing to do is go back to your surgeon and ask him about it, or go to your family doctor; ask the Mastectomy Association if you have difficulties. The nipple is usually affected by the cancer and therefore removed, but it may be possible to build a new one.

Talk to your surgeon before your first operation if you know in advance that you want reconstruction; he may be able to operate in such a way as to make it easier.

Mastectomy organizations The Mastectomy Association (25 Brighton Road, South Croydon, CR2 6EA; tel: 01-654 8643) is a strictly non-medical group which provides support for mastectomy patients, and practical advice on how to get help, on how to avoid depression, and how to find out about prostheses, bras, and swimsuits. Telephone for immediate help, or preferably write with a stamped, addressed envelope. The Association will send you a range of leaflets with information and advice. After the operation it can arrange for you to meet and talk privately to another mastectomy patient.

For information about cancer, and about help and services available for cancer patients, *see* page 99.

Mastectomy books

- *Living with the Loss of a Breast*, a free booklet for mastectomy patients produced jointly by the Health Education Council and the Mastectomy Association, provides basic advice and information.
- Nancy Robinson and Ian Swash, *Mastectomy: A Patient's Guide to Coping with Breast Surgery* (Thorsons, 1977) goes into much greater detail. It is extremely helpful on the feelings of mastectomy patients, and on how to handle the painful emotions. It also provides masses of information about the different types of prosthesis, which manufacturers produce them, and organizations and books to which you can turn.
- *Breast Biopsy and Mastectomy*, another free booklet published by the Mastectomy Association, describes all that is involved in simple language.
- Angela Phillips and Jill Rakusen, *Our Bodies Ourselves* (Penguin, 1978) provides information about breast cancer and the types of treatment that are actually available, and also discusses the psychological problems that arise.
- Michael Baum, *Breast Cancer: The Facts* (Oxford University Press, 1981) is informative, though rather medical in approach.
- Betty Ford, *The Times of My Life* (W. H. Allen, 1979), an entertaining autobiography of the wife of the former American President, includes a frank account of her mastectomy and how she coped with it.

Illnesses other than breast cancer Of course mastectomy is not the only treatment where the patient can sometimes feel isolated or neglected. Other chapters in this book deal specifically with other conditions – look in the index for details. Organizations such as the Mastectomy Association include:

- The Coeliac Society of Great Britain and Northern Ireland, PO Box 181, London NW2 2QY; tel: 01-459 2440.
- The Colostomy Welfare Group, 38 Ecclestone Square, London SW1V 1PE; tel: 01-828 5175.
- The British Polio Fellowship, Bell Close, West End Road, Ruislip, Middlesex HA4 6LP; tel: 71 75515.
- The Ileostomy Association of Great Britain and Northern Ireland, Amblehurst House, Chobham, Woking, Surrey.
- The National Association of Laryngectomee Clubs, 4th Floor, Michael Sobell House, 30 Dorset Square, London NW1 6QL; tel: 01-402 6007.
- The Leukaemia Society, Hamlyns View, St Andrew's Road, Exeter EX4 2AF; tel: 0392 30032.
- The Multiple Sclerosis Society of Great Britain and Northern Ireland, 286 Munster Road, London SW6 6AP; tel: 01-381 40220.
- The Patients Association (11 Dartmouth Street, London SW1H 9BN; tel: 01-222 4992) provides an information and advice service by letter or telephone, and has a list of self-help organizations.

Locally, the Citizens Advice Bureau and the Marriage Guidance Council will know of helpful organizations (see your telephone directory or page 218).

How to get help

We all experience problems from time to time. Some are worse than others, and occasionally they seem to be unbearable. But however low you feel, you have to decide what to do. You may need help to find a good plan, and one of the organizations below may be able to provide that help, either directly or by pointing you in the right direction. There are references throughout this book to specific sources of help. Look in the index in case your particular problem is mentioned in the book.

Local newspapers, especially the smaller ones, usually have an information column that tells you which hospitals have emergency departments, where to find a family planning clinic, how to reach the Samaritans and the Citizens Advice Bureau (CAB), and so on. You could perhaps cut this out and stick it up by your telephone; even if you never need it your next-door neighbour might.

Immediate help In a medical emergency telephone your doctor, or another doctor in his group. Or go direct to the nearest hospital casualty department; if possible telephone first to make sure that it is open and tell them what has happened, if you know. Or dial 999 and ask for an ambulance, but remember that it could take some time to get to you if you live some distance from the ambulance station; you will probably get to hospital more quickly by driving yourself.

In a non-medical crisis call the *Samaritans* (see your telephone directory). They are always there, twenty-four hours a day, all over the country. They are non-legal and non-religious, and will listen sympathetically to your problems and do all they can to help. You do not have to give your name, or tell them where you live; they will not criticize you, nor call in the authorities, nor put the telephone down. They were originally set up to help anyone who felt suicidal, and this is still one of their main aims, but they will also help you through any sort of crisis. For example if you are worried about going to court, or to a doctor, a Samaritan will support you, and if you wish may even be able to accompany you. You can call them from a hospital bed. If you want to meet a Samaritan you can go to their office, or you can usually arrange to meet at your home or in some other place, such as a pub. They also have an extensive list of other organizations that may be able to provide direct assistance.

Women facing a crisis such as rape, or attack by a partner, should telephone the *Rape Crisis Centre* (see the telephone directory under 'Rape'), or *WIRES* (0742 755290), or the Samaritans. Most towns have refuges with space available for women and children who are in danger. You can go direct to the Samaritans, or the police.

There may be a local family crisis telephone service; look in the telephone

directory under 'Family' for *Family Network* or *Family Crisis Centre*, or get their number from the CAB.

Information For medical information go to your family doctor, to the nurse at his surgery, to the health visitor, to the welfare clinic, or to the family planning clinic. You can ask at a post office where the clinics are, or look in the teleohone directory under the District or Area Health Authority), or in the yellow pages under 'Clinics' or 'Physicians'. Any family doctor in your area should be prepared to give you emergency treatment. If you want to register with a doctor go to the most convenient surgery and ask to be taken on; you can ask your friends or neighbours first for advice about a helpful doctor. If you have difficulty write to the local Family Practitioner Committee (see address in the telephone directory under the District or Area Health Authority) or to the *Patients Association* (11 Dartmouth Street, London SW1H 9BN; tel: 01-222 4992). If you want to change your doctor, *see* page 189.

For any other information try the *Citizens Advice Bureau* (*CAB*); look in the telephone directory under 'Citizens', or ask at a post office. You can telephone, or visit the bureau in person. It is generally open during office hours, and when you go there is likely to be a queue, especially on Mondays. The staff will listen with sympathy to any problems you have; they will advise you of your rights and tell you what services and benefits you may be entitled to, and how to get them. They will help you with financial and legal problems, without charge, and they will tell you how to get help of various kinds.

There may also be a local advice bureau closer to your home or work. Look in the local newspaper, or under 'Information' in the yellow pages, or ask the CAB or the post office.

Counselling When you have an emotional problem, whether it seems to be inside yourself or whether it involves other people, you may want to talk to someone about it. If you have a friend or relative who can help that is fine, but you might prefer to talk to someone neutral, someone who does not know you or your circle of friends, someone who is confidential and unbiased. In that case you might like to try a professional counsellor, like those in the *Marriage Guidance Council (MG)* or the *Catholic Marriage Advisory Council* (see your telephone directory under 'Marriage').

You do not have to have a marriage problem to go to MG; in fact you do not have to be married. They are ready to talk about any personal problem; to listen, to try and understand, to clear away dead wood, and to help you sort out your difficulties.

Telephone in the first place to make an appointment. MG does not attempt to offer immediate service, although a brief interview can sometimes be arranged the same day. Generally you will have to wait at least a few days before your first session at their office. Then you will meet your counsellor in private and in complete confidence, for at least an hour each week for for as long as you both feel it is useful. Whether your problem is over sex, or divorce, a difficult grandparent, or a death in the family, you will be given understanding and support. Because they are impartial, counsellors are often particularly helpful in simplifying problems, in helping you to understand what really matters, and in finding out how your upbringing, or the things that you feel you ought to do, are making your decisions more difficult.

MG do not charge fees, but they will as you to make a contribution – if you can afford it – towards their costs. If you do not like your counsellor, telephone and ask for another.

There may also be a family advice or counselling service in your area (*see* above); or you can try social workers – go to your Social Service office and ask for the Duty Officer (*see* pages 34 and 87) – health visitors, welfare staff, or the county Probation Service.

Finally, if you are worried about your personality, or the mental health of someone in your family, you can try *MIND* (look in the telephone directory under 'MIND', or contact the Head Office at 22 Harley Street, London W1N 3ED; tel: 01-637 0741). MIND is the National Association for Mental Health, and provides, for all types of people with mental illness or handicap, a variety of services such as accommodation, day centres, companionship, work experience, self-help ventures, transport, and educational events. They can often arrange counselling, and sometimes group therapy. They are there to help, and you can find out what is actually available by contacting your nearest branch. In addition they publish books, leaflets, and a magazine called *Mind Out*.

Self-help groups Many personal problems are hard to understand without direct experience; we cannot easily comprehend the terror of a phobic or the isolation of someone who is depressed unless we have actually felt the same way. The success of self-help organizations, where groups of people with a particular problem come together to help others, depends on their experience and understanding. Sharing experiences can greatly relieve the feeling of being cut off from the rest of society, and self-help groups are also an excellent source of information about treatment.

You will find references to self-help groups throughout this book, and you can obtain a list from the Patients Association (*see* above), or from one of the other sources mentioned on page 166.

Many of these organizations are national, but there are often local branches. A great majority of them are short of money; but when you approach them you may well find that what they lack in financial resources they make up for in enthusiasm and hope.

Illustration Acknowledgments

The producers of this book would like to thank all those listed below who have allowed us to reproduce photographs.

Mike Abrahams/Network, 149
Associated Newspapers, 108
Steve Benbow/Network, 126
Daily Telegraph Colour Library (Photo: David Redfern), 73
Sally and Richard Greenhill, 20, 24 (posed by a model), 47, 62, 112, 122 (posed by models)
John Harrison, 147
Adam Hart-Davis, 14, 18 (below), 26, 38, 41 (left and right), 48 (posed by a model), 55, 56, 58, 64, 70, 76 (posed by a model), 79, 84, 94, 100, 103, 106, 115, 128, 131, 138 (posed by a model), 141, 152 (posed by a model), 161, 163, 171, 182, 185, 195, 199, 208, 215
John Hillelson Agency (Photos: Michael Hardy), 22, 97, 202
Barry Lewis/Network, 165
Medical Defence Union, 180
MIND, 150
NSPCC, 34
Pictorial Press, 12, 21
Pictor International, 88
Ron Reid, 43
John Sturnock/Network, 134
Homer Sykes, 71, 98
John Topham Picture Library, 86, 219
Understanding Women, 121
Vision International, 190; (Photos: Anthea Sieveking) 36, 180 (posed by models)
Yorkshire Television, 107
Zefa, 2–3, 168, 206

The following photographs were contributed by those whose stories are reproduced in the book: 16, 18 (above left and right), 27 (left and right), 28 (left and right), 31, 51, 52, 65, 67, 80, 91, 92, 116, 154 (left and right), 155, 157, 159, 172, 175, 187, 193 (left and right), 210

Index

In entries that include several page numbers those for the main sources of help, advice, or information are picked out in **bold** type.